Private Cities

Urban Development Series

The Urban Development Series discusses the challenge of urbanization and what it will mean for developing countries in the decades ahead. The series aims to delve substantively into a range of core issues related to urban development that policy makers and practitioners must address.

Previous titles in the series

What a Waste 2.0: A Global Snapshot of Solid Waste Management to 2050 (2018) by Silpa Kazo, Lisa C. Yao, Perinaz Bhada Tata, and Frank Van Woerden

East Asia and Pacific Cities: Expanding Opportunities for the Urban Poor (2017) by Judy Baker and Gauri U. Gadgil

Regenerating Urban Land: A Practitioner's Guide to Leveraging Private Investment (2016) by Rana Amirtahmasebi, Mariana Orloff, Sameh Wahba, and Andrew Altman

Financing Transit-Oriented Development with Land Values: Adapting Land Value Capture in Developing Countries (2015) by Hiroaki Suzuki, Jin Murakami, Yu-Hung Hong, and Beth Tamayose

East Asia's Changing Urban Landscape: Measuring a Decade of Spatial Growth (2015) by World Bank Group

Transforming Cities with Transit: Transit and Land-Use Integration for Sustainable Urban Development (2013) by Hiroaki Suzuki, Robert Cervero, and Kanako Iuchi

Urban Risk Assessments: Understanding Disaster and Climate Risk in Cities (2012) by Eric Dickson, Judy L. Baker, Daniel Hoornweg, and Asmita Tiwari

The Economics of Uniqueness: Investing in Historic City Cores and Cultural Heritage Assets for Sustainable Development (2012) by Guido Licciardi and Rana Amirtahmasebi

Climate Change, Disaster Risk, and the Urban Poor: Cities Building Resilience for a Changing World (2012) by Judy L. Baker

Cities and Climate Change: Responding to an Urgent Agenda (2011) by Daniel Hoornweg, Mila Freire, Marcus J. Lee, Perinaz Bhada-Tata, and Belinda Yuen

All books in the Urban Development Series are available free at
http://hdl.handle.net/10986/2174.

URBAN DEVELOPMENT SERIES

Private Cities

Outstanding Examples from Developing Countries and Their Implications for Urban Policy

Yue Li and Martin Rama, Editors

 **WORLD BANK GROUP**

Contents

Tables

Foreword

Urbanization is the cornerstone of economic development in low- and middle-income countries. In cities, firms can exploit economies of scale as they have access to large markets, while fierce competition triggers innovation. Rural workers move to cities in pursuit of higher wages and a better quality of life, while urban schools raise skill levels. Cities are the drivers of economic growth as agglomeration effects increase productivity, while cities in low- and middle-income countries continue to attract more firms and more workers.

To materialize the positive externalities of agglomeration, public goods must be provided: urban planning, efficient urban infrastructure, and a broad range of services, from education to health care and waste disposal. These public goods are ultimately funded by tax income (including real estate taxes) and land sales.

In South Asia also, urbanization is the main driver of growth. But its potential is underutilized. Most cities in South Asia are messy, with poor urban planning, under-developed urban infrastructure, large slums, congestion, and pollution. Especially the megacities suffer from this messiness, and there are too few secondary cities to alleviate the congestion in the megacities.

Past research has pointed to several causes of the inefficiency of many cities in South Asia: lack of empowerment of local governments, a too narrow tax base, difficulties in the administration of real estate taxes and, in several cases, insufficient institutional capacity. The current book doesn't add to the analysis of these causes but points out that in the absence of effective local governments, private cities may emerge.

Private cities are built and operated by significant nongovernment actors that not only build the houses, factories, offices, and roads, but also provide public services. These unconventional players can provide public goods without collecting taxes because the value of the land and the buildings they own increases when cities are operating more efficiently and the quality of urban life improves. Private actors, often powerful and well connected, can be quite successful in attracting dynamic companies to their cities.

This book is not advocating for private cities or for the privatization of existing cities. It discusses several potential dangers of private cities, from exclusion of disadvantaged groups to lack of transparency and unreliable environmental commitments. However, the book also does not dismiss the advantages of private cities out of hand. With this open mind, the book analyzes the development of past and present private cities. One lesson that emerges is that an optimal cooperation exists between local governments and private actors. That optimum improves when the capacity of local governments is strengthened. These local governments can learn from the planning and execution of existing private cities.

We hope this book triggers debate in South Asia and elsewhere. And hopefully that debate leads to better-functioning cities, generating higher productivity and improved quality of life. Even if private cities are not the solution, they may well provide invaluable insights.

Although this book, led by former South Asia Chief Economist, Martin Rama, and our former colleague Yue Li, started in the Office of the Chief Economist for South Asia at the World Bank from concerns about urban development in South Asia, by drawing on the expertise of the Urban, Resilience and Land Global Practice, it gradually added examples from many other parts of the world as global experiences provide the best insights. We are grateful to Martin and Yue for continuing to work on this book long after they assumed other responsibilities and to the numerous colleagues who researched case studies in many parts of the world.

Bernice K. Van Bronkhorst
Global Director
Urban, Resilience and Land Global Practice
The World Bank

Hans Timmer
Chief Economist, South Asia
The World Bank

Acknowledgments

This book summarizes the findings of several years of analytical work involving World Bank staff as well as academicians and practitioners in both developing countries and advanced economies. Funding was provided by the research project on Private Cities (P166738), which was led by Yue Li and Martin Rama, at a time when both were affiliated with the World Bank. The core World Bank team behind this work also included Virgilio Galdo, who coauthored the synthesis piece in the book, as well as Sohaib Athar and Mark Roberts, who made substantive contributions to country-level components of the project.

The research greatly benefited from guidance and encouragement by Hans Timmer, Chief Economist for South Asia, and by Sameh Wahba, then Global Director for Urban, Resilience and Land Global Practice at the World Bank.

The peer reviewers for the book were Gilles Duranton (University of Pennsylvania), Somik V. Lall (World Bank), and Siqi Zheng (Massachusetts Institute of Technology). Their valuable inputs and constructive suggestions are gratefully acknowledged.

The team also benefited from very useful comments by Erik Berglof (Asian Infrastructure Investment Bank), Edward Glaeser (Harvard University), Pierre Picard (University of Luxembourg), and Anthony Venables (University of Oxford).

The research built on a review of historical experience with private cities and on country-level inventories of such cities in the Arab Republic of Egypt, India, Indonesia, and Pakistan. Kun Cheng prepared the historical review. Mulya Amri, Balakrishnan Balachandran, Tamer Elshayal, Kareem Ibrahim, Arjun Joshi, Yue Li, Nadia Qureshi, and Tony Hartanto Widjarnarso were responsible for the inventories.

In-depth reviews of 14 outstanding private cities in developing countries were another important building block. While some of the reviews are based on existing literature, several of them summarize rich case studies especially prepared for this project by Mulya Amri, Sohaib Athar, Balakrishnan Balachandran, Tamer Elshayal, Kareem Ibrahim, Arjun Joshi, Yue Li, Nadia Qureshi, Mark Roberts, Arturo Villegas Limas, and

Tony Hartanto Widjarnarso. In the case of East Dhaka, the review is based on a previous study jointly written with Julia Bird, Hossain Zillur Rahman, and Anthony J. Venables. In the case of Gu'an, China, it is based on a collaboration with Kun Cheng and Siqi Zheng.

Productive discussions of preliminary findings from this research helped tighten the analysis. Special thanks for their constructive suggestions go to participants at the "Private Cities: Authors' Workshop" organized by the World Bank on May 20–21, 2020; at the consultation workshop "Leveraging the Private Sector's Role in Urban Development," jointly organized by the World Bank and Indonesia's Ministry of National Development Planning (BAPPENAS) on March 25, 2021; and at a research seminar at the Asian Infrastructure Investment Bank on July 29, 2021.

Sincere gratitude is extended to the Directorates of Regional Development and Development of Urban, Housing and Settlement Areas of BAPPENAS for their engagement with the research team and their openness to discuss the implications of this project for the design of urban development and affordable housing policies in Indonesia.

Engagement and insights by Quang Hong Doan, Thomas Farole, Jaafar Sadok Friaa, Jessica Carolina Grisanti Bravo, Nancy Lozano-Garcia, Catalina Marulanda, Barjor Mehta, Megha Mukim, Frederico Gil Sander, Harris Selod, and Ming Zhang, all with the World Bank, are also gratefully acknowledged.

Logistical support for the project was provided by Ahmad Khalid Afridi, Neelam Chowdhry, Rana Damayo AlGazzaz, Jacqueline Larrabure Rivero, Betelihem Tsegaye Nigatu, and Agnes R. Yaptenco. Cindy A. Fisher, Amy Lynn Grossman, and Jewel McFadden managed the publication process. Editors from Publications Professionals LLC edited the book and Melina Yingling Rose prepared its design.

About the contributors

The editors

Yue Li has been a senior economist at the Asian Infrastructure Investment Bank since 2021, leading the research and data unit in its Economics Department. Previously a senior economist at the World Bank, she also served in the World Bank's research department, economists' network, Office of the Chief Economist for South Asia, and global investment climate unit. Her research centers on international economics, firm dynamics, economic geography, and urban economics. She holds a PhD in economics from Rutgers University, a master's degree in economics and political science from Syracuse University, and a bachelor's degree from Peking University.

Martin Rama has been a consultant to the World Bank's presidency since 2021. Previously, he served as a member of the World Bank's research department (1992–2002), as the lead economist for Vietnam (2002–10), as the director of its *World Development Report* (2011–12), and as chief economist for South Asia (2013–19) and Latin America and the Caribbean (2019–21). He earned his economics degree from the Universidad de la República in Uruguay, where he also worked for Centro de Investigaciones Económicas—an independent think tank. He received his PhD in economics from the University of Paris, where for 15 years he taught as a visiting professor in the graduate program in development economics.

The authors

Mulya Amri is a researcher in urban development and public policy based in Jakarta, Indonesia, and is currently affiliated with Katadata Insight Center and the World Benchmarking Alliance.

Sohaib Athar is a senior urban economist at the World Bank, with a focus on the Middle East and North Africa Region.

Balakrishnan Balachandran is an urban planning researcher and consultant based in Dallas, Texas, with a PhD in regional planning from the University of Illinois at Urbana-Champaign.

Julia Bird is a senior engagement manager at Vivid Economics, a McKinsey Company, based in London, and was previously with the Department of Economics at the University of Oxford.

Kun Cheng is a researcher with the Department of Urban Studies and Planning at the Massachusetts Institute of Technology in Cambridge, Massachusetts.

Tamer Elshayal is an urban policy and planning consultant based in Cairo, Arab Republic of Egypt, is affiliated with Takween Integrated Community Development, and is a PhD candidate in urban planning at Harvard University.

Virgilio Galdo is a research analyst with the Office of the Chief Economist for Latin America and the Caribbean at the World Bank.

Kareem Ibrahim is an urban development consultant based in Cairo, Arab Republic of Egypt, chief executive officer of Takween Integrated Community Development, and a graduate of Cairo University.

Arjun Joshi is an architect and urban planner based in Ahmedabad, India, a director at Urbintarch, and a visiting faculty member in the Faculty of Planning, CEPT University in Ahmedabad, India.

Nadia Qureshi is an architect and urban planner based in Lahore, Pakistan, a senior urban development specialist with The Urban Unit in Pakistan, and a graduate of the University of Michigan in Ann Arbor.

Hossain Zillur Rahman is the founder and chairman of the Power and Participation Research Centre and the chairperson of BRAC-Bangladesh, based in Dhaka, Bangladesh.

Mark Roberts is a lead urban economist with the Global Practice for Urban, Disaster Risk Management, Resilience and Land at the World Bank.

Anthony J. Venables is a professor of economics at the University of Manchester and the research director of its Productivity Institute. Previously he was a professor of economics at the University of Oxford and the chief economist at the UK Department for International Development, among other positions.

Arturo Villegas Limas is a research associate at the American Institutes for Research, based in Washington, DC.

Tony Hartanto Widjarnarso is an urban planning analyst based in Jakarta, Indonesia, and a consultant with the World Bank.

Siqi Zheng is STL Champion Professor of Urban and Real Estate Sustainability and Faculty Director of the Center for Real Estate and Sustainable Urbanization Lab at the Massachusetts Institute of Technology, in Cambridge, Massachusetts.

Abbreviations

ADB	Asian Development Bank
AfDB	African Development Bank
AFGRE	Al Futtaim Group Real Estate
BIDA	Batam Industrial Development Authority
CC	city corporation
CCIC	Chamber of Commerce and Industry of Cortés
CEO	chief executive officer
CFLD	China Fortune Land Development
CT&D	Central Trading and Development
DHA	Defense Housing Authority
DLF	Delhi Lease and Finance
EPZ	export processing zone
GDP	gross domestic product
GLC	government-linked company
GMDA	Gurugram Metropolitan Development Authority
HUDA	Haryana Urban Development Authority
IBRA	Indonesian Bank Restructuring Agency
JUSCO	Jamshedpur Utilities and Services Co. Ltd.
MAASP	Ministry of Agrarian Affairs and Spatial Planning
MPWH	Ministry of Public Works and Housing
NIMBY	not in my backyard
NUCA	New Urban Communities Authority
PMHC	Phu My Hung Corporation
PPP	public-private partnership
SCCI	Sialkot Chamber of Commerce and Industry

SEDFZE   South Energyx Development F.Z.E
SEZ   special economic zone
SIJORI   Singapore-Johor-Riau [Growth Triangle]
TISCO   Tata Iron and Steel Company
WIC   Waterfall Investment Corporation

Private cities in developing countries

Yue Li and Martin Rama

W eak local governments are at the root of some of the most serious urbanization challenges faced by the developing world. In low- and middle-income countries, cities are often messy and disconnected. There are simply not enough of them, but the few that emerge—capital cities in particular—become oversized. By now the majority of the megacities in the world can be found in developing countries, where underurbanization and overcrowding appear to be the norm (Duranton and Puga 2020; Lall et al. 2021; United Nations 2018).

The assessment obviously has nuances across developing regions, but the challenges are not exclusive to any of them. In Sub-Saharan Africa, investments in infrastructure have not kept pace with the concentration of people, with cities developing as collections of small and fragmented neighborhoods that limit job opportunities and prevent reaping agglomeration benefits (Lall, Henderson, and Venables 2017). In South Asia, the widespread existence of slums and sprawl has been found to constrain the potential of agglomeration forces to bring about faster improvements in prosperity (Ellis and Roberts 2016). In parts of East Asia, the elasticity of income per capita to the urbanization rate has been substantially lower than the global average (Roberts, Sander, and Tiwari 2019). And in Latin America and the Caribbean, the productivity of cities seems to be driven by the attraction of more qualified households rather than by strong agglomeration effects (Ferreyra and Roberts 2018).

These poor outcomes reflect the limited capacity of local governments to plan, finance, build, and manage cities. To begin, the assembly of unbuilt land with clear titles is challenging. Property rights are not always well defined, and they may involve ownership by the army and other entities not subject to the authority of local governments. Cadastral records and titling tend to be incomplete, and land regulations are most often cumbersome. In addition, governments in developing countries are hampered by legal and organizational constraints that typically do not encumber the private sector (López-de-Silanes 1997).

Some of the most severe institutional constraints facing local authorities arise from the constitutional arrangements in force. By now, in almost every country, there is a hierarchy of administrative jurisdictions—such as provinces, departments, and communes—each subject to one level of government. However, "not all agglomerations have single proactive autonomous local governments. Local autonomy may not be part of the national constitution; many local governments may not or cannot be proactive; and not all agglomerations are governed by a single local government or by a set of township governments that coordinate well" (Henderson and Becker 2000, 471).

Strengthening urban authorities is therefore a key priority in most developing countries. However, political economy constraints make the reform of urban governance an arduous and at times frustrating task. Progress often requires changes at the constitutional level. This agenda is thus of the utmost importance but delivering on it is bound to take time.

Meanwhile, rural-urban migration is proceeding at an unabated pace, especially in some of the poorest countries. Between 1960 and 2000, the number of metropolitan areas with a population of more than 100,000 inhabitants almost tripled in the developing world. Going forward, Asia's urban population is expected to increase by 1,359 million between 2015 and 2050, that of the Middle East and North Africa by 224 million, and that of Sub-Saharan Africa by 883 million (United Nations 2018).

With these developing regions needing to accommodate almost 2.5 billion additional urban dwellers in barely more than three decades, only focusing on addressing weak urban governance could result in missed opportunities. Given the contribution cities make to economic development, improving the technical and institutional capacity of local governments may be conceptually ideal but in practice it could slow down economic growth and poverty reduction if not accompanied by other urban policies.

* * *

The flip side of weak local governments is the disproportionate role played by significant private actors in the development of major urban agglomerations. In fact, there are important precedents of privately built or managed cities in the history of today's advanced economies. For example, medieval Paris was run by the Seine River boatmen's corporation. Florence, one of the most extraordinary urban agglomerations of the Renaissance, was arguably the city of the Medici family. And during the industrial revolution, company towns were pervasive in the United States, the United Kingdom, and other parts of Europe.

Private actors play a similar or even bigger role in the urbanization process of the developing world nowadays. There, many major cities encompass large built-up areas that host households or firms but are built, run, and serviced with limited intervention by local governments.

On the household side, private residential areas—or gated communities—are increasingly common at the high end, whereas megaslums—such as Dharavi in India or Kibera in Kenya—illustrate the urbanization challenges faced at the low end. On the firm side, industrial parks and business improvement districts offer better infrastructure and support services than those provided by local governments. Depending on the case, real estate developers, civil society organizations, firms specializing in logistics, or business associations are behind these unusual urban developments.

However, what is truly remarkable is the emergence of entire urban agglomerations that are totally or partially built and managed by nongovernment actors. These agglomerations bring together households and firms—that is, people and jobs, not just one side of the equation—which is the defining feature of cities. And they often do so on a scale without historic precedents in today's advanced economies.

An inventory of such unusual urban agglomerations was conducted for this book in four large developing countries—the Arab Republic of Egypt, India, Indonesia, and Pakistan. The exercise aimed at identifying all cities associated with at least one significant private actor with a footprint of at least 2.5 square kilometers and mixed land use. In all, 86 cities hosting 15.5 million people were uncovered, corresponding to 4 percent of all officially recognized cities in the four countries and 2 percent of their urban population.

The book also builds on a detailed review of 14 outstanding urban agglomerations associated with at least one significant private actor, from all around the developing world (figure O.1). Taken together, they account for 1 percent of all officially recognized cities in the 11 countries concerned, and for 0.6 percent of their urban population.

The 11 countries touched by this detailed review have different income levels, varied cultural backgrounds, and diverse political systems. The ubiquity of major urban agglomerations associated with at least one significant private actor suggests that their emergence responds to untapped urbanization needs more than to specific country characteristics.

Some of these outstanding urban agglomerations were associated with a major private company—similar to the company towns of advanced economies during the industrial revolution—or with a large developer. Others involved a complex interplay between local governments and significant private actors. Some emerged in response to the authorities' weak capacity or deliberate neglect, while others were the result of their strategic actions to crowd in large investors.

Several of them were the brainchild of a greater-than-life entrepreneur whose legacy carries into urbanization today. Some were initially run by corporations or through joint ventures with local governments. Yet others were managed by business or citizen associations, reminiscent of the trade guilds that used to run urban centers in medieval Europe.

During the emergence phase, significant private actors not only built residential or commercial structures: they assembled land on a large scale, drew plans for its use, built transport infrastructure, and even provided services to local households and firms, much the same as local governments would have been expected to do. Some of the

FIGURE O.1 **Selected outstanding urban agglomerations shaped by significant private actors in the developing world**

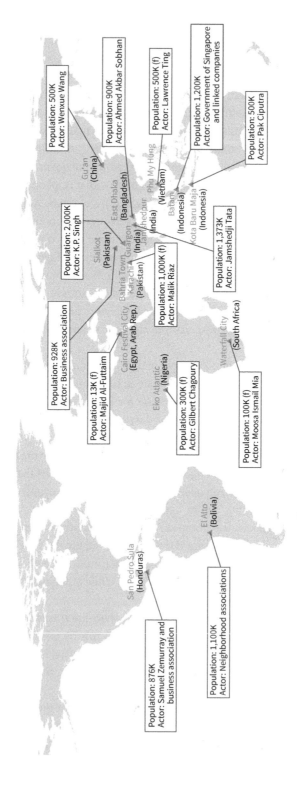

Population: 500K
Actor: Wenxue Wang

Population: 900K
Actor: Ahmed Akbar Sobhan

Population: 500K (f)
Actor: Lawrence Ting

Population: 1,200K
Actor: Government of Singapore and linked companies

Population: 500K
Actor: Pak Ciputra

Population: 2,000K
Actor: K.P. Singh

Population: 928K
Actor: Business association

Population: 13K (f)
Actor: Majid Al-Futtaim

Population: 1,000K (f)
Actor: Malik Riaz

Population: 1,373K
Actor: Jamshedji Tata

Population: 300K (f)
Actor: Gilbert Chagoury

Population: 100K (f)
Actor: Moosa Ismail Mia

Population: 876K
Actor: Samuel Zemurray and business association

Population: 1,100K
Actor: Neighborhood associations

Gu'an
(China)

East Dhaka
(Bangladesh)

Phu My Hong
(Vietnam)

Batam
(Indonesia)

Jamshedpur
(India)

Kota Baru Maja
(Indonesia)

Sialkot
(Pakistan)

Bahria Town
(Pakistan)

Gurgaon
(India)

Karachi

Cairo Festival City
(Egypt, Arab Rep.)

Eko Atlantic
(Nigeria)

Waterfall City
(South Africa)

San Pedro Sula
(Honduras)

El Alto
(Bolivia)

Source: Original figure for this book, based on chapters 9–22.
Note: K stands for thousand and (f) for forecasted.

significant private actors also went beyond the traditional functions of local govern-ments by embracing strategic economic development orientations for their cities or by influencing national governments and tilting public policies in their favor.

However, after a few decades, many of them became conventional cities run by a local government. Such institutional fluidity is not surprising, given that the very success of these unusual urban agglomerations ended up creating large political constituencies.

* * *

Major urban areas in whose development and management at least one significant nongovernment actor has played an important role are designated in what follows as *private cities*—the title of this book. The reference to major urban areas is intended to distinguish these agglomerations from gated communities, megaslums, industrial parks, and business improvement districts. The reference to a significant nongovern-ment actor, in turn, emphasizes that the agency behind the emergence of private cities is not exclusively—or not even mainly—associated with the public sector.

The term "private cities" itself is not new. It has been used before in relation to major urban agglomerations in India and even more broadly (Tabarrok and Rajagopalan 2015; Lutter 2014, respectively). However, its meaning, associated typolo-gies, and policy implications have remained relatively vague so far—knowledge gaps that this book tries to fill.

Some of the unusual urban agglomerations described above have also been dubbed *new cities*, in both Africa and Asia (van Noorloos and Kloosterboer 2018; Jo and Zheng 2020, respectively). The term fits well with an emerging trend in middle-income coun-tries, whereby local governments mobilize large developers in support of their urban-ization strategies. The implicit vision is one in which the design, construction, and potentially servicing of a city is outsourced, under well-specified terms, to a private actor that has a comparative advantage in spatial planning, finance mobilization, proj-ect implementation, and the like.

However, the term "new cities" could be too narrow. To begin with, not all large urban agglomerations built and managed by significant private actors are new; some of the 14 outstanding private cities mentioned above go back around one century, or even more. More importantly, many of these unusual urban agglomerations emerged because private actors took initiative on their own, with local governments being mostly reactive followers rather than strategic leaders.

Charter cities is another potentially relevant term in this context. The defining fea-ture of such cities is the introduction of local governance arrangements that differ from national laws, in a way that supports greater economic dynamism. For example, liti-gation on contract breaches in a charter city could, in principle, be conducted in the courts of an advanced economy (Fuller and Romer 2012).

Yet, using this term is problematic as well. The focus of the charter cities concept is on the legal or regulatory framework applying to the locality rather than on the pro-cess through which land is assembled, street layouts are designed, urban infrastructure is built, and local services are provided. And while some of the unusual urban agglomerations mentioned above do have idiosyncratic business regulations, they are not the norm.

Finally, these unusual urban agglomerations could also be called *competitive cities*, a term intended to capture a deliberate focus by local authorities on attracting, retaining, and supporting private sector firms (World Bank 2015). Cities built and managed by private actors with significant planning and implementation capacity clearly have an edge in this respect relative to the sprawling, congested, and messy cities that emerge when local governments are weak. Some of the private actors may even target specific firms or sectors of activity, tilting the local playing field as needed.

However, the term "competitive cities" may be questionable too. Some of the unusual urban agglomerations discussed above do have an explicit sectoral focus, but often the agents behind it are private actors, not local governments, as is assumed by the literature on competitive cities. And their decisions are closer to investment bets than to urban policy.

The term "private cities" is thus more accurate than new cities, charter cities, or competitive cities. It emphasizes the agency of significant nongovernment actors in urban development, rather than specific features, such as the strategic behavior of local governments, the exceptional nature of the legal framework, or the deliberate focus of local authorities on specific sectors of activity.

* * *

The term "private cities" may seem to clash with the generally accepted division of roles between government and markets in a modern economy, according to which the production of goods and services is better left to the private sector, whereas the public sector should play a coordinating role. Cities undoubtedly coordinate economic activity in a specific area, a typical government role. However, they are not very different in nature from a large firm. And as noted by Stiglitz (1977), a large firm can, in principle, do anything that a centralized government can do.

Analyzing the potential and pitfalls of private cities can therefore be interpreted in connection with a broader question that has motivated economic analysis for more than a century, namely whether administrative decisions or market mechanisms are more efficient in guiding resource allocation. The answer obviously depends on whether institutional failures or market imperfections are a greater concern. In the urban context, local externalities—known as agglomeration and congestion effects—are not just an interesting qualification of the market equilibrium but rather its very foundation. But in the case of developing countries, the weak capacity of local governments to plan, build, and service cities should also be factored in.

Simplifying, the government-versus-markets question has received three different answers, with their modern articulation taking shape roughly around the same time. The most widely accepted answer comes from welfare economics (Pigou 1932). In this approach, the government can ensure efficiency by taxing activities that generate negative externalities and subsidizing those with positive externalities. The government can also use tax revenue to modify the allocation of resources across agents in a way that is considered socially desirable—for instance, from rich to poor.

A fundamentally different answer comes from socialist economics (Lange and Taylor 1938). Instead of tilting prices through taxes and subsidies, the government could directly guide the allocation of resources across different uses in the same way a large firm would do it across departments or tasks. Industries could simply be nationalized, with central planners monitoring supply and demand through inventories for goods and capacity utilization for services. Proceeding this way would allow mimicking the outcomes of a market economy but also adjusting them to correct for socially undesirable effects.

Finally, a third answer comes from the law and economics approach (Coase 1937, 1960). In this case, the focus is on the compensatory payments needed to offset the externalities and make everybody better off. An easement is an obvious legal arrangement to consider in this respect, but other ways to trade property rights could work as well. Coase (1974) illustrated this point in his study of lighthouses, which seem ideally suited to the public sphere given the externalities involved. Yet, in nineteenth-century Great Britain—the greatest maritime power of the time—lighthouses were managed by the offspring of a medieval seamen's guild and funded through the collection of fees from ships docking at British ports.

These three approaches have radically different implications in the case of cities. In the socialist economics approach, land-use planning, infrastructure development, and the delivery of services would be entirely in the hands of central planners. In the welfare economics approach, a significant private actor—say, a large developer—could be in charge, provided that adequate subsidies and taxes align the actor's interests with those of society at large. And a nongovernment actor could hold the rights to the city in the law and economics approach, provided that the compensation it pays to acquire these rights is sufficient for no one else to be worse off.

These stark differences are often presented as a choice regarding the *size* of government, from very large in the socialist economics approach to minimal in the law and economics approach, with the welfare economics approach occupying an intermediate position. However, it is more accurate to say that the three approaches entail different *roles* for government.

In the welfare economics approach, the government essentially taxes and redistributes, with the tax code and the budget as its key tools to steer the economy. In the socialist economics approach, the government makes investment decisions and sets production plans, as the chief executive officer of a large firm would do. And in the law and economics approach, the government runs a judiciary system, one able to ensure that the social optimum can still be attained when bargaining between the parties fails.

Seen this way, the real choice is between the government as a regulator, as an entrepreneur, or as a judge. There may be questions on how effectively a bureaucracy can perform each of these three roles, and many would doubt that the government can be a successful entrepreneur—especially in developing countries. Yet, this is exactly what is expected in the urban context.

Indeed, standard urban policy recommendations are predicated on the assumption that cities are planned, built, and managed by local governments (O'Sullivan 2007). This assumption is understandable, given that modern constitutions typically subject each jurisdiction to one level of government. This is true both in advanced economies and in developing countries, and therefore, the policy messages are very similar in both cases (World Bank 2019). The received wisdom, is that it is up to local governments to assemble land, design urban layouts, build infrastructure, and provide services. It may not be by chance that key decision-makers at the local level are called urban planners, reminiscent of the central planners of the socialist economics approach.

However, in a world of imperfect tax instruments, ineffective public management, and weak property rights the urbanization process is more likely to result from varying mixes of public and private decisions. Understanding how such mixes work in practice is important because the resulting insights may help tailor urban policy recommendations to better offset the institutional failures and market imperfections of developing countries.

In the words of Coase (1960, 18), "economists need to study the work of the broker in bringing parties together, the effectiveness of restrictive covenants, the problems of the large-scale real estate development company, the operation of government zoning and other regulating activities."

An important hypothesis of the law and economics approach is that property rights evolve endogenously in response to the circumstances. In the presence of a large, untapped surplus, it is in the interest of the parties involved to establish property rights or introduce compensatory payments that reduce transaction costs to a point where all can benefit (Demsetz 1967).

Based on this hypothesis, innovative arrangements for city development are more likely in countries where the urbanization potential is sizeable, but local governments are weak. Private cities would thus be a manifestation of such innovative arrangements.

* * *

This book documents and analyzes the way outstanding private cities emerged in the developing world, how local governments and significant private actors interacted along the way, to what extent these cities generated a sizeable economic surplus, and how the surplus was shared among key stakeholders. It also considers the performance of private cities on key nonmonetary outcomes, including environmental degradation, social segregation, and institutional secession.

The book combines three methodological approaches to assemble the necessary evidence and make sense of it. First, a simple analytical framework treats the urban equilibrium characterizing a specific location as the outcome of a game between the local government and a significant private actor. The former is benevolent and seeks to maximize welfare, but its capacity to plan, build, and service a city is limited. The latter is technically competent, but its objectives are not aligned with those of society at large. The game can be played in different ways depending on whether decisions by the two actors are simultaneous or sequential.

Among other insights, this analytical component of the research yields an urban typology. At one end, a conventional city emerges when the capacity of the local government is high. At the other end, when its capacity is low, a company town—built and run by the private actor—may arise. In between these two polar cases, the locality may become a mixed city, where each of the two players develops urban land on its own.

Or it can be a strategic city, in which the local government deliberately crowds in the more capable private actor.

The second methodological approach used in the book is the already-mentioned assembly of four country-level inventories of private cities. These inventories reveal that in all four countries, there are cities whose development was shaped by at least one significant private actor, although their relative importance and characteristics vary. The inventories also confirm the relevance of the urban typology emerging from the analytical framework. Indeed, some of their entries can be characterized as company towns and a few as strategic cities. Most of them are mixed cities, hence intrinsically messy.

The most important contribution of the book arguably stems from its third methodological approach, the detailed review of the experience of 14 outstanding private cities from 11 developing countries, also mentioned above. For each of these outstanding private cities, a snapshot is assembled using the same template. The snapshot provides background information on the relevant private actor, describes its interaction with the government, characterizes the location and connectivity of the private city, lists the key milestones in its development, chronicles how its institutional status evolved, describes the land assembly process, assesses the city's performance across monetary and nonmonetary outcomes, and analyzes how land value was captured by key stakeholders.

Whereas the concrete circumstances surrounding the emergence of these outstanding private cities were diverse, four conditions were always met. First, their location was particularly advantageous, especially in terms of access to markets. The median population of the closest major agglomeration is 14.8 million, and the median distance to it is barely 33 kilometers. Second, in almost all cases, the capacity of the local government was weak, if not necessarily in absolute terms, at least compared to that of the significant private actor (figure O.2, panel a). Third, the latter was never an ordinary player. Depending on the case, greater-than-life entrepreneurs, companies with innovative business models and capacity to implement at scale, or unusually cohesive associations were involved (figure O.2, panel b). And, finally, there was an institutional environment that allowed the emergence of a private city.

At the same time, the significant private actors behind these outstanding private cities did not always take on all the traditional functions of a local government. Based on standard urban recommendations, local authorities are supposed to assemble land, improve transport connectivity, decide on land use, and deliver urban services. Depending on their goals, private actors performed only some of these functions. On the other hand, several of them went further and took on unconventional roles, such as being an industrial champion to attract business to the city or a political actor to tilt policies and public investments to the city's advantage (figure O.2, panel c).

Despite this diversity of functions, the outstanding private cities reviewed tend to be more dynamic than their conventional city counterparts. Many of them display a strong performance relative to other cities within their countries, including above-average population growth, income per capita, or export volumes. Some of them also have better urban amenities and are overall more livable. Improved economic opportunities and in some cases higher livability typically result in higher land prices.

FIGURE O.2 **Main features of selected outstanding private cities in the developing world**

a. Characteristics of the local government

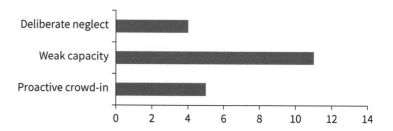

b. Characteristics of the private actor

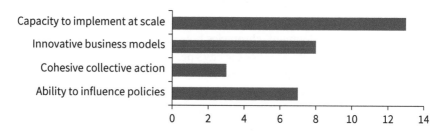

c. Functions taken on by the private actor

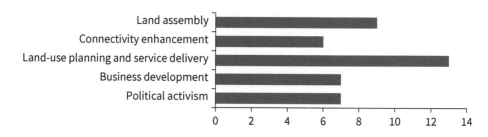

d. Land value capture mechanisms

Source: Original figure for this book, based on chapters 9–22
Note: Numbers indicate how many of the 14 outstanding cities reviewed in this book match each category.

One important question is who captured the land value appreciation triggered by the development of outstanding private cities? Some of the economic surplus generated by the urbanization process ended up in the hands of the significant private actors involved, as seizing as much of it as possible was presumably their main objective.

Governments also captured some of the gains, with taxation as their main instrument to do so. However, it is worth noting that general taxes raised from the city were a much more significant source of revenue than property taxes raised from its landowners. Land value capture by the government also relied on the direct sale of land concessions to significant private actors. And in some cases, it involved the creation of joint ventures with them to develop the cities and share the proceeds.

Some of the land value generated by these private cities was directly appropriated by key stakeholders, without government intervention. In some cases, private actors allowed the traditional villages of the area to remain in the private cities so that they could benefit from the overall land appreciation around them. In others, they invited the original residents to convert their land into shares of the urban development projects being implemented. Direct land value capture also happened spontaneously on the fringes of private cities, as their economic dynamism led to higher land prices—and even to new urban developments—in the surrounding areas.

Finally, there were also cases in which land value capture was the subject of social conflict. General strikes, court litigation, and defaults on obligations ended up shifting the distribution of the economic surplus generated by specific private cities (figure O.2, panel d).

While the economic performance of the outstanding private cities from developing countries reviewed in this book is generally strong, their nonmonetary outcomes are more mixed. Environmental sustainability is not always assured, with uncoordinated profit-seeking even creating serious disaster risks. There is also social tension from well-functioning private cities that cater to higher income groups but are segregated from their poorer and messier surroundings. In some cases, private cities directly eschew democratic governance, enforcing regulations that are not supported by the country's legal environment or violating constitutional freedoms and rights.

* * *

This book does not advocate for private cities. It only brings to the surface and carefully documents a reality that has been mostly ignored by urban economics. In doing so, the book shows that major urban agglomerations associated with at least one significant private actor have become a fact of life in the developing world. The question then is what, if anything, should governments do in relation to them? At this stage, the answer is bound to be tentative. However, several important insights emerge from combining the three methodological approaches used in this book.

The simple analytical framework proposed allows not only the identification of what kind of city emerges in a specific context but also how far that city is from the ideal urbanization that local circumstances would allow. While the empirical review shows that private cities tend to have sizeable populations and be economically dynamic, their locations could well support an even larger number of inhabitants and a stronger overall performance. Conceptually deriving this ideal benchmark makes it possible to assess whether private cities lead to efficient urbanization.

The answer is no. The analytical framework shows that private cities do not generate as much economic surplus as would be socially optimal. This is because the objectives of the private actor are different from those of society at large. The private actor wants to maximize the profit it derives from urbanization, not the overall surplus of the locality. Such profit depends on the price of urban land, which is determined by the output the last developed plot generates. Aiming for a bigger city would thus increase the supply of land and reduce the price of all the plots the private actor had previously developed. Much the same as a monopolist maximizes its profit by producing less output than is socially optimal, a significant private actor maximizes its profit by not developing the socially optimal amount of urban land.

Additional sources of inefficiency are at play when the local government also develops urban land, as in mixed cities and strategic cities. Weak government capacity implies that the economic surplus per unit of urban land is lower when the public sector is the developer instead of the private sector. The bigger the share of the city the government develops, the lower the average surplus per unit of land. And then, on top of that, the noncooperative nature of the interaction between the two players makes the problem worse, as the sum of the amounts of urban land each of them wants to develop generally differs from the socially optimal amount of urban land.

The simple analytical framework proposed in this book also allows simulating how changes in the values of key parameters would affect the surplus of the locality. In particular, it shows that just building government capacity—the standard urban policy recommendation—may not lead to better local outcomes. Indeed, with an increased ability to assemble land, conduct urban planning, build infrastructure, and provide services, a local government may be able to develop more urban land and do it better than before. But as long as the quality of public urban land is lower than that of private urban land, the net outcome could be a lower economic surplus of the locality, despite a potentially bigger city.

The analytical framework also shows that banning significant private actors from participating in the urbanization process could be counterproductive too. In countries where local government capacity is very low, localities with a substantial urbanization potential could remain rural. Private cities may have serious shortcomings, but no urbanization at all is arguably an even worse outcome.

Taken together, the insights from this book suggest that a different approach is needed to improve urbanization outcomes in developing countries. In this new approach, the role of urban authorities must be broadened, from planning, building, and servicing cities to also regulating, incentivizing, and overseeing large private actors with the technical expertise and coordination capacity that is needed to deliver. But which instruments to use in practice would very much depend on the circumstances.

In some cases, local governments may themselves lead the urban development process, as in the socialist economics approach. In others, they may use subsidies and taxes to align the incentives of a significant private actor with those of society at large, as in the welfare economics approach. And yet in others, they may allocate total or partial rights to the city, in line with the law and economics approach.

If—and only if—involving a significant private actor is deemed appropriate, then a deal in the spirit of a public-private partnership (PPP) for urban development could be considered. As in other agreements of this sort, it is essential to agree on the functions and responsibilities of the two parties. It is also important to allocate the returns—in this case, to structure the land value capture—in a way that incentivizes not only the private actor to do its part but also benefits all other key stakeholders. And specific incentives and regulations are needed to address the environmental, social, and governance downsides potentially associated with private cities.

Some of the biggest challenges in designing PPPs for urban development stem from their potential time inconsistency. Contracts may be written, but not all contingencies may be foreseen, not all quality issues can be specified, and strict enforcement may not be feasible. Over the long course of city development, the government may not deliver on its commitments, may withdraw its support for the private city approach, or could even seize urban assets. Conversely, the private actor may free ride on public goods provided by the government or underinvest in public goods needed for an efficient city to emerge.

The magnitude of the sunk investments associated with a large city and the uncertainty on whether it will be successful, amplify the time-inconsistency challenges normally associated with PPPs. This may explain why there are not more private cities in the developing world.

More research is needed on the mechanisms that would allow governments to contract out urban development in ways that are both incentive compatible and socially desirable. But in the meantime, insights from this book can be used to guide decisions in this respect. Those insights can be organized under the form of a protocol (box O.1).

The steps in this protocol will certainly have to be refined as more research becomes available. For now, however, they may provide a useful checklist to decision-makers in developing countries. And in doing so, they may stimulate a rich debate on urban policies, regardless of whether in the end significant private actors are mobilized or not.

Beyond the specifics, private cities should only be seen as one more instrument in the urban policy toolkit. This instrument is more likely to be useful when the capacity of the local government to steer the urbanization process is low and when significant private actors with sufficient expertise and integrity can be mobilized for the task. Even so, private cities are bound to have downsides and not only upsides. Minimizing the former and maximizing the latter should be a central objective of a government that considers using this alternative instrument.

BOX O.1 **A tentative protocol for urban policy in relation to private cities**

The implications of the analyses in this book can be organized under the form of a series of sequential questions, as follows:

1. *LOCATION POTENTIAL. Does the area or jurisdiction considered have characteristics that make it especially well suited for urban development?*

   Such characteristics may include the availability of natural resources of particular interest for some sectors of activity or natural scenery that makes it a touristic asset. Most importantly, the location needs to be well connected to a major urban agglomeration. If such is not the case, there is a risk that a private city in that area or jurisdiction will become a white elephant.

2. *PRIVATE ACTORS. Are there firms or associations with the technical expertise, coordination capacity, and business integrity to be entrusted with the development of the locality?*

   The capacity of the private actors who could conduct spatial planning, build connecting infrastructure, and deliver urban services should be substantially higher than that of the local government. They should also have a track record of delivering at scale and not be suspected of corrupt practices or political tinkering. Actors not meeting these criteria should be ruled out.

3. *GOVERNMENT FUNCTIONS. Where does the comparative advantage of the identified private actor lie relative to the local government?*

   To develop a city, it is necessary to assemble land, build connecting infrastructure, and deliver urban services. Technical and institutional constraints may result in one of the two players being better placed than the other to take on each of these functions. This comparative advantage should guide the allocation of responsibilities for urban development.

4. *LAND VALUE CAPTURE. How will the economic surplus generated by the city be distributed among key stakeholders?*

   Building the right type of city must be profitable for the private actor, and the local government may have to provide additional incentives to that effect. But the surplus generated by urbanization must benefit society at large. General taxation, land concessions, or a joint venture with the private actor can be used as tools for land value capture and redistribution.

5. *INCENTIVES AND REGULATION. Could the allocation of key functions to the private actor result in environmental damage, social exclusion, or institutional secession?*

   If so, mechanisms should be found to align the incentives of the private actor with those of society at large. Such mechanisms may take the form of mandates, for example in relation to environmental protection or individual freedoms. They could also take the form of economic incentives such as subsidies for affordable housing.

(Box continues on next page)

BOX O.1 **A tentative protocol for urban policy in relation to private cities** (continued)

6. *CONTRACT ENFORCEMENT. Could the private actor default on its commitments or be reluctant to engage because the local government cannot credibly commit?*

Even well-specified contracts may not foresee all the uncertainties related to urban development or be robust enough to deter opportunistic behavior by the signing parties. Specifying credible mechanisms for the settlement of disputes and possibly involving reputable foreign partners—such as cities from more advanced economies or international financial institutions—may help.

References

Coase, Ronald Harry. 1937. "The Nature of the Firm." *Economica* 4 (16): 386–405.

Coase, Ronald Harry. 1960. "The Problem of Social Cost." In *Classic Papers in Natural Resource Economics,* edited by Chennat Gopalakrishnan, 87–137. London: Palgrave Macmillan.

Coase, Ronald Harry. 1974. "The Lighthouse in Economics." *Journal of Law and Economics* 17 (2): 357–76.

Demsetz, Harold. 1967. "Towards a Theory of Property Rights." *American Economic Review* 57 (2): 347–59.

Duranton, Gilles, and Diego Puga. 2020. "The Economics of Urban Density." *Journal of Economic Perspective* 34 (3): 3–26.

Ellis, Peter, and Mark Roberts. 2016. *Leveraging Urbanization in South Asia: Managing Spatial Transformation for Prosperity and Livability*. Washington, DC: World Bank.

Ferreyra, María Marta, and Mark Roberts, eds. 2018. *Raising the Bar for Productive Cities in Latin America and the Caribbean*. Washington, DC: World Bank.

Fuller, Brandon, and Paul Romer. 2012. *Success and the City: How Charter Cities Could Transform the Developing World*. Ottawa: Macdonald-Laurier Institute for Public Policy.

Henderson, J. Vernon, and Randy Becker. 2000. "Political Economy of City Sizes and Formation." *Journal of Urban Economics* 48 (3): 453–84.

Jo, Angie, and Siqi Zheng. 2020. "New Planned Cities as Economic Engines: Global Trend and Our Conceptual Framework." In *Toward Urban Economic Vibrancy: Patterns and Practices in Asia's New Cities,* edited by Siqi Zheng and Zhengzhen Tan. Cambridge, MA: Massachusetts Institute of Technology.

Lall, Somik Vinay, Vernon J. Henderson, and Anthony J. Venables. 2017. *Africa's Cities: Opening Doors to the World*. Washington, DC: World Bank.

Lall, Somik, Mathilde Lebrand, Hogeun Park, Daniel Sturm, and Anthony Venables. 2021. *Pancakes to Pyramids: City Form to Promote Sustainable Growth*. Washington, DC: World Bank.

Lange, Oskar, and Fred M. Taylor. 1938. *On the Economic Theory of Socialism*. Government Control of the Economic Order, vol. 2. Edited by Benjamin E. Lippincott. New York: University of Minnesota Press.

López-de-Silanes, Florencio. 1997. "Determinants of Privatization Prices." *Quarterly Journal of Economics* 112 (4): 965–1025.

Lutter, Mark. 2014. "Private Cities 101." Foundation for Economic Education, Atlanta, GA, June 11, 2014.

O'Sullivan, Arthur. 2007. *Urban Economics*. Chicago, IL: Irwin-McGraw-Hill.

Pigou, A. Cecil. 1932. *The Economics of Welfare*. London: Macmillan.

Roberts, Mark, Frederico Gil Sander, and Sailesh Tiwari. 2019. *Time to ACT: Realizing Indonesia's Urban Potential*. Washington DC: World Bank.

Stiglitz, Joseph E. 1977. "The Theory of Local Public Goods." In *The Economics of Public Services*, 274–333. London: Palgrave Macmillan.

Tabarrok, Alex, and Shruti Rajagopalan. 2015. "Designing Private Cities, Open to All." *New York Times*, March 16, 2015.

United Nations. 2018. *World Urbanization Prospects: The 2018 Revision*. United Nations Department of Economic and Social Affairs, Population Division, Online Edition. https:// population.un.org/wup/Download. Reported as of February 11, 2019.

Van Noorloos, Femke, and Marjan Kloosterboer. 2018. "Africa's New Cities: The Contested Future of Urbanisation." *Urban Studies* 55 (6): 1223–41.

World Bank. 2015. *Competitive Cities for Jobs and Growth: What, Who, and How*. Washington, DC: World Bank.

World Bank. 2019. "Urban Development," accessed February 11, 2019. http://www.worldbank .org/en/topic/urbandevelopment/overview#2.

Part I: The reality of private cities and its policy implications

Yue Li, Martin Rama, and Virgilio Galdo

CHAPTER 1

Empirical regularities from a global review

The applied research available on urban agglomerations shaped by large private actors refers mostly to advanced economies and especially to the United States. A review of such research was commissioned for this book (Cheng 2020). Together with more descriptive work by urban planners, urban sociologists, and journalists, such review serves as the basis for a brief account of the role played by private cities in the development of today's advanced economies.

The history of private cities in developing countries is less well documented and analyzed. Their disclosure of land records, development plans, and infrastructure projects is more limited than that of conventional cities. Private cities also interact less frequently with government budget offices, national development banks, and multilateral development agencies, which are among the most reliable oversight mechanisms in low- and middle-income countries.

Advanced economies

Active private participation in urban development has a long history, and significant precedents can be found in today's advanced economies. Together with organic city formation and government-driven urban development projects, these outstanding private cities have shaped the urban landscape as it is known today. Some of these important precedents have stood the test of time and remain a source of economic dynamism. Others have become conventional cities but are still admired for what they accomplished when they were run for private gain.

In medieval times, *merchant and craft guilds* played a critical role in the economy of cities (Jacobs 1969). Societies of businesspeople held exclusive rights on doing business in these cities. For example, since the end of the Roman period, the city of Paris was run by the Seine River boatmen's corporation, a powerful guild that resembled a municipal government more than a trade. The motto of the corporation, 'fluctuat nec mergitur' (tossed by the waves but not sinking), remains emblazoned in the city's coat of arms to this day, together with the image of a medieval boat (Hillairet 1977).

This often-underplayed history has carried over to modern times. For example, the primary decision-making body for London's financial district, in the United Kingdom, is the Court of Common Council, whose members must belong to the Guild of Freemen of the City of London. Additionally, its Lord Mayor and its Sheriffs must be elected by the liverymen, who must belong to the Guild as well (City of London 2018; The Guild of Freemen of the City of London, n.d.).

The *garden city movement* also provides some early examples of private cities. The concept of a garden city was developed and advocated in the late nineteenth century by social reformer Ebenezer Howard. A garden city was both a method of urban planning and a system of community management. Its goal was to promote orderly, self-contained communities that would contain proportionate areas of residences, industry, and agriculture and be located in a greenbelt of open countryside. The concept also included a "rate-rent" system to finance the city (Howard 1898). This system combined financing for community services (rates) with a return for those who had invested in the development of the city (rent).

The first two garden cities in the world, Letchworth and Welwyn, were founded by Ebenezer Howard in the UK through private finance and were managed by private entities for decades (figure 1.1). Both are small cities with 30,000–40,000 inhabitants on less than 20 square kilometers of land in Hertfordshire, England, within the 50-kilometer ring of London. In order to attract investors to buy land and to create the first garden city of Letchworth, Howard founded the Garden Cities Association, which created First Garden City, Ltd. Professional planners were hired through a competition on the town design.

Letchworth was built with the town in the center, surrounded by a large greenbelt, exactly as Howard envisaged in his books. The city slowly attracted residents who were mostly skilled middle-class workers. Industry was also slow to arrive but gradually reached a large scale. Eventually, Letchworth became profitable, and after a decade or so it started paying dividends to its investors. The management of Letchworth has remained under a private entity handling many planning and grant-making functions. An elected local government body has existed separately from the private entity, complementing it on the governance front (International Garden Cities Institute, n.d.; Letchworth Garden City Heritage Foundation, n.d.).

Company towns are the most straightforward example of urban development entirely led by a private actor. A company town is a place where the main employer owns the land, builds the infrastructure, develops almost all commercial and residential housing

FIGURE 1.1 **Private cities in advanced economies: Letchworth Garden City, United Kingdom**

Source: © Air Video UK/Alamy Stock Photo. Used with permission of Alamy Stock Photo. Further permission required for reuse.

stocks, and requires its employees to reside. Such urban settings were common during the Industrial Revolution in the US, the UK, and other parts of Europe. At one point, there were reportedly over 2,500 company towns in the US alone (Crawford 1995; Garner 1992).

Early mining camps and villages were the first incarnations of company towns. Driven by the geographic distribution of mining resources, mining sites were remote and often in the wild. The logic of building mining company camps and villages was to provide housing and living amenities to attract sufficient labor to the area. However, both housing and amenities were quite primitive. For example, in the US most early coal mining company towns were characterized by uniformity and repetition in town plans and workers' housing (Metheny 2007; Sharpless and Miller 1985).

Model company towns emerged in the late nineteenth century, reflecting the paternalistic views—and at times, the utopian aspirations—of the industrial champions behind them. These model towns usually consisted of both factories and dwellings. They were characterized by their systematic planning and fast execution and were financed by a single investor. Outstanding examples include Hershey (chocolate) in Pennsylvania and Morgan Park (steel) in Minnesota.

One of the largest and most significant company towns was developed in the 1880s by George Pullman for his railroad car company, just outside the city of Chicago (figure 1.2). In addition to increasing production capacity by building a new factory, Pullman wanted to use his model company town to instill in workers his vision of a paternalistic American society. He quietly acquired land near Lake Calumet and assigned it to his company's subsidiary, the Pullman Land Association. Professional architects were hired to plan and implement the town development.

Land and buildings were entirely owned by the company, which provided housing, markets, a library, churches, and entertainment for its 6,000 employees and their dependents. Employees were required to live in the town as renters. George Pullman firmly believed that he had brought tangible improvements to his employees' lives by providing comfortable rowhouses, investing in amenities such as gas, roads, water and sewers, and setting high behavioral standards. It was reported about this model company town that even before Pullman's first residents settled in 1881, visitors came to admire its beauty, which stood in stark contrast to other working-class areas in industrial cities, and to marvel at the success of its social planning (Ely 1885).

Over time, the declining profitability of the Pullman company as the automobile revolution gained momentum, together with a series of labor strikes, led to a state Supreme Court order requesting that the company divest itself of residential property. The town became another Chicago neighborhood by the end of the first decade of the twentieth century (Buder 1967; Electronic Encyclopedia

FIGURE 1.2 **Private cities in advanced economies: The Pullman company town, United States**

Source: Chicago History Museum, https://commons.wikimedia.org/wiki/File:Greenstone_and_Arcade_Pullman.jpg.

of Chicago 2022; Ely 1885; Historic Pullman Foundation 2022; Scarlett and Walton 2017).

The decline of the Pullman company town was not exceptional. Advances in transportation technology and improvements in social welfare systems gradually reduced the relevance of model company towns in the US. Some still remain, such as Hershey Chocolate company town, where many properties are still controlled by Hershey School Trust, and Walt Disney World, established and still run by the Walt Disney Company.

However, in most cases, governments eventually took control of city management, even if the fate of these former company towns continued to depend on that of their founding companies for decades. For example, after all residential properties were sold to its employees by the United States Steel company in 1947, the residents of Morgan Park remained dependent on the employment opportunities the company provided until it shut in 1971 (Alanen 2007; Kurie 2018).

Edge cities are a more modern form of private-led urban development that emerged in the late twentieth century. Around 1990 there were 123 established and 77 emerging edge cities in the largest metropolitan areas of the US. By then, more people lived in these places than in traditional city cores. The edge cities in this count met the following criteria: 465,000 square meters of leasable office space or more; 56,000 square meters of retail space or more, more offices than bedrooms, a local perception as a single end-destination for mixed use, and a history in which the site was overwhelmingly residential or rural in character three decades earlier (Garreau 1992; Jonas 2003; Stanback 1991). Similar urban areas outside of city cores also emerged during the same period in Europe (Bontje and Burdack 2005).

These large urban areas outside of core cities are organized around vast tracts of mixed-use land, often developed by a single, large private actor. In the words of Henderson and Mitra (1996, 613), they "are complete cities, offering jobs, residences, shopping and services for their inhabitants. They are not simply bedroom communities or a product of urban decentralization and sprawl. They are the creation of strategically controlled office development, by large-scale developers."

At least in the early phases, the edge cities of the US were most often the out-come of market forces rather than government intervention. The land was usually privately owned, leading to unincorporated areas with no political representation. This reality substantiated the claim that "there is no zoning, only deals" (Bontje and Burdack 2005).

Like model company towns, many edge cities reflect the vision of a single person or a single family. For example, significant portions of the Washington, DC, metropolitan area, including Crystal City and Tyson's Corner, were developed by John T. "Til" Hazel (Hiatt 1983). Because of the personal imprint he left on the spatial configuration of the nation's capital, Hazel has been compared with Pierre L'Enfant, who designed the original street layout of the city (Garreau 1991). Today, both Crystal City and Tyson's Corner are vibrant urban centers in their own right (figure 1.3).

FIGURE 1.3 Private cities in advanced economies: Crystal City, Tyson's Corner, and Reston edge cities, United States

a. Crystal City

b. Tyson's Corner

c. Reston

Sources: Panel a: Carol M. Highsmith, photographer. Retrieved from Library of Congress, https://www.loc.gov/item/2011633695/. Panel b: © Rob Crandall/Alamy Stock Photo. Used with permission of Alamy Stock Photo. Further permission required for reuse. Panel c: © La Citta Vita is licenced under CC BY-SA 2.0, https://commons.wikimedia.org/wiki/File:Aerial_shot_of_Tysons_Corner,_Virginia_2010.jpg.

Recently, Amazon selected Crystal City as the site of its second headquarters out of an open competition among over 200 urban agglomerations in Canada, Mexico, and the US.

Another case in point is Reston, the largest edge city in the Washington, DC, metropolitan area. Reston's development was guided by the "live, work, play" principles articulated by Robert Simon Jr. in the 1960s. These principles emphasize mixed-use, mixed-density, and flexible development. The land was originally privately owned and was purchased by Simon from the Bowman family. The urban layout was designed by professional planners. Simon also provided financing in the early stages. Later, due to financial constraints, the city project and management were transferred several times, but they have always been under private control, with Reston remaining an unincorporated area in Fairfax County. Today, Reston provides abundant employment opportunities—management, scientific, and financial services are its core businesses—and offers many public amenities to its residents and visitors (figure 1.3).

Finally, private cities in advanced economies are also associated with NIMBY-ism, with the abbreviation standing for "Not in My Backyard"—a term used to describe the ability of local communities to block initiatives that are desirable for society at large. Saclay, in France, meets this description. An agricultural plateau that is just 30 minutes away from downtown Paris by car and surrounded by urbanized valleys, the Saclay area hosts roughly 800,000 inhabitants.

Saclay's rural nature is a legacy of the massive hydrological works undertaken in the seventeenth century to fetch water to the fountains of the nearby Versailles palace. Canals and drainage boosted agricultural productivity, with the byproduct being a dozen farming families powerful enough to block urbanization. The success of this group was reflected in a 2013 parliament decision to protect 41 square kilometers of land in the area, of which 24 were to be exclusively devoted to agriculture (figure 1.4).

The availability of land attracted a scientific community that was increasingly living nearby, thanks to a nineteenth-century train line that connected the south of the plateau to the left bank of Paris, where some of the country's top tertiary education institutions sit. Saclay's development started in earnest after World War II, with the establishment of France's atomic research center. But over time, a myriad of universities, elite schools, corporate research centers, and biotech firms followed (Cheng 2020). Some are public or semipublic; many are private. Collectively, these institutions account for 15 percent of France's research output, both public and private. Since the 1960s they have jointly won two Nobel Prizes in physics, seven Field Medals in mathematics, and one Turing Award in computer science (Veltz 2015).

However, the Saclay area is not a city, but rather 49 juxtaposed communes, each one fully empowered to decide on territorial matters affecting it. Attempts to coordinate these communes have been numerous, with 10 of them getting together in 1991, 9 in

FIGURE 1.4 **Private cities in advanced economies: Research campuses in Saclay, France**

Source: Desvigne, Geyter, and Askemade 2009.

2002, 14 in 2007, and 18 in 2010. But not much came of these efforts. And in the meantime, NIMBY-ism managed to block the development of a major satellite city north of the plateau, the construction of an expressway intended to connect Paris to the south of France, and the building of several light train and metro lines.

The justification for the opposition to these projects was the fear of unchecked urbanization. As a result, however, no direct public transport connection to downtown Paris exists or is even planned. At some point, the atomic research center was running 92 private bus lines. And even today, private cars remain the most convenient way to get there. As noted by Veltz (2015, 104), "there is a clear contrast between the success of labs and the scientific community, which confirms its power, and the collective failure of institutions."

Confronted with this reality, in 2010 France's government decided to treat Saclay as a strategic priority, regrouping 27 of its communes under a task force, with a CEO appointed by the nation's president for a period of five years. The proposed institutional arrangement was criticized as antidemocratic during its discussion in parliament.

Saclay's CEO has no power to affect planning decisions by the 27 communes but counts with a budget of about US$2 billion for strategic investments in the area, including 1.7 million square meters of office and housing space. In his own words, "the context is that of what exists, a network of sites that can only function as an archipelago: sites that are very leafy but not very lively because of their low density and poor connectivity to cities" (Veltz 2015, 132). With the rise of NIMBY-ism, other private cities like Saclay could gradually emerge in advanced economies.

Developing countries

To address the limited information available on private cities in developing countries, detailed reviews of 14 of them were conducted for this book. Spanning 11 countries across all developing regions, these are significant cities (some very large) whose development was shaped by at least one significant private actor (figure 1.5). The reviews are presented in the form of snapshots in the second part of this volume, using a standardized format that facilitates comparative analysis. Despite being cursory, these snapshots yield important insights.

Much the same as advanced economies during the Industrial Revolution, developing countries host *urban agglomerations developed without much government participation*. Thus, the steel company town of Jamshedpur was founded in 1907 in the backwaters of eastern India by Jamshedji Tata, an entrepreneur often referred to as the father of Indian industry. From being an experiment in green and social urbanism, Jamshedpur evolved into a large-scale, award-winning city. Along the way, its economic activity diversified from steel to other sectors but always in connection with Jamshedji Tata's group of companies. To this day Jamshedpur is yet to be run by a local government (chapter 15).

San Pedro Sula, the second largest city in Honduras, also started developing a century ago, in this case as a byproduct of investments in land clearance and railway infrastructure by Samuel Zemurray, a US entrepreneur. His fruit-processing company had been granted a vast agricultural area in concession by a president that he had helped establish by funding mercenaries and staging a coup, coining by the same token the expression "banana republic." Over time, local industrialists became the key players, leveraging national economic reforms to transform what was by then a declining plantation town into Central America's biggest manufacturing hub (chapter 13).

Some private cities have been driven by citizens' associations, reminiscent of the trade guilds that used to run urban centers in medieval Europe. El Alto in Bolivia was a mostly rural highland until the mid-twentieth century, when large numbers of mostly indigenous migrants—displaced by land reform first and then by the downsizing of state-owned tin mines—started settling in. This spontaneous urbanization, driven by the proximity of the capital city, was neglected by the authorities. Yet a vibrant civil society led to the creation of hundreds of neighborhood associations that fought, sometimes literally, for better urban services and economic opportunities, in a context of interethnic tensions (chapter 10).

Over time, however, it is large developers who have become the key private actors. Malik Riaz is one of Pakistan's biggest real estate investors. After having successfully built several large-scale gated communities, in 2015 his company launched the construction of Bahria Town Karachi. With a surface larger than Manhattan, at the edge of one of the biggest agglomerations in the world, this private city could host one million

FIGURE 1.5 **Selected outstanding private cities in developing countries**

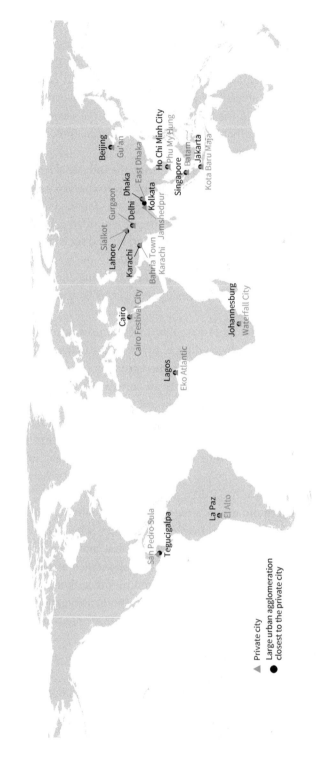

Source: Original figure for this book, based on chapters 9–22.

people. Its developer has unusual planning and implementation autonomy and a strong track record in providing high-quality urban amenities, but its land assembly methods have been controversial (chapter 19).

Eko Atlantic in Nigeria is associated with a large developer too. Currently being built on a vast reclaimed peninsula off the coast of sprawling Lagos, Eko Atlantic aspires to be a tidy, Dubai-style city. Its name evokes ecology in reference to the project's massive oceanic wall to stop coastal erosion, a feature that has earned it international recognition. The private actor in this case is Gilbert Chagoury, a well-connected Nigerian entrepreneur with Lebanese roots. Planning and building are in the hands of a Chinese construction firm specializing in dredging and landfilling. By contrast, involvement by local authorities has been minimal (chapter 18).

Some outstanding private cities in developing countries have resulted from *a complex interplay between local governments and large private actors*. Sialkot, also in Pakistan, was a well-known manufacturing center for centuries and became a city under British rule. But its economic activity collapsed with the partition of the subcontinent, and its proximity to India made the national government reluctant to invest in it. Since then, a remarkably cohesive business community took charge of urban development, building major infrastructure—including an international airport and a dry port—and transforming the city into one of Pakistan's most important economic hubs (chapter 20).

East Dhaka, in Bangladesh, is a vast area next to the city center that is flood-prone; a planned embankment was never built by the authorities, and water retention canals and ponds were neglected. Urbanization there is thus proceeding through sand-filling by large developers, with the powerful real estate group founded by Ahmed Akbar Sobhan in the lead. Its project not only offers residential accommodation for the upper-middle class but also is home to hospitals, universities, and other services with high value added. The economic potential of East Dhaka's organic urbanization is thus significant but so are earthquake risks with a loose and segregated soil structure (chapter 9).

Economic potential has undoubtedly been realized already in the case of Gurgaon, a major urban agglomeration outside India's capital city. With a fully privately financed metro, gleaming skyscrapers, and shopping malls, Gurgaon has indeed become a major hub of information technology and an aspirational destination for India's fast-growing middle class. Its emergence was associated with K.P. Singh, a large developer who seized the opportunities created by the unusual territorial development policies of the host state—opportunities that were not available in Delhi itself. K.P. Singh was also instrumental in attracting major foreign investors to outsource their business operations to India and settle in Gurgaon (chapter 14).

The interplay between local governments and private actors is often shaped by political developments. The emergence of Waterfall City, South Africa's largest private real estate project, is linked to Apartheid and its demise. In the 1930s Moosa Ismail Mia managed to assemble and then retain a vast amount of land next to Johannesburg, despite being a non-White migrant from India. The urban potential of the area increased significantly after Apartheid ended, as crime rates surged in cities while new major connectivity investments were being made to counter race-based spatial segregation. Waterfall City tapped this potential through a "basket of rights" negotiated with the city of Johannesburg (chapter 21).

In Indonesia, similarly, the rapid growth of Kota Baru Maja owes much to the "big bang" decentralization policies of the late 1990s and early 2000s. The new local governments recognized the role the private sector could play in urban development, but they were also supported by nationwide urban policies mandating service provision by large developers and helping keep housing affordable. In Kota Baru Maja's case, Pak Ciputra—a major developer with projects in multiple countries—managed to build a city across three districts in two provinces, an institutional challenge that the corresponding local governments would have had trouble addressing (chapter 17).

Finally, other outstanding private cities in the developing world involve a *deliberate crowding in of private investments by the government*, for strategic reasons. One of the precursors of this approach was Batam, a large Indonesian island city across from Singapore. The government had initially handed the responsibility to boost its development to a large state-owned enterprise, but progress was limited. In 1989, Singapore's government made the case that Batam was ideally suited to accommodate its industrial parks. An agreement was reached whereby companies affiliated with the Singaporean government would be in charge of master plans and overall industrial park development, whereas the Indonesian government would contribute infrastructure investments and ensure regulatory certainty (chapter 16).

Almost at the same time, Vietnam was embarking on the transition from socialist planning to market economy. Leading reformers were keen to test the possibilities opened by new land-use rights. Their focus was Phu My Hung, a salted marshland at the edge of Ho Chi Minh City that had been left mostly untouched due to a strong Vietcong presence during the Vietnam War. After several false starts, in 1991 a deal was reached with Lawrence Ting, a businessman from Taiwan, China, in whose company the Kuomintang had a stake. Under its terms, his company would build key infrastructure and develop Phu My Hung into a full-fledged city, one that is nowadays touted as an urban model in Vietnam (chapter 22).

The legal framework to involve large developers in urban development had been introduced in the Arab Republic of Egypt as early as 1979. The approach was viable thanks to the availability of large tracts of government-owned desert land, but it only gained momentum with the market-oriented reforms the government embraced in the 1990s. In the year 2000, a decree was issued to develop Cairo Festival City on the outskirts of the nation's capital. The private counterpart chosen for the project was the United Arab Emirates–based real estate company of Majid Al Futtaim, whose business model included incurring the full cost of infrastructure development and service delivery upfront, instead of proceeding incrementally (chapter 12).

In China, finally, the weak capacity of many local governments to build new cities had resulted in widespread overindebtedness, prompting the national government to instead encourage public-private partnerships (PPPs) for urban development. This opportunity was seized by Gu'an, a locality next to one of China's most dynamic agglomerations. Relying on a national PPP template introduced in 2004, its local government contracted a company created by Wenxue Wang whose strength was to combine urban planning and infrastructure development with the attraction of private businesses. The resulting city was a resounding success, but the company now teeters on the brink of bankruptcy (chapter 11).

Three stylized facts

The review above reveals three important stylized facts. First is the *ubiquitous nature* of private cities, as they were common in the history of advanced economies and can now be found across multiple parts of the developing world. In particular, the developing countries where these cities are located nowadays have different political systems, they range from low- to middle-income in economic terms, and their legal and cultural traditions are very diverse. This ubiquity implies that the economic forces and policy choices at play transcend the specificities of individual countries.

The second stylized fact is the *large size* of private cities relative to other urban agglomerations in the same countries and periods. Medieval Paris and Renaissance Florence were among the biggest and wealthiest cities of their time.

As for the 14 outstanding private cities just discussed, they represent 1 percent of all officially recognized cities in the 11 countries they belong to. And when completed they will account for 0.6 percent of the combined populations of those countries. Taken together they will host 11.3 million inhabitants and will have a median population of 888,000.

Most importantly, the 14 outstanding cities reviewed occupy a much higher position in the urban ranking of their countries than the most significant private cities in today's advanced economies (table 1.1). For example, Reston is probably one of the biggest private cities in the US. Its population is about 60,000, but this is in a country where there are more than 300 cities with a population above 100,000. By contrast, the majority of the 14 private cities reviewed are—or will be, if built as planned—among the largest urban agglomerations in their countries.

Closely connected to this sharp contrast, the third stylized fact is the *institutional fluidity* of private cities over time. Medieval Paris and Renaissance Florence were built and managed by private actors, but they are now under the jurisdiction of their local governments. With a few exceptions, the company towns of the Industrial Revolution have either vanished or become conventional cities. And a similar dynamic is under way in developing countries, with outstanding private cities from El Alto in Bolivia to Gurgaon in India gradually becoming government-run cities, with constituencies to report to. This institutional fluidity implies that different modes of urbanization may be more appropriate in different phases of the development process.

TABLE 1.1 **The size of selected outstanding private cities in developing countries**

Country	City	Land area in sq. km	Population in thousands		Population in percent of city with indicated rank		
			Current	Forecasted	Rank 1	Rank 10	Rank 20
Bangladesh	East Dhaka	28	900	—	4.6	293.1	486.2
Bolivia	El Alto	370	1100	—	80.6	1259.9	3934.1
China	Gu'an	170	500	—	1.9	6.3	11.0
Egypt, Arab Rep.	Cairo Festival City	3	—	13	0.1	2.9	5.3
Honduras	San Pedro Sula	840	876	—	80.6	1536.8	5475.0
India	Gurgaon	406	2,000	—	10.9	65.7	118.7
India	Jamshedpur	244	1,373	—	7.5	45.1	81.5
Indonesia	Batam	715	1,200	—	13.4	99.6	201.5
Indonesia	Kota Baru Maja	155	500	—	5.6	41.5	84.0
Nigeria	Eko Atlantic	10	—	300	2.1	22.6	46.5
Pakistan	Bahria Town Karachi	72	25	1,000	6.7	99.9	256.1
Pakistan	Sialkot	32	928	—	6.2	92.7	237.7
South Africa	Waterfall City	22	—	100	2.0	24.6	88.4
Vietnam	Phu My Hung	33	278	500	3.1	132.0	182.8
All (Median)		**114**	**888**		**5.9**	**79.2**	**150.8**
United States	Reston	**41**	**60**		**0.7**	**5.8**	**9.0**

Sources: Original figure for this book, based on chapters 9–22; master plans; cities' websites; LandScan Global 2018; and World Population Review 2021.
Note: Sq. km=square kilometer. — = not applicable. Median population is computed using expected figures whenever the city is still under development and current figures otherwise.

These three stylized facts also have an important analytical implication. Modern urban economics emerged in today's advanced economies, where it has blossomed as a specialized field over the last few decades. This is a time when a vast majority of urban agglomerations in advanced economies were run by local governments, regardless of whether this was so in early stages of their development. Not surprisingly, many of the policy recommendations emerging from this study field relate to ways in which local governments could become better planners, be more effective at mobilizing finance, or improve their capacity to deliver social services. But a capable local government is assumed almost by default, and the possible role of significant private actors in the urbanization process is neglected.

As a result, attempts to conceptualize private cities have been rare, and in developing countries policy engagements by multilateral organizations and development partners have mostly ignored significant private actors. The rare studies on private cities draw their conclusions from limited information, often focusing on cities that are still in the planning stage.

For example, it has been noticed that "while these projects are beginning to receive academic attention, the majority of studies have a limited capacity to explain why and how they are produced" (Percival and Waley 2012). Questions have been raised on "whether there are also ways in which new planned cities can create new, broader economic and societal value" (Jo and Zheng 2020). But these explorations are the exception more than the rule.

References

Alanen, Arnold R. 2007. *Morgan Park: Duluth, U.S. Steel, and the Forging of a Company Town.* Minneapolis: University of Minnesota Press.

Bontje, Marco, and Joachim Burdack. 2005. "Edge Cities, European-style: Examples from Paris and the Randstad." *Cities* 22 (4): 317–30.

Buder, Stanley. 1967. *Pullman: An Experiment in Industrial Order and Community Planning, 1880–1930.* New York: Oxford University Press.

Cheng, Kun. 2020. "Private Involvement in City Making: A Preliminary Historical Review." Background paper, *Private Cities: Outstanding Examples from Developing Countries and Their Implications for Urban Policy*, World Bank, Washington, DC.

City of London. 2018. "Freedom of the City." https://www.cityoflondon.gov.uk/about-the-city /history/Pages/freedom-of-the-city.aspx.

Crawford, Margaret. 1995. *Building the Workingman's Paradise: The Design of American Company Towns.* London and New York: Verso.

Desvigne, Michel, Xaveer de Geyter, and Floris Askemade. 2009. "Paris Saclay, Campus Sud." PowerPoint presentation, accessed August 15, 2022. http://micheldesvignepaysagiste.com/en /paris-saclay-campus-sud.

Electronic Encyclopedia of Chicago. 2022. "Pullman," accessed October 11, 2022. http://www .encyclopedia.chicagohistory.org/pages/1030.html.

Ely, Richard Theodore. 1885. "Pullman: A Social Study." *Harper's Magazine* 70: 452–66.

Garner, John. 1992. *The Company Town: Architecture and Society in the Early Industrial Age.* Oxford: Oxford University Press.

Garreau, Joel. 1991. "Til Hazel, King of the New Frontier." *Washington Post*, July 21, 1991.

Garreau, Joel. 1992. *Edge City: Life on the New Frontier.* New York City: Anchor.

Guild of Freemen of the City of London. n.d. "Freedom of the City," https://www.guild-freemen -london.co.uk/freedom-of-the-city.

Henderson, J. Vernon, and Arindam Mitra. 1996. "The New Urban Landscape: Developers and Edge Cities." *Regional Science and Urban Economics* 26 (6): 613–43.

Hiatt, F. 1983. "Hazel Saw Land of Opportunity in Fairfax." *Washington Post*, April 18, 1983.

Hillairet, Jacques. 1977. *Connaissance du Vieux Paris.* Paris: Éditions Princesse.

Historic Pullman Foundation. 2022. "The History of Pullman," accessed October 11, 2022. https://www.pullmanil.org/the-history-of-pullman/.

Howard, Ebenezer. 1898. *To-morrow: A Peaceful Path to Real Reform*. London: Swan Sonnenschein & Co.

International Garden Cities Institute. n.d. "Letchworth Garden City." Accessed October 11, 2022. https://www.gardencitiesinstitute.com/resources/garden-cities/letchworth-garden-city.

Jacobs, Jane. 1969. *The Economy of the Cities*. New York: Random House.

Jo, Angie, and Siqi Zheng. 2020. "New Planned Cities as Economic Engines: Global Trend and Our Conceptual Framework." In *Toward Urban Economic Vibrancy: Patterns and Practices in Asia's New Cities*, edited by Siqi Zheng and Zhengzhen Tan. Cambridge, MA: MIT Press.

Jonas, A. E. 2003. "Making Edge City: Post-Suburban Development and Life on the Frontier in Southern California." In *Changing Suburbs: Foundation, Form, and Function*, edited by Richard Harris and Peter Larkham, 218–37. London: Routledge.

Kurie, Peter. 2018. *In Chocolate We Trust: The Hershey Company Town Unwrapped*. Philadelphia: University of Pennsylvania Press.

LandScan Global. 2018. dataset, Oak Ridge National Laboratory. https://doi.org/10.48690/1524213.

Letchworth Garden City Heritage Foundation. n.d. "Letchworth Garden City Heritage Foundation: Who We Are," accessed October 11, 2022. https://www.letchworth.com/who-we-are/about-us.

Metheny, Karen Bescherer. 2007. *From the Miners' Double House: Archaeology and Landscape in a Pennsylvania Coal Company Town*. Knoxville: University of Tennessee Press.

Meyer, Eugene L. 2016. "Crystal City, Once Cast Off by Washington, Reboots Itself." *New York Times*, April 19, 2016.

Percival, T., and P. Waley. 2012. "Articulating Intra-Asian Urbanism: The Production of Satellite Cities in Phnom Penh." *Urban Studies* 49 (13): 2873–88.

Scarlett, Timothy J., and Steven A. Walton. 2017. "Archaeological Overview and Assessment: Pullman National Historical Monument, Town of Pullman, Chicago, Illinois." Technical report, Michigan Technological University.

Sharpless, Richard E., and Donald L. Miller. 1985. *The Kingdom of Coal: Work, Enterprise, and Ethnic Communities in the Mine Fields*. Philadelphia: University of Pennsylvania Press.

Stanback, Thomas M. 1991. *The New Suburbanization: Challenge to the Central City*. Boulder, CO: Westview Press.

Veltz, Pierre. 2015. *Petite ensaclaypédie*. Paris: Éditions La Découverte.

World Population Review, 2021. dataset. https://worldpopulationreview.com/world-cities.

CHAPTER 2

A simple analytical framework

A conceptual framework is needed to identify the key economic and institutional features that drive city formation. The one proposed here highlights the critical role of two often-neglected institutional dimensions: the capacity of the local government and the clout of the private actor. A typology of cities arises, with the two institutional dimensions determining the role (if any) of the private actor. The framework also helps to assess the efficiency and equity implications of the various equilibria and to discuss how urban policies could lead to better overall outcomes.

A blend of two traditions

The conceptual framework presented in this chapter can be interpreted as a blend of two different bodies of literature on urban development. One of them is economic in nature, focusing on resource allocation and its implications for efficiency and equity. The other is more political, emphasizing the way key private actors—typically, large developers, business groups, and civil society representatives—influence decision-making by local authorities at the city level.

In the *urban economics* tradition, city formation is driven by entrepreneurial coordinators of urban sites. These coordinators compete to attract the number of firms and workers that maximizes the local surplus. Through land zoning and incentives, they overcome the coordination failures that would arise if firms and workers gathered spontaneously across locations. These entrepreneurial coordinators do not need to be local governments, but it is generally assumed that they are. The resulting urbanization process is shown to be efficient when land can be assembled for urban development at no cost and when both capital and labor can move freely across localities (Henderson 1974; Henderson and Venables 2009).

The potential role of large private actors as planners, builders, and managers of cities has long been recognized in urban economics. However, with the notable exception of Henderson and Mitra (1996), the interplay between local government and private actors in the city formation process has not received much attention. There is also a rich literature on private developments such as gated communities and business improvement districts (Glasze, Webster, and Franz 2016; Helsley 2003; Helsley and Strange 2000; Moroni 2014; Webster 2001). However, the scale of these units tends to be small relative to that of the city, questioning the idea that these developments deal with urbanization—a process of spatial rearrangement that brings together people, jobs, and amenities.

In contrast with the urban economics tradition, *urban political science* stresses the important role played by the private sector in city development, criticizing the biases that arise when local governments are seen as the only or the main decision-maker. In this other tradition, a city is the areal expression of special interests that seek to benefit from the way in which land is used in the area (Logan and Molotch 1987; Molotch 1976). In the context of the United States, in particular, it has been argued that landowners and developers drive urban development policy along with their allies, including utility companies, the media, and politicians (Stoker 1998).

The urban political science literature is organized around the role of power, understood as the capacity to provide leadership and a mode of operation that enables significant tasks to be done in cities. Public and private actors may have different objectives, but they build long-term coalitions to establish a near-monopoly of decision-making over the critical choices facing their locality. The theory further predicts that to be effective, governments must blend their capacities with those of various nongovernmental actors to facilitate action and achieve significant goals (Stoker 1998; Stone 1989, 1993).

The *proposed analytical framework* blends some of the interpretations of the urban political science tradition into the urban economics tradition (Li and Rama 2022). It does so by explicitly relying on a political economy approach. While such an approach is not common in the urban economics tradition, there are a few important precedents to consider (Helsley 2003; Helsley and Strange 1994, 2000).

Building on these precedents, it is assumed here that the local government of a specific jurisdiction struggles to assemble and develop a large tract of urban land, while a significant private actor may have the capacity to do so. The jurisdiction is supposed to be small relative to the size of the country, which allows ignoring broader spillover effects (Scotchmer 2002).

With two major actors involved, the urbanization process can be interpreted as a policy game. Because this game can be played in different ways, depending on whether decisions are simultaneous or sequential, multiple types of cities can emerge, with the private actor having a different role in each.

Proceeding this way does not amount to dismissing the key forces that have been shown to drive urbanization across localities. Key among them is their *economic potential (*denoted as α), which encompasses location advantages, agglomeration economies, and self-selection (Behrens and Robert-Nicoud 2015; Duranton and Puga 2004; Glaeser 2012). Location advantages are shaped by fundamentals such as geography and climate but can also be improved through infrastructure investments. Agglomeration economies derive from better labor matching, greater product diversification, and stronger knowledge spillovers. As for self-selection, both households and firms are diverse in their mixture of skills, energy, and entrepreneurship, and the most productive ones often find themselves drawn to urban areas.

There are also forces constraining the urbanization process, with the strength of *congestion effects (γ)* being the most obvious one. Bringing people together makes them more productive, but cities do not keep growing indefinitely because being together in large numbers also gives rise to negative local externalities, from clogged traffic to increased crime to contagious disease. For example, other things equal, hilly terrain and recurrent flooding may make traffic congestion more likely. The other obvious force constraining the growth of cities is *the cost of capital (i)*, because it determines how expensive it is to convert agricultural land into urban land.

However, the blend of urban economics and urban political science traditions leads to emphasizing the role of institutions, in addition to economic forces. Two key institutional parameters stand out in this respect. First is the *capacity of the local government (θ)* to assemble land for urban development, plan the layout of the city, build its infrastructure, and provide the necessary services. In the urban economics tradition, it is assumed that local governments can handle these tasks smoothly, as an entrepreneur would do, but the urbanization experience of developing countries suggests that this may be an overly optimistic assumption.

The second key institutional parameter is the *clout of the private actor (μ)*, understood as its ability to effectively develop a city in the locality. In this case, the constraints do not arise from limited managerial capacity, but rather from the difficulties to secure land conversion permits, acquire land, decide on its zoning, and the like. Unlike the capacity of the local government, which carries a positive connotation, the sizeable clout of the private actor may not be seen as socially desirable. Such large clout could derive, for instance, from unofficial payments to public officials, or from undue pressure on the farmers who originally lived and worked in the locality.

For ease of interpretation, these two institutional parameters are defined so that they range from 0 to 1. When the capacity of the local government reaches the upper bound of this range, its ability to develop high-quality urban land is as high as the most optimistic urban economist could hope for. And when the clout of the private actor reaches the upper bound, its capacity to acquire land for urban development at no cost is as high as the most pessimistic urban political scientist could fear.

A typology of cities

City formation can be interpreted as the provision of urban land as a public good at the local level (Henderson 1974; Stiglitz 1977). In response to the newly available local public good, large numbers of atomistic households and firms choose where to locate. Capital and labor can typically move quite freely across locations within a country. Households and firms thus settle in the new urban land until their net incomes match what they could earn elsewhere in the country. The more that high-quality urban land is developed, the more capital and labor migrate to the area and the bigger the new city becomes.

In the traditional conceptualization of city formation, localities are either urban or rural. But when city formation is analyzed as a game, more than just two equilibria may arise. The locality may become urban in several of these equilibria, but even so, the relationship between the local government and the private actor may be different across them. The size of the city and the surplus of the locality may vary as a result, and the distribution of the surplus between the private actor and the rest of society could vary as well.

Urban land can in principle be developed by both the local government (L_g) and the private actor (L_p). The sum of the two (L) provides a measure of the size of the city that emerges in the locality. However, any of the two players could choose not to develop any land, even if the potential of the locality is high, congestion effects are manageable, and the cost of capital is affordable. Such favorable conditions are assumed here so that failure to urbanize can only be attributed to the low capacity of the local government and the limited clout of the private actor.

How much land each of the two players develops depends on the decisions the other player makes. Game theory considers different ways in which the players can interact. When both players are reactive, each of them takes the amount of urban land developed by the other as given; this corresponds to what is known as a simultaneous game. However, one of the two players could be proactive, explicitly recognizing the way the other player would react and taking advantage of it. For example, the local government could choose to develop a limited amount of urban land to crowd in land development by the private actor. Such strategic interactions between the players are known as sequential games.

A local equilibrium is sustainable when the amount of land developed by a player is optimal from its point of view given the amount of land developed by the other player. In the parlance of game theory, this self-reinforcing mechanism is called a Nash equilibrium.

Decisions by the two players are determined by their objectives (box 2.1). In line with the urban economics tradition, it is assumed that the local government is benevolent, meaning that it aims to maximize *the surplus* (Y) of its jurisdiction. This surplus is the output the locality generates once urbanized, net of the cost of developing the required urban land. Such cost does not include the payments made to the original occupants

BOX 2.1 A sketch of the underlying analytical model

The size of the city L is the sum of urban land developed by the local government and the private actor (L_g and L_p respectively). In line with the urban economics tradition, the output of the locality $F(L)$ is supposed to grow with the size of the city, but at declining rates ($F'(L) > 0$ and $F''(L) < 0$). For tractability, the output of the locality is assumed to verify $F'(L) = \alpha(1 - \gamma L)$, hence $F''(L) = -\alpha\gamma$, with parameters α and γ capturing the strength of agglomeration and congestion effects respectively.

The surplus of the locality Y is the difference between this output and the amount of resources devoted to developing the land, which depends on the cost of capital i. Because the local government is not fully effective ($\theta < 1$), the cost it incurs to develop urban land is higher than that faced by the private actor:

$$Y = F(L) - \frac{i}{\theta}L_g - iL_p \tag{1}$$

The rent of the private actor R, in turn, increases with the value of the land it develops. The small size of the jurisdiction and the mobility of capital and labor across localities ensure that the value of land is equal to its marginal product $F'(L)$. From the private actor's perspective, the unit cost of developing urban land is higher than the cost of capital, because of the expenses it incurs to secure permits from the local government and to acquire land from the original residents of the locality:

$$R = \left[F'(L) - \frac{i}{\mu} \right] L_p \tag{2}$$

Each of the two players chooses the amount of urban land it develops to maximize its objective function. When the amount of land developed by the other player is taken as given, the first-order condition of this optimization problem can be interpreted as a reaction function, indicating how much urban land each player develops for every unit of urban land developed by the other player.

In a simultaneous game, both players decide according to their reaction function. The equilibrium can then be analyzed as the solution of a problem with two equations and two unknowns (L_g and L_p). This problem has, in principle, four possible solutions, depending on whether L_g and L_p are strictly positive or nil. In a sequential game, the player that moves first maximizes its objective function taking the reaction function of the other player into account. The solution encompasses the previous equilibria when only one of the players develops land. But when both do, the size of the city and the share of it developed by each player do not coincide with the solution of the simultaneous game.

The difference between the surplus of the locality and the rent of the private actor is the windfall from urbanization that accrues to the rest of society (H):

$$H = Y - R \tag{3}$$

(Box continues on next page)

BOX 2.1 **A sketch of the underlying analytical model** *(continued)*

This windfall can be interpreted as the change in the value of the land in the locality. However, in a setting with taxes and transfers, the windfall may accrue to taxpayers, beneficiaries of public services, and government contractors both in the locality and in the rest of the country.

In the social optimum, urban land would be developed by a fully effective local government at unit cost i. The urbanization process would then proceed up to the point L^* where the output of the last unit of urban land $F'(L^*)$ equals its development cost i. Subtracting the total cost of urban land development iL^* from the total output $F(L^*)$ yields the optimal surplus of the locality Y^*. Given the absence of rent, this surplus also represents the windfall from urbanization for society at large (figure B2.1.1, panel a).

When only the local government is active, and it is partially effective, the unit cost of developing urban land is i/θ. Because this cost is higher than in the social optimum, and the output function $F(L)$ is concave, a smaller city emerges. This underurbanization implies that the surplus of the locality is necessarily smaller than in the optimum. But in addition, resources are wasted because land is developed at cost i/θ instead of i (figure B2.1.1, panel b). This smaller surplus accrues entirely to society at large though, as there is no private land development in this case and hence no rent.

The analysis is similar when only the private actor develops urban land. From its perspective, the marginal cost of developing urban land is i/μ. Again, this cost is higher than the social optimum, which results in a smaller city emerging in the locality. But in addition, the concavity of the output function creates an incentive for the private actor to develop even fewer units of land. This is because every additional unit reduces the marginal output $F'(L)$, hence the value of privately developed land. Replacing $L = L_p$ in equation (2), the rent is maximized for $F'(L) = i/\mu - F''(L)L$, with this condition determining the size of the city (figure B2.1.1, panel c).

Despite the resulting underurbanization, the surplus of the locality is positive in this case, because the output function is concave and the marginal output from urban land $F'(L)$ exceeds its development cost i/μ. The windfall H is positive as well, for two reasons. First, the rest of society appropriates the difference $F(L) - (i/\mu)$ on each unit of urban land developed. But in addition, there is a gap between the private cost i/μ and the social cost, which remains i because the private actor is an effective developer of land. This gap corresponds to the payments the private actor needs to make to secure permits and purchase land, and those payments are part of the windfall.

The analysis is slightly more cumbersome when both players develop land. How the size of the city is determined in this case requires going through the model, but it can be shown that $L < L^*$. In this case, however, there is both waste and rent. Their representation follows the same criteria as in the previous equilibria, except that the waste is now represented to the right of the figure rather than on the vertical axis, as shown by the vertical bars in bold, to facilitate the comparison with the surplus (figure B2.1.1, panel d).

(Box continues on next page)

BOX 2.1 **A sketch of the underlying analytical model** (*continued*)

FIGURE B2.1.1 **The size of the city, the surplus of the locality, and its distribution in equilibrium**

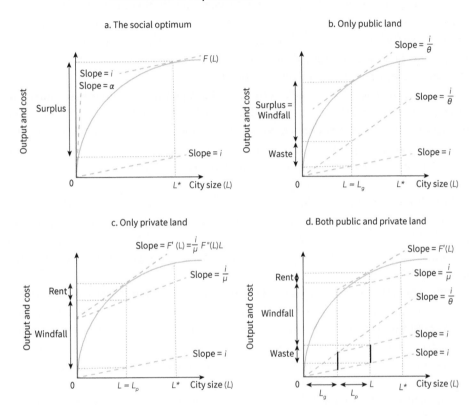

Source: Adapted from Li and Rama 2022.
Note: L_g = urban land developed by the local government; L_p = urban land developed by the private actor; L^* = optimal city size; $F(L)$ = total output of the locality; $F'(L)$ = output of an additional unit of urban land; α = initial agglomeration effect; i = cost of capital; θ = capacity of the local government; μ = clout of the private actor.

of the land—say, the farmers who used to live and work there—because those payments represent an income for them. From a social welfare perspective, the land-acquisition costs and land-related income simply cancel out.

The private actor, in turn, seeks to maximize *the rent* (R) it derives from its investment in the locality. This rent is the difference between the market value of the land it develops and the cost it incurs to secure the necessary permits, acquire land, and develop it. With free mobility of capital and labor across localities, the market value of urban land should be equal to the output that can be generated by the marginal unit the private actor develops. But unlike the local government, the private actor sees the payments it needs to make to the original residents of the locality as a cost.

A typology of potential equilibria emerges when considering whether each of the two players develops any urban land and if it does, whether its decisions are merely reactive or proactive (table 2.1). If none of the players develops urban land, the locality remains rural. It becomes a conventional city when only the local government develops urban land and a company town when only the private actor does.

There are also potential equilibria in which both players develop urban land. If the local government and the private actor develop urban land in reaction to the decisions by the other (that is, if they play simultaneously), a mixed city emerges. However, if the local government is proactive (in other words, if the government moves first) it may induce the private actor to develop more land, to tap its greater capacity. In that case, a strategic city emerges in the locality.

The absence of an equilibrium in which the private actor is proactive and the local government reactive may come as a surprise. However, in the conceptual framework proposed here, such a combination would not be sustainable as a Nash equilibrium. Indeed, it can be shown that when the private actor is proactive, the locality—if it ever urbanizes—becomes either a company town or a conventional city.

This typology can be approximately matched to the grouping of private cities in developing countries that was presented in the previous chapter. Thus, the company town equilibrium corresponds to urban agglomerations developed without government participation, mixed cities reflect a complex interplay of local governments and private actors, and strategic cities can be associated with a deliberate crowding in of private investments in urban development by the local government.

The nature of the equilibrium that emerges in the locality critically depends on the values of the five parameters of the model. Three of them—the potential of the locality, congestion effects, and the cost of capital—are shaped by the context, from geography to weather to finance. The other two parameters—the capacity of the local government

TABLE 2.1 **A range of potential local equilibria**

Private actor	Local government		
	Inactive	**Reactive**	**Proactive**
Active	Company town	Mixed city	Strategic city
Inactive	Rural area	Conventional city	

Source: Original figure for this book.

and the clout of the private actor—are institutional in nature. The proposed analytical framework allows "mapping" the equilibrium that prevails in the locality to the values of these two institutional parameters.

In practice, this amounts to dividing the institutional space into "regions," corresponding to a rural area, a company town, a mixed city, a strategic city, or a conventional city. It can be shown that in both the simultaneous and sequential games there is a unique Nash equilibrium associated with each pair of values of the institutional parameters of the model. The lines separating two contiguous regions in the institutional space can be interpreted as "frontiers" between equilibria. Crossing those frontiers, by modifying either the capacity of the local government or the clout of the private actor, amounts to switching from one Nash equilibrium to another.

The results have a relatively straightforward interpretation. When the game is played simultaneously, a conventional city emerges if government capacity is high, a company town if the clout of the private actor is substantial, and a mixed city in between. The locality remains rural if both capacity and clout are weak (figure 2.1, panel a).

When the game is played sequentially, the scope for a company town increases whereas that for a conventional city decreases. Overall, a greater share of urban land is developed by the private actor, and this is so regardless of which of the two players moves first. This paradoxical outcome is due to the private actor being a more effective developer of urban land than the local government.

When the local government is the first mover, it is in its interest to crowd in investments by the private actor, because that leads to a larger surplus of the locality. Compared to the simultaneous game, this new partition expands the scope for a company town while reducing the likelihood that a conventional city will emerge (figure 2.1, panel b). Conversely, when the private actor moves first, it can attain a higher rent if it crowds out the local government. The region supporting the conventional city equilibrium remains the same, but the mixed city equilibrium disappears with a company town emerging in its place (figure 2.1, panel c).

Urbanization efficiency and equity

An important property of the simple analytical framework proposed is that the size of the city that emerges in the locality, measured as the sum of urban land developed by the two players, is always suboptimal. Given the potential of the locality, the strength of congestion forces, and the cost of developing urban land, a bigger city should emerge. Underurbanization is most blatant when the locality remains rural despite its potential, but it happens to varying degrees in all the equilibria.

It follows that the surplus of the locality is not maximized either. This is due to both underurbanization and wasteful land development. Underurbanization implies that the output generated by the locality is not as large as it should be. Wasteful land

FIGURE 2.1 **How institutional parameters affect the nature of the local equilibrium**

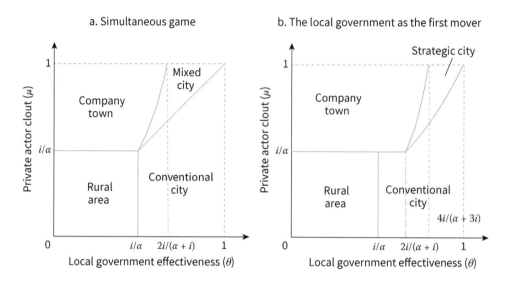

a. Simultaneous game

b. The local government as the first mover

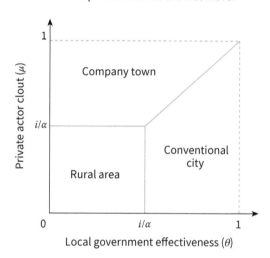

c. The private actor as the first mover

Source: Adapted from Li and Rama 2022.
Note: α = initial agglomeration effect; i = cost of capital.

development happens in all equilibria in which the local government is an active player because its low capacity makes it spend more resources to deliver a unit of urban land than would be strictly necessary.

The windfall from urbanization for the rest of society may be further reduced by the rent of the private actor. However, it would be wrong to assume that for a given city size the windfall is always smaller when the private actor develops urban land. The windfall could be larger as well because the private actor develops urban land more efficiently than the local government, and therefore its involvement reduces the waste of resources.

The distributional implications of participation by private actors in the urbanization process are therefore ambiguous. By maximizing their rent, private actors may reduce the share of the pie that accrues to their fellow citizens. At the same time, by being more efficient land developers than the local government, they may also increase the size of the pie. The balance of these two opposite effects depends on the values of the key economic and institutional parameters driving urbanization.

With urbanization being inefficient, a relevant question is whether urban policy options exist that could lead to better outcomes. The standard recommendation in the urban economics literature is to *increase the capacity of the local government* to plan, build and manage cities. The analytical framework above confirms that a fully capable government is associated with the maximum surplus for the locality. However, it does not follow that increasing government capacity from a low level would always lead to better outcomes.

In the proposed analytical framework, city size is a nondecreasing function of the capacity of the local government, and this is so regardless of whether the players move simultaneously or one of them moves first. However, it is important to keep in mind that a bigger city is not necessarily a more productive city. Other things equal, a sprawling urban area may generate a smaller surplus than a more compact counterpart.

The impact of greater local government capacity on the surplus of the locality is in fact ambiguous. In the mixed-city equilibrium, a greater capacity can encourage the local government to engage in more wasteful urban land development, thus crowding out the more effective private actor. A greater capacity of the local government may also trigger a switch from a company town to a bigger but less efficient conventional city when the private actor is the first mover. Overall, the impact can be negative when the initial capacity of the local government is very low.

Other urban policy options could involve *modifying the incentives faced by the private actor*. As discussed in the overview of this book there are three alternative resource allocation mechanisms, and they have different implications on how to tilt incentives. One way to do so, in the spirit of socialist economics, is to ban urban land development by the private actor so that the responsibility for urbanization falls exclusively in the hands of the local government. A second possibility, aligned with welfare economics, is to rely on fiscal instruments to incentivize the private actor and to redistribute the surplus to the rest of society. And the third possibility, in line with the law and economics approach, is to transfer the rights to the city to the private actor, collecting a sizeable fee in exchange.

Banning the private actor could be justified on the grounds that the noncooperative nature of the game it plays with the local government is one of the reasons why urbanization is inefficient. A Nash equilibrium is optimal for each of the two players, in the sense that the amount of urban land they each develop is optimal given the amount developed by the other player. But it is generally suboptimal from a social point of view. Besides, given the potentially large rent the private actor appropriates, a ban on its activities could also be popular, making this first option politically appealing.

However, the socialist economics approach could make the urbanization process even more inefficient. With a low government capacity, the locality could just remain rural, whereas a private actor with sufficient clout could transform it into a company town. The latter is not socially optimal, as was discussed above. But at least it generates a windfall for the rest of society, which a rural area does not.

In the welfare economics approach, two sources of inefficiency need to be addressed. First, the private actor values the urban land it develops by pricing it to market or, equivalently, it values each of those units of land based on the output the marginal unit of land generates. But with the output function being concave, this is less than the average output supported by the urban land the private actor develops, which is what matters from a social point of view. And second, the private actor sees the expenses it incurs to secure the necessary government permits and to acquire land from the original residents of the locality as a cost. Yet, from a social point of view, these expenses amount to a redistribution of resources among members of society and not to a real cost.

These two sources of inefficiency can be corrected by subsidizing urban land development by the private actor, a result that is often referred to as the Henry George Theorem, in reference to his insightful analyses of urban development in the early twentieth century (George 1879; Stiglitz 1977). However, the amount of resources that need to be transferred to the large developer is very large, as it has to offset both the cost of land acquisition and the gap between the average and marginal output that urban land generates. In the analytical approach presented here, the subsidization needed is so large that the rest of society would be unambiguously worse off.

This concern can in principle be addressed by clawing back some of the rent of the private actor and distributing it to the rest of society. To avoid undermining the incentives for the private actor to develop urban land, a lump-sum tax would have to be used. However, the taxation required to increase the windfall from urbanization for the rest of society is extremely high. And it is dubious that a local government with limited capacity would be able to redistribute resources on the scale needed for the welfare economics approach to ensure efficient and equitable urbanization—especially when confronted with a private actor with sizeable clout.

Finally, if the rights to the jurisdiction were transferred to the private actor, it would be in its interest to maximize the surplus of the locality. By relinquishing its rights, the local government would allow the private actor to appropriate the full output generated by the land it develops, and not only on its marginal output. Also, having acquired the locality, the private actor would not need to secure government permits anymore or purchase land plots from original residents. But under such conditions, there would be no windfall from urbanization for the rest of society.

The way to address this concern is to sell the rights to the city for a price at least equal to the windfall associated with the Nash equilibrium that could have otherwise prevailed, given the values of the relevant economic and institutional parameters. If the fee the private actor pays for the rights to the city exceeds this threshold, then the optimal city size would be attained, and society at large would be better off. Such outsourcing could be interpreted as an urbanization public-private partnership.

References

Behrens, Kristian, and Frederic Robert-Nicoud. 2015. "Agglomeration Theory with Heterogeneous Agents." In *Handbook of Regional and Urban Economics.* Vol. 5, edited by Gilles Duranton, J. Vernon Henderson, and William C. Strange, 175–245. Amsterdam: Elsevier, North-Holland.

Duranton, Gilles, and Diego Puga. 2004. "Micro-foundations of Urban Agglomeration Economies." In *Handbook of Regional and Urban Economics: Cities and Geography*, Vol. 4, edited by J. Vernon Henderson and Jacques-François Thisse, 2063–117. Amsterdam: Elsevier, North-Holland.

George, Henry. 1879. *Progress and Poverty: An Inquiry into the Cause of Industrial Depressions, and of Increase of Want with Increase of Wealth. The Remedy*. New York: D. Appleton.

Glaeser, Edward. 2012. *Triumph of the City: How Our Greatest Invention Makes Us Richer, Smarter, Greener, Healthier, and Happier*. New York: Penguin.

Glasze, Georg, Chris Webster, and Klaus Frantz, eds. 2016. *Private Cities: Global and Local Perspectives*. London and New York: Routledge.

Helsley, Robert W. 2003. "Urban Political Economics." In *Handbook of Regional and Urban Economics: Cities and Geography*, Vol. 4, edited by J. Vernon Henderson and Jacques-François Thisse, 2381–421. Amsterdam: Elsevier, North-Holland.

Helsley, Robert W., and William C. Strange. 1994. "City Formation with Commitment." *Regional Science and Urban Economics* 24 (3): 373–90.

Helsley, Robert W., and William C. Strange. 2000. "Potential Competition and Public Sector Performance." *Regional Science and Urban Economics* 30 (4): 405–28.

Henderson, J. Vernon. 1974. "The Sizes and Types of Cities." *American Economic Review* 64 (4): 640–56.

Henderson, J. Vernon, and Arindam Mitra. 1996. "The New Urban Landscape: Developers and Edge Cities." *Regional Science and Urban Economics* 26 (6): 613–43.

Henderson, J. Vernon, and Anthony J. Venables. 2009. "The Dynamics of City Formation." *Review of Economic Dynamics* 12 (2): 233–54.

Li, Yue, and Martin Rama. 2022. "Private Cities: Implications for Urban Policy in Developing Countries." Policy Research Working Paper 9936, World Bank, Washington, DC.

Logan, J., and H. Molotch. 1987. *Urban Fortunes: The Political Economy of Place.* Berkeley: University of California Press.

Molotch, Harvey. 1976. "The City as a Growth Machine: Toward a Political Economy of Place." *American Journal of Sociology* 82 (2): 309–32.

Moroni, Stefano. 2014. "Towards a General Theory of Contractual Communities: Neither Necessarily Gated, nor a Form of Privatization." In *Cities and Private Planning Property Rights, Entrepreneurship and Transaction Costs*, edited by Daniel Edward Andersson and Stefano Moroni, 38–65. Cheltenham, UK: Edward Elgar Publishing.

Scotchmer, Suzanne. 2002. "Local Public Goods and Clubs." In *Handbook of Public Economics.* Vol. 4, edited by Alan J. Auerbach and Martin Feldstein, 1997–2042.

Stiglitz, Joseph E. 1977. "The Theory of Local Public Goods." In *The Economics of Public Services,* edited by Martin S. Feldstein and Robert P. Inman, 274–333. London: Palgrave Macmillan.

Stoker, Gerry. 1998. "Theory and Urban Politics." *International Political Science Review* 19 (2): 119–29.

Stone, Clarence. 1989. *Regime Politics: Governing Atlanta 1946–1988.* Lawrence: University Press of Kansas.

Stone, Clarence. 1993. "Urban Regimes and the Capacity to Govern: A Political Economy Approach." *Journal of Urban Affairs* 15 (1): 1–28.

Webster, Chris. 2001. "Gated Cities of Tomorrow." *Town Planning Review* 72 (2): 149–70.

CHAPTER 3

Country-level inventories of private cities

Private cities are mostly absent from urban economics or urban planning, implying that there is no ready-made database to build upon. To fill this gap, detailed information was gathered about private cities in four major developing countries—the Arab Republic of Egypt, India, Indonesia, and Pakistan. The cities are classified, following the typology from the proposed analytical framework, into company towns, mixed cities, and strategic cities. Their characteristics are summarized with reference to the key features of the proposed analytical framework.

Data sources and summary statistics

The construction of this partial inventory relied on substantive contributions by urban experts from the respective countries who have a deep knowledge of the local context. Information on the identified cities was collected through desk research and interviews. Key sources included company websites, annual reports, academic journals, and news articles. Official city boundaries, satellite images, and information on transportation networks were also gathered along the way. The collection process took place between October 2019 and February 2020 for Indonesia and Pakistan, between December 2019 and August 2020 for Egypt, and between August 2020 and March 2021 for India.

Consistent with the definition of private cities retained for this book, the selection was limited to urban agglomeration meeting three key criteria. First, urban development was led by at least one private actor or happened through a public-private collaboration with significant contributions from private actors. Second, the area covered by the agglomeration exceeds 2.5 square kilometers. And third, mixed land use is observed within the urban area. The first criterion involves a dose of subjective judgment, whereas the third one is constrained by the varying quality of land-use information across locations. Therefore, the three criteria are not applied in a totally consistent way, despite the best efforts to this effect.

The resulting inventory of private cities across the four countries is only a starting point. There are many more private cities in other developing countries and, potentially, even in the selected countries. Nonetheless, this partial inventory provides valuable information on a rich set of city characteristics, including the year of launching, the identity of the main private actors, land and population size, distance to the nearest major urban agglomeration, distance to transportation hubs and networks, land-use composition, and average land price.

Six private cities were identified in Egypt (table 3A.1). The number is the smallest across all four countries considered, in part because mixed land use is less common than elsewhere, thus breaching the second criterion (Ibrahim, Elshayal, and Athar 2021). The list is longer in the other three countries, comprising 17 private cities in India (table 3A.2), 47 in Indonesia (table 3A.3), and 16 in Pakistan (table 3A.4).

This is potentially an undercount, as the initial inventories compiled for India, Indonesia, and Pakistan in the background studies by Balachandran, Joshi, and Li (2021), Amri, Roberts, and Li (2021), and Qureshi and Li (2021), respectively, were considerably longer. Had any of the three criteria been looser than considered here, up to 136 private cities could have been reported for just India, Indonesia, and Pakistan.

Private cities by type

The private cities in these country-level inventories can be classified based on the typology from the proposed analytical framework. Again, depending on the role played by the local government, three broad categories can be considered. In *company towns*, the local government plays no role. In *mixed cities*, both the local government and a large private actor develop urban land, but they do so in an uncoordinated manner. Finally, in *strategic cities* the local government develops urban land but also deliberately crowds in urban investments by private actors.

The exercise shows that mixed cities are the most prevalent type of private cites (figure 3.1). But there are important differences across countries:

- Four of the six private cities in Egypt are mixed cities. They are all located in the greater Cairo area and are mostly residential townships, complemented with non-negligible commercial areas and public spaces. One exception is El-Gouna, a self-sufficient resort and tourism destination established by a major private investor on the Egyptian Red Sea Coast. The other exception corresponds to Cairo Festival City, whose emergence reflects a strategic decision by the local government to tap the know-how and resources of a major foreign large developer.

FIGURE 3.1 **Private cities by type**

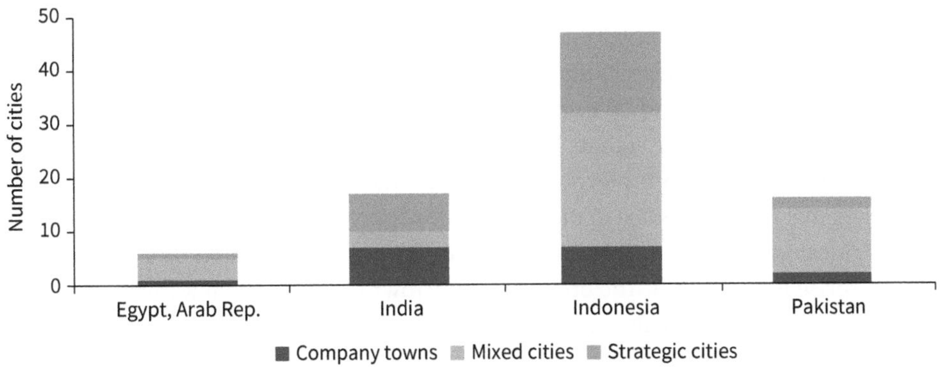

Sources: Original figure for this book, based on Amri, Roberts, and Li 2021; Balachandran, Joshi, and Li 2021; Ibrahim, Elshayal, and Athar 2021; and Qureshi and Li 2021.

- Mixed cities account for 3 of 17 private cities in India. Gurgaon is the biggest, but the others are also relatively large-scale suburban or off-central city developments, combining residential townships with considerable commercial and even industrial uses. There are also seven company towns, mostly established by companies (some state-owned) to serve as the base for their business. Five of these are steel company towns, one is a resort town, and one transitioned from manufacturing to a focus on high-end education services. The remaining seven Indian cases are strategic cities, initiated by the government with the intention to spur economic growth in the locality. Four of them are service-oriented, while one (Mundra) focuses on industrial activities. The other two are a broad-based new town development project (Rajarhat) and a special investment region championed by the state of Gujarat (Dholera).

- In Indonesia, 25 out of 47 private cities can be classified as mixed cities. They are all in the spirit of edge cities, mainly set up by private real estate developers and targeting mostly residential demand but still offering considerable commercial, industrial, and public spaces. There are also seven company towns, all established by private firms as the base for their operations. Many are related to extractive industries. Some, such as Sawahlunto, have over time become conventional cities. The remaining 15 private cities fall in the category of strategic cities, but they comprise two clearly distinct groups. Some were designed to boost economic development, such as Batam and several other special economic zones (SEZs). Others were planned as new administrative capitals for provinces or the country, such as the new national capital city. Both types of strategic cities are developed and managed in collaboration with private entities or state-owned enterprises.

- Pakistan has the second highest share of mixed cities—12 out of a total of 16 private cities—with some involving unusual actors. The local business community has been responsible for major urban infrastructure investments and management in Sialkot. The Pakistan Army, through its Defense Housing Authorities (DHAs), has built and managed major urban projects such as DHA Karachi and DHA Lahore. It can be argued that the DHA is one of the largest developers in Pakistan, operating in parallel with local governments. There is a steel company town, operated by a state-owned enterprise near Karachi. The other company town—Bahria Town Karachi, a city the size of Manhattan and also in Karachi's outskirts—is an investment project by one the country's largest real estate developers. The two strategic cities of Gwadar and Hunza were designed by the government in collaboration with international actors to boost economic development and meet social and political goals. Both are still works in progress.

Main features of private cities

Land size varies substantially by country and by type of city, but overall, mixed cities appear to be the smallest (figure 3.2). In Egypt, the mixed cities of the greater Cairo region cover on average 14 square kilometers, significantly less than the 37 square kilometers of the only company town. The median surface of mixed cities in India is 19 square kilometers. Company towns have a much larger area, reaching an average of 155 square kilometers. There is less variation in Indonesia, where median land sizes by city type range from 14 to 19 square kilometers, with strategic cities being the largest. Batam registers the biggest surface among all Indonesian private cities. In Pakistan, army-built cities and Bahria towns occupy much larger parcels than the rest of the mixed cities. The two strategic cities are situated on large tracts of land (over 600 square kilometers), which puts them on a different scale compared to the other private cities.

Private cities tend to be within close distance of a major urban agglomeration (figure 3.3, panel a). They also enjoy relatively good connectivity by being near airports or train stations (figure 3.3, panel b). Thus, all four mixed cities in Egypt are less than 50 kilometers away from Cairo, as is the only company town in relation to Hurghada.

The median distance to the closest major urban agglomeration is only 27 kilometers for India's mixed cities. A case in point is Gurgaon, a major agglomeration in its own right that sits less than 30 kilometers away from Delhi. Similarly, half of India's strategic cities are within 26 kilometers of a major urban agglomeration. Dholera stands out as an outlier, being 108 kilometers away from Ahmedabad, the largest city in Gujarat. In contrast, all company towns are located far away from major urban agglomerations. The median distance is 130 kilometers, and the mean is about 171 kilometers.

FIGURE 3.2 **Land size of private cities**

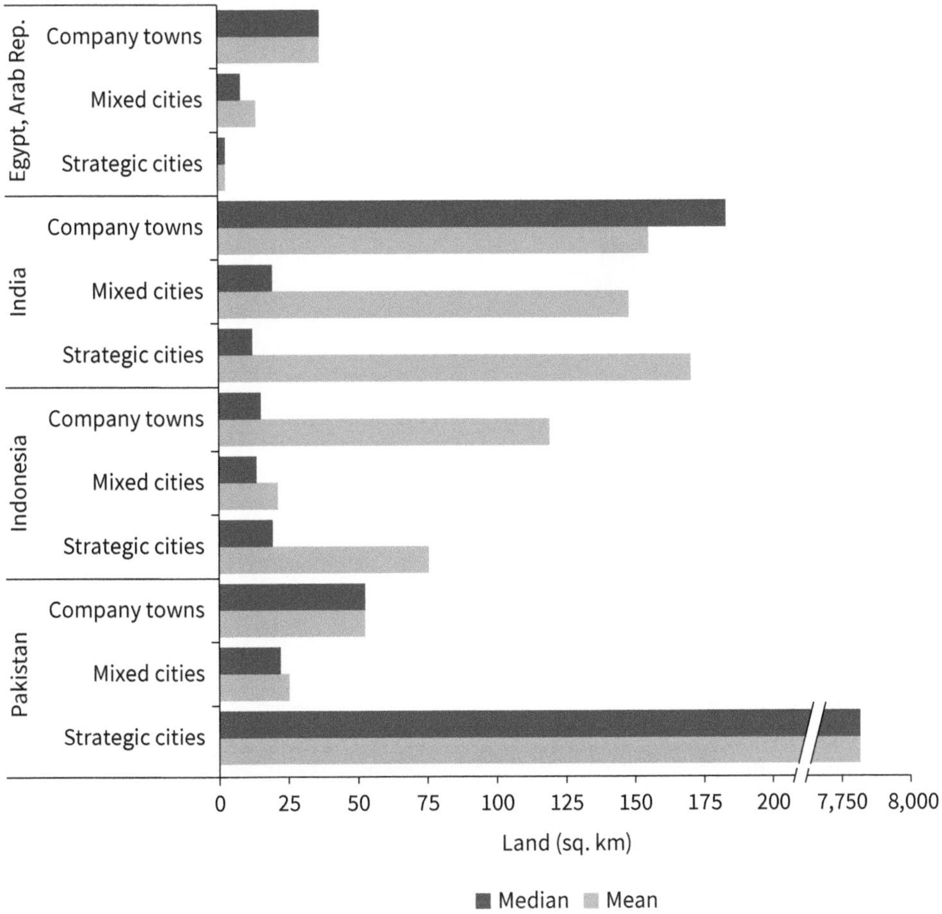

Sources: Original figure for this book, based on Amri, Roberts, and Li 2021, Balachandran, Joshi, and Li 2021; Ibrahim, Elshayal, and Athar 2021; and Qureshi and Li 2021.

Greater distance is understandable in the case of almost autonomous company towns, especially if their location is driven by the availability of natural resources.

Patterns are similar in Indonesia, where the majority of the mixed cities are located within 25 kilometers of the nearest major urban agglomeration. Company towns and strategic cities are much farther away, with the median distance to the nearest major agglomeration being 83 and 170 kilometers respectively. Being an archipelago may partially explain their more limited access to markets. Company towns tend to be located near natural resource reservoirs, and these may lie in outer islands. But in addition,

FIGURE 3.3 **Access to markets of private cities**

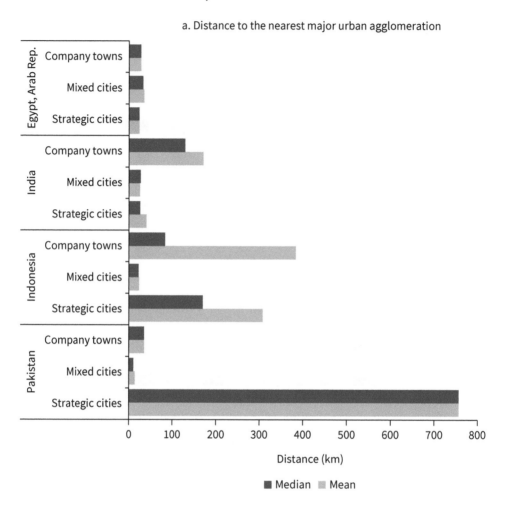

a. Distance to the nearest major urban agglomeration

(Figure continues on next page)

strategic cities have often reflected the government's motivation to encourage development in lagging areas or to improve public administration in specific regions.

As in the other three countries, mixed cities in Pakistan are located near major urban agglomerations. Distance is less than 15 kilometers for most of them, and none is more than 50 kilometers away. On the other hand, the two company towns of Pakistan have good access to train stations. Finally, the only two strategic cities are far from major urban agglomerations and accessible through airports.

FIGURE 3.3 **Access to markets of private cities** (*continued*)

b. Distance to the nearest airport or train station

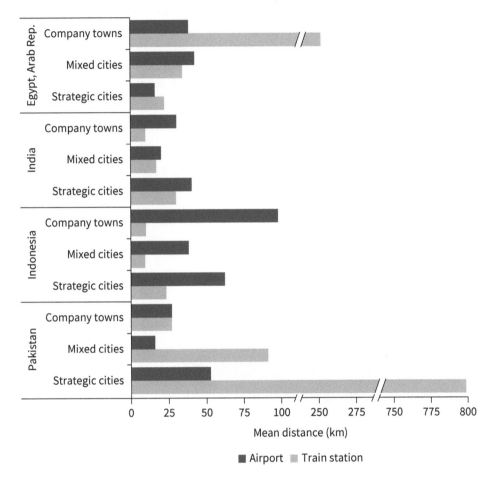

Sources: Original figure for this book, based on Amri, Roberts, and Li 2021, Balachandran, Joshi, and Li 2021; Ibrahim, Elshayal, and Athar 2021; and Qureshi and Li 2021.

Private cities exhibit very diverse population sizes across countries and city types (figure 3.4, panel a). However, population density is consistently higher among mixed cities in all countries covered, suggesting that overcrowding is the norm in their case (figure 3.4, panel b).

Overall variation in population size is small in Egypt, where all private cities range from 10,000 to 40,000 inhabitants. But the population density of the four mixed cities is much higher than that of El-Gouna, the only company town. On average, an

Egyptian mixed city hosts 2,176 inhabitants per square kilometer, compared to 462 for the company town.

In India, mixed cities are significantly larger than company towns and strategic cities. The median population sizes are 500,000, 156,000, and 140,000 respectively. Once again, mixed cities are denser, hosting on average a striking 11,224 inhabitants per square kilometer. The population densities of company towns and strategic cities are more in line with international patterns, with their medians reaching 3,096 and 2,222 people per square kilometer respectively. Across the four countries considered in this inventory, the private cities of India are the largest, and its mixed cities are the densest.

FIGURE 3.4 **Population of private cities**

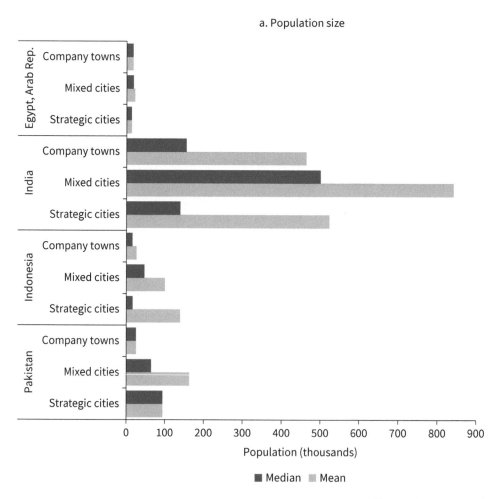

a. Population size

Population (thousands)

■ Median   ■ Mean

(Figure continues on next page)

FIGURE 3.4 **Population of private cities** (*continued*)

b. Population density

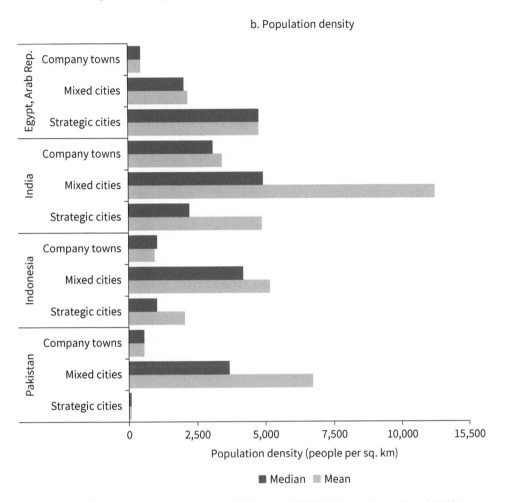

Sources: Original figure for this book, based on Amri, Roberts, and Li 2021, Balachandran, Joshi, and Li 2021; Ibrahim, Elshayal, and Athar 2021; and Qureshi and Li 2021.

With a mean population of 140,000 inhabitants, strategic cities are Indonesia's largest private cities. They are followed by mixed cities, with an average of 100,000 inhabitants. The ranking is reverted if median population is considered instead, but company towns are the smallest regardless of the metric used. The density of mixed cities is the highest, with the mean reaching 5,171 inhabitants per square kilometer, and the median 4,191. Both the strategic cities and company towns exhibit lower population densities, with the corresponding average at around 2,000 and 1,000 inhabitants per square kilometer respectively.

Finally, there is also variation in land use across private cities. A vast majority of them feature mixed land use, with specific areas to host service and commercial activities. And about three-fourths offer urban amenities in the form of community facilities including schools, hospitals and clinics, shopping malls, commercial areas, office space, parks, and sports facilities, among others.

In Egypt, all six private cities have a relatively balanced land-use distribution. However, the mixed cities are centered around services such as high-end retail, business and finance, or education and health, whereas the only company town circles around tourism.

Mixed land use is also the norm in India, but the smaller cities are tilted toward residential buildings and company towns toward industrial activities—especially steel mills. Mixed cities and strategic cities are the most diversified of the lot.

In Indonesia, while all 47 private cities display mixed land use, the smaller ones have a higher share of residential buildings and a weaker balance between uses. All company towns engage in natural resource extraction, even after they have been transformed into conventional cities. Strategic cities tend to be the most diversified with their main economic activities ranging from manufacturing to business to hospitality.

Mixed land use characterizes the 16 private cities of Pakistan as well. But army-built cities and Bahria towns support a wider range of services, such as business, finance, education, health, retail, and recreation. Conversely, Sialkot focuses mainly on manufacturing industries and logistic services to support exports. The smaller mixed cities mostly concentrate on residential property development.

References

Amri, Mulya, Mark Roberts, and Yue Li. 2021. "Private Cities in Indonesia." Background paper, *Private Cities: Outstanding Examples from Developing Countries and Their Implications for Urban Policy*, World Bank, Washington, DC.

Balachandran, Balakrishnan, Arjun Joshi, and Yue Li. 2021. "Private Cities in India." Background paper, *Private Cities: Outstanding Examples from Developing Countries and Their Implications for Urban Policy*, World Bank, Washington, DC.

Ibrahim, Kareem, Tamer Elshayal, and Sohaib Athar. 2021. "Private Cities in Egypt." Background paper, *Private Cities: Outstanding Examples from Developing Countries and Their Implications for Urban Policy*, World Bank, Washington, DC.

Qureshi, Nadia, and Yue Li. 2021. "Private Cities in Pakistan." Background paper, *Private Cities: Outstanding Examples from Developing Countries and Their Implications for Urban Policy*, World Bank, Washington, DC.

Annex 3A Country-level inventories of private cities

TABLE 3A.1 A country-level inventory of private cities: Arab Republic of Egypt

Typology	City	Land size (km²)	Population size (thousands)	Density (people per km²)	Distance to nearest major agglomeration (km)	Distance to nearest airport (km)	Distance to nearest train station (km)	Land use	Economic activities	Urban amenities
Company town	El-Gouna	37	17	462	28	39	253	M	Tourism	Yes
Mixed city	Al-Rehab City	10	40	4,000	30	17	28	M	Services	Yes
Mixed city	Madinaty	32	20	625	47	31	43	M	Services	Yes
Mixed city	New Giza	7	10	1,538	27	60	30	M	Services	Yes
Mixed city	SODIC West	6	16	2,540	35	63	38	M	Services	Yes
Strategic city	Cairo Festival City	3	13	4,779	24	16	23	M	Services	Yes

Source: Original table for this book, based on Ibrahim, Elshayal, and Athar 2021.
Note: M = mixed land use. The assessment of urban amenities is based on the existence of community facilities including schools, hospitals or clinics, shopping malls, commercial areas, office space, parks, and sports facilities, among others.

TABLE 3A.2 A country-level inventory of private cities: India

Typology	City	Land size (km²)	Population size (thousands)	Density (people per km²)	Distance to nearest major agglomeration (km)	Distance to nearest airport (km)	Distance to nearest train station (km)	Land use	Economic activities	Urban amenities
Company town	Aamby Valley	33	156	4,718	50	55	14	M	Tourism	Yes
Company town	Bhilai Township	357	1,000	2,801	145	40	7	M	Industry	Yes
Company town	Bokaro Steel City	183	560	3,060	130	4	9	M	Industry	Yes
Company town	Jamshedpur	244	1,370	5,627	107	4	5	M	Industry	Yes
Company town	Modinagar	263	130	494	85	65	4	M	Serv./Manuf.	Yes
Company town	Reliance Greens	3	13	4,223	350	18	26	M	Industry	Yes
Company town	Vidyanagar Township	3	10	3,096	330	28	5	M	Industry	Yes
Mixed city	Gurgaon	406	1,308	3,222	27	13	28	M	Serv./Manuf.	Yes
Mixed city	Lodha Palava City	18	500	27,457	16	24	6	M	Commercial	Yes
Mixed city	Sriperumbudur	19	25	1,289	33	24	17	M	Industry	Yes
Strategic city	Dholera	920	2,000	2,175	108	122	96	M	Serv./Manuf.	Yes
Strategic city	Electronic City	4	51	13,998	16	39	10	M	Serv./Manuf.	Yes
Strategic city	GIFT City, Ahmedabad	4	—	—	26	11	17	M	Services	Yes
Strategic city	Mahindra World City, Chennai	6	24	3,934	47	33	2	M	Serv./Manuf.	Yes
Strategic city	Mahindra World City, Jaipur	12	—	—	22	16	19	M	Serv./Manuf.	Yes
Strategic city	Mundra SEZ	180	400	2,222	50	53	53	M	Industry	Yes
Strategic city	New Town Rajarhat	60	140	2,333	13	9	14	M	Services	Yes

Source: Original table for this book, based on Balachandran, Joshi, and Li 2021.

Note: M = mixed land use; Manuf. = manufacturing; S = services; — = not available. The assessment of urban amenities is based on the existence of community facilities including schools, hospitals and clinics, commercial areas, office space, parks, and sport facilities among others.

TABLE 3A.3 A country-level inventory of private cities: Indonesia

Typology	City	Land size (km²)	Population size (thousands)	Density (people per km²)	Distance to nearest major agglomeration (km)	Distance to nearest airport (km)	Distance to nearest train station (km)	Land use	Economic activities	Urban amenities
Company town	Bontang	498	92	185	80	77	—	M	Mining	Yes
Company town	Duri	15	16	1,033	83	47	—	M	Oil and gas	Yes
Company town	Muara Enim	20	30	1,534	137	138	7	M	Mining	Yes
Company town	Rumbai	12	23	1,887	6	113	—	M	Oil and gas	Yes
Company town	Sawahlunto	273	5	18	53	55	13	M	Mining	Yes
Company town	Sorowako	11	13	1213	361	208	—	M	Mining	Yes
Company town	Tembagapura	4	3	715	1,965	48	—	M	Mining	Yes
Mixed city	Alam Sutera	8	86	10,738	22	13	9	M	Commercial	Yes
Mixed city	Bintaro Jaya	25	213	8,531	18	13	7	M	Commercial	Yes
Mixed city	Bukit Semarang Baru	10	40	3,960	11	8	11	M	Manufacturing	Yes
Mixed city	Bumi Serpong Damai	60	331	5,565	24	20	3	M	Commercial	Yes
Mixed city	Citra Maja Raya	30	10	346	55	40	—	M	Commercial	Yes
Mixed city	Citra Land Talassa	7	2	277	9	9	—	M	Commercial	Yes
Mixed city	Citra Raya Tangerang	28	85	3,076	38	21	21	M	Commercial	Yes
Mixed city	Harvest City	14	34	2,519	27	21	14	M	Commercial	Yes
Mixed city	Kendal Industrial Park	22	29	1,335	17	12	4	M	Industry	Yes
Mixed city	Kota Baru Parahyangan	13	39	3,092	19	14	3	M	Commercial	Yes
Mixed city	Kota Deltamas	32	129	4,034	41	36	19	M	Manufacturing	Yes
Mixed city	Kota Jababeka Cikarang	56	396	7,066	34	30	8	M	Commercial	Yes
Mixed city	Lippo Cikarang	55	231	4,191	34	29	15	M	Manufacturing	Yes

(Table continues on next page)

TABLE 3A.3 A country-level inventory of private cities: Indonesia *(continued)*

Typology	City	Land size (km²)	Population size (thousands)	Density (people per km²)	Distance to nearest major agglomeration (km)	Distance to nearest airport (km)	Distance to nearest train station (km)	Land use	Economic activities	Urban amenities
Mixed city	Lippo Karawaci (Lippo Village)	33	32	963	29	14	2	M	Commercial	Yes
Mixed city	Millenium City	10	43	4,259	32	27	2	M	—	—
Mixed city	Pakuwon City	6	47	7,813	7	269	9	M	Commercial	Yes
Mixed city	Pakuwon Indah	4	32	7,943	10	253	6	M	Commercial	Yes
Mixed city	Pantai Indah Kapuk	8	90	11,212	17	10	10	M	Commercial	Yes
Mixed city	Sentul City	30	84	2,807	39	34	15	M	Commercial	Yes
Mixed city	Summarecon Bandung	8	11	1,361	10	15	3	M	Services	Yes
Mixed city	Summarecon Kelapa Gading	6	106	17,011	8	12	2	M	Commercial	Yes
Mixed city	Summarecon Mutiara Makassar	4	7	1,865	12	7	—	M	Commercial	Yes
Mixed city	Summarecon Serpong	25	218	8,728	26	15	9	M	Commercial	Yes
Mixed city	Suvarna Sutera	26	165	6,360	39	17	28	M	Commercial	Yes
Mixed city	Tanjung Bunga Township	10	42	4,233	4	21	—	M	Hospitality	Yes
Strategic city	Batam	715	1,756	2,456	294	11	—	M	Industry/Trade	Yes
Strategic city	Kota Baru Bandar Kemayoran	5	65	14,350	8	14	5	M	Commercial	Yes
Strategic city	Kota Baru Maja	26	75	2,883	57	43	1	M	Commercial	Yes
Strategic city	Metro Lampung	69	177	2,574	37	187	21	M	Commercial	Yes
Strategic city	New Indonesian Capital	30	31	1,021	31	34	—	M	Commercial	Yes
Strategic city	SEZ—Arun	26	48	1,824	196	184	20	SEZ	—	—
Strategic city	SEZ—Galang Batang	23	3	120	303	12	—	SEZ	Industry	Yes

(Table continues on next page)

TABLE 3A.3 A country-level inventory of private cities: Indonesia (continued)

Typology	City	Land size (km²)	Population size (thousands)	Density (people per km²)	Distance to nearest major agglomeration (km)	Distance to nearest airport (km)	Distance to nearest train station (km)	Land use	Economic activities	Urban amenities
Strategic city	SEZ—Mandalika	10	14	1,384	124	16	—	SEZ	Hospitality	Yes
Strategic city	SEZ—MBTK	6	0	39	170	168	—	SEZ	Industry	Yes
Strategic city	SEZ—Palu	16	8	474	305	23	—	SEZ	Industry	Yes
Strategic city	SEZ—Sei Mangkei	19	17	879	89	75	5	SEZ	Industry	Yes
Strategic city	SEZ—Sorong	5	1	149	1,393	19	—	SEZ	Manufacturing	Yes
Strategic city	SEZ—Tanjung Lesung	15	8	544	124	118	88	SEZ	Hospitality	Yes
Strategic city	Sofifi	28	11	374	1,117	24	—	M	Commercial	Yes
Strategic city	Tanjung Selor	8	16	2,053	372	9	—	M	Commercial	Yes

Source: Original table for this book, based on Amri, Roberts, and Li 2021.
Note: M = mixed land use; SEZ = Special Economic Zone; — = not available. The assessment of urban amenities is based on the existence of community facilities including schools, hospitals and clinics, shopping malls, commercial areas, office space, parks, and sport facilities among others.

TABLE 3A.4 A country-level inventory of private cities: Pakistan

Typology	City	Land size (km²)	Population size (thousands)	Density (people per km²)	Distance to nearest major agglomeration (km)	Distance to nearest airport (km)	Distance to nearest train station (km)	Land use	Economic activities	Urban amenities
Company town	Bahria Town Karachi	72	25	347	40	33	50	M	Commercial	Yes
Company town	Steel Town Karachi	33	25	760	30	21	3	M	Industry	Yes
Mixed city	Bahria Town Lahore	16	38	2,363	18	36	17	M	Commercial	Yes
Mixed city	Bahria Town Rawalpindi	28	48	1,711	18	21	19	M	Commercial	Yes
Mixed city	DHA Bahawalpur	7	134	18,148	1	1	15	M	Commercial	Yes
Mixed city	DHA Karachi	36	81	2,290	6	22	8	M	Commercial	Yes
Mixed city	DHA Lahore	87	378	4,343	7	2	6	M	Commercial	Yes
Mixed city	DHA Multan	36	132	3,615	4	3	4	M	Commercial	Yes
Mixed city	DHA Peshawar	3	13	3,736	17	17	17	M	Commercial	Yes
Mixed city	DHA Rawalpindi	35	134	3,863	7	19	9	M	Commercial	Yes
Mixed city	Lake City	10	34	3,547	15	30	4	M	Pharma	Yes
Mixed city	Model Town	6	28	4,693	5	16	6	M	Manufacturing	Yes
Mixed city	Naval Anchorage	6	20	3,357	14	20	990	M	Commercial	Yes
Mixed city	Sialkot	32	928	29,000	51	3	2	M	Manufacturing	Yes
Strategic city	Gwadar	604	91	150	914	6	980	M	Trade/Services	Yes
Strategic city	Hunza	15,031	98	7	600	99	614	M	Tourism	Yes

Source: Original table for this book, based on Qureshi and Li 2021.

Note: DHA = Defense Housing Authority; M = mixed land use; Pharma = pharmaceuticals. DHA: Defense Housing Authority. The assessment of urban amenities is based on the existence of community facilities including schools, hospitals and clinics, shopping malls, commercial areas, office space, parks, and sport facilities among others.

CHAPTER 4

Necessary conditions for private cities to emerge

The proposed analytical framework helps organize ideas about private cities, including the conditions for their existence, their characteristics, and their outcomes. At the same time, the review of outstanding private cities in the developing world shows that the concrete circumstances surrounding their emergence and development can be very diverse. This greater granularity can be tapped to better understand what lies behind the emergence of private cities in practice. Four shared features stand out: a particularly advantageous location, a weak or removed local government, an extraordinary private actor, and an enabling institutional environment. These preconditions had been approached from a high level of abstraction in the analytical framework but gain considerable texture thanks to the empirical review.

Particularly advantageous locations

In the proposed analytical framework the *potential of the locality* (α) is a critically important parameter in determining the type of equilibrium that arises. The higher that potential is, the more likely that the locality will urbanize. Indeed, not all locations are equally suitable for urban development, even when facing the same policy environment. Only some of them make it possible for businesses to tap into the markets for labor, goods, and services offered by the regional, national, or even international economy. A key question is what makes such locations advantageous. The review of outstanding private cities in the developing world provides some hints in this respect.

In some cases, the advantage of a location comes directly from nature. Company towns, in particular, tend to emerge in places where highly valuable mineral resources are abundant. In India, for example, due to the local availability of the raw materials needed for steelmaking—coal, iron ore, and limestone—Jamshedpur was built away from existing economic hubs in what is now the lagging state of Jharkhand. The villages around also hosted large numbers of blacksmiths with indigenous knowledge of local mineral resources (chapter 15).

In other cases, the economic potential resulted from a major economywide shock, such as structural transformation, global integration, a political disruption, or a technological breakthrough. Regardless of its specific form, the shock affected the spatial equilibrium of the country, making some previously backwater locations suddenly attractive for urbanization. This change in fortunes may generate a new local dynamic.

Start with structural transformation. Urbanization is associated with a shift from agricultural activities to manufacturing and services, with changes in the sectoral and spatial composition of economic activity being two facets of the same phenomenon. The result of this transformation is a steady rise in the demand for denser industrial, commercial, and residential land. If conventional cities cannot satisfy this demand, private actors may step in.

In Bangladesh, almost 35 million more people are expected to live in cities over the next two decades. Dhaka itself is at the center of this transformation, having gone from a population of 3 million in 1980 to 18 million today. With 29,000 inhabitants per square kilometer, Bangladesh's capital has already become one of the most densely populated cities in the world. But a huge spatial imbalance creates enormous opportunities for East Dhaka; with a surface area comparable to that of a major European city, it sits next to the city center, but only hosts 900,000 inhabitants.

The area has remained mostly rural because a major river embankment planned decades ago was never built, which makes it flood prone. This is changing rapidly as major private developers are filling vast tracts of land with sand to build their real estate projects (chapter 9).

The urbanization potential of locations is also affected by global integration. In India, the trade and market liberalization reforms adopted in 1991 were associated with unprecedented private sector dynamism. This was at a time when large companies in advanced economies were actively seeking opportunities to outsource some of their back-office business operations to developing countries.

With its large numbers of English-speaking engineers, India was particularly well placed to seize the new opportunities. The country saw a rising tide of foreign direct investment, which, in turn, boosted the demand for commercial real estate. However, existing major cities, such as Delhi, failed to accommodate such demand. Against this background, a nearby locality like Gurgaon stood out as the second-best solution to investors (chapter 14).

Major political disruptions have been at play as well. In Bolivia, indigenous villages had been subsumed into large estates until the 1950s, when radical land reforms unsettled the traditional agricultural system. Growing demographic pressure combined with local inheritance practices led to a repeated division of land plots, pushing many in the young rural cohorts to migrate. El Alto, the edge of the plateau overlooking the capital city of La Paz, was a natural destination for migrants to secure a livelihood. Subsequently, the closing of overstaffed, state-owned tin mines also drove thousands of laid-off miners to El Alto, further accelerating its urbanization process (chapter 10).

In Vietnam, Phu My Hung is barely 4 kilometers away from the center of Ho Chi Minh City, the country's main economic hub. However, the area had remained mostly a salty marshland until the fall of the southern regime in 1975, arguably one of the last century's most significant political events. One important reason for such an anomaly was the strong presence of Vietcong guerrillas during the Vietnam War, which deterred investments and economic activity.

Phu My Hung's economic potential remained untapped during the relatively brief period under central planning that followed. But the advantages of such proximity to the center of Ho Chi Minh City were magnified after Vietnam embarked on a fast-paced transition from central planning to a market economy in the 1980s (chapter 22).

In other cases, technological breakthroughs radically changed spatial fortunes and created new opportunities for urban development. In Honduras, San Pedro Sula emerged as a plantation hub thanks to the success of frigorific shipping, which allowed taking refrigerated bananas—at the time, an exotic delicacy—to markets before they would rot. Until a century ago, the area had been used mostly as commons for cattle grazing, with a government-led attempt to convert it into coffee production being largely unsuccessful. But its potential for banana growing, combined with the proximity of a port, made it attractive to fruit production companies (chapter 13).

In Nigeria, the building of Eko Atlantic was made possible only by sea dredging and sand filling on a massive scale. About 10 square kilometers of land are being reclaimed from the ocean, which requires moving 140 million tons of sand and bordering it with a sea defense barrier made of 100,000 five-ton concrete blocks. When completed, this structure will be 8.5 kilometers long, stand 8.5 meters above sea level, and comprise a wave deflector. In the absence of the technical and logistical capability to do all this, Eko Atlantic would simply not exist (chapter 18).

Regardless of whether the impetus for urbanization came from the geography of natural resources or a shock affecting the spatial distribution of economic potential, the review of outstanding private cities in developing countries shows that most of them emerged in the vicinity of major urban agglomerations (table 4.1).

The major urban agglomerations closest to the 14 outstanding private cities considered have a median population of 14.8 million, and a median GDP of US$77 billion. And the median distance between the centroids of these 14 private cities and those of the major urban agglomerations in their vicinity is barely 33 kilometers.

TABLE 4.1 **Major urban agglomerations near selected outstanding private cities**

Country	Private city	Nearest major urban agglomeration			
		City name	Distance (km)	Population (million)	GDP (US$, billions)
Bangladesh	East Dhaka	Dhaka	1	20	65
Bolivia	El Alto	La Paz	7	2	11
China	Gu'an	Beijing	50	22	634
Egypt, Arab Rep.	Cairo Festival City	Cairo	24	20	91
Honduras	San Pedro Sula	Tegucigalpa	180	1	5
India	Gurgaon	Delhi	27	17	293
	Jamshedpur	Kolkata	107	15	150
Indonesia	Batam	Singapore	294	5	424
	Kota Baru Maja	Jakarta	57	33	304
Nigeria	Eko Atlantic	Lagos	10	18	43
Pakistan	Bahria Town Karachi	Karachi	40	15	79
	Sialkot	Lahore	51	11	38
South Africa	Waterfall City	Johannesburg	20	5	76
Vietnam	Phu My Hung	Ho Chi Minh City	4	9	62

Sources: Original table for this book, based on chapters 9–22 and other publicly available resources; LandScan Global 2018; and World Population Review 2021.

Weak or removed local governments

Another critically important parameter in the proposed analytical framework is the *capacity of the local government* (θ). And one of the insights from this framework is that private cities (of any type) are more likely to emerge when such capacity is low. The review of outstanding private cities in developing countries confirms this prediction.

Private cities are indeed more likely to emerge when the ability of local governments to assemble land, build infrastructure, and provide services does not meet the standards assumed by urban textbooks. In many developing countries, local governments do not have the authority to convene a myriad of institutions with overlapping functions in the jurisdiction. They often find it difficult to mobilize the necessary financial resources and lack the capacity to implement urban plans and land regulations.

In Bangladesh, for example, expanding the increasingly congested capital city eastward would have required the construction of a major river embankment and the maintenance of retention ponds and canals, which the local government proved unable to do. With most of East Dhaka remaining flood prone, Ahmed Akbar Sobhan and other large real estate developers took on the urbanization process through massive sand-filling of low-lying land (chapter 9).

In Nigeria, similarly, the sprawling capital city of Lagos has become one of the biggest and messiest agglomerations in the world. By reclaiming a peninsula as large as Manhattan just across from the city center and by developing it as Eko Atlantic—a city with a tidy Dubai-like urban design—Gilbert Chagoury is tapping the largely unmet needs for urban infrastructure and service delivery of high-end firms and affluent segments of society (chapter 18).

However, the review of outstanding private cities in developing countries also reveals other reasons why local governments may not lead the urbanization process (figure 4.1). Deliberate neglect—if not outright discrimination—is one of them. In colonial India, Jamshedji Tata preferred to build his massive steel mill away from cities managed by British rulers. By choosing a setting in the gray area between colonial governance and the purview of local landlords, he could navigate between the two systems and ensure greater control over his project. His model city of Jamshedpur was also an affirmation of what India would accomplish if it could take its destiny into its own hands (chapter 15).

Similarly, in South Africa, where Apartheid policies had resulted in dramatic spatial segregation along racial lines. The demise of Apartheid, in turn, was accompanied by a surge of crime in cities, but also by a massive government effort to improve connectivity and bring disadvantaged populations and job opportunities closer together. These two trends combined made the vast tract of land assembled by Moosa Ismail Mia on the outskirts of Johannesburg especially well suited for urban development. His descendants did not miss the chance to tap it and build Waterfall City (chapter 21).

Finally, other outstanding private cities in developing countries emerged as the result of governments becoming aware of their capacity constraints and in response, tapping the greater capacity of private actors in support of urban development. This was accomplished in practice by mobilizing reputable firms—often from more advanced

FIGURE 4.1 Key characteristics of the local government in selected outstanding private cities

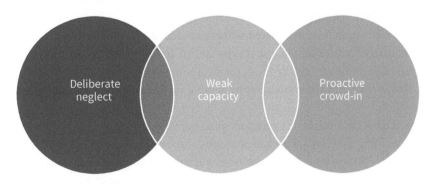

Source: Original illustration for this book.

economies—and by experimenting with new institutional arrangements to split respon-sibilities and benefits with them.

For example, until the turn of the century, urban development in the Arab Republic of Egypt had been primarily government-led. But progress in developing new cit-ies in desert areas around major metropolitan centers turned out to be much slower than anticipated. Acknowledging this reality, the government increasingly relied on regulatory power and land concessions to catalyze private sector participation. Cairo Festival City—where the chosen developer was United Arab Emirates–based Majid Al Futtaim—embodies the new approach (chapter 12).

In Indonesia, the government had entrusted the development of Batam island to one of its major state-owned enterprises, but progress was modest at best. The locality only took off after 1989, when the government of nearby Singapore proposed a deal to develop it into a major industrial park area where it could relocate its factories. Under the terms of this deal, urban development was successfully put in the hands of reputable Singapore-based corporations (chapter 16).

In Vietnam, the leading reformers in the country's transition from central planning to a market economy were keen to experiment with the possibilities opened by newly established land-use rights. Phu My Hung was selected as the pilot for the approach, and the company of Lawrence Ting, a businessman from Taiwan, China, as the private partner. The government contributed land, whereas Lawrence Ting's company built major export-processing zones, energy and transport infrastructure, and especially, a new model city (chapter 22).

Extraordinary private actors

Another important institutional parameter in the proposed analytical framework is the *clout of the private actor* (μ), interpreted as its ability to assemble and develop large tracts of urban land. The framework suggests that such clout needs to reach some mini-mum threshold for a private city to emerge, a result that the review of outstanding private cities in developing countries seems to confirm.

These cities are indeed associated with extraordinary levels of agency. The private actors associated with them use a diverse set of levers to influence and coordinate investments, including visionary ideas, financial strength, implementation capacity, and political networks. But there is also considerable variation in what makes them special (figure 4.2).

Some of these remarkable private actors stand out for their planning and implementation capacity, building cities on a scale and at a speed that would be out of reach for most local governments. Often, they even engage in several large urban projects at once.

In Indonesia, for example, the main actor behind the rapid emergence of Kota Baru Maja is Pak Ciputra, a descendant of Chinese merchants who became the coun-try's most significant real estate developer. His holding company has been involved in

FIGURE 4.2 **Key characteristics of private actors in selected outstanding private cities**

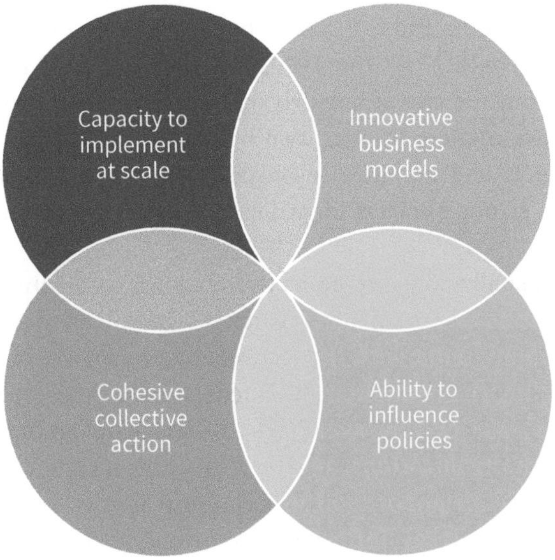

Source: Original illustration for this book.

close to 50 urban projects at home and abroad. Kota Baru Maja's population already exceeds 500,000 and is expected to reach 1.5 million by 2035 (chapter 17).

Something similar happens in Pakistan, where Bahria Town Karachi is being developed by a large real estate company owned by Malik Riaz, one of the country's wealthiest persons. With more than 50,000 employees and a major financial institution affiliated with it, the company is working simultaneously on several major urban development projects, which are at different stages of completion. Bahria Town Karachi stands out as the most ambitious of all, with a surface comparable to that of Manhattan and the capacity to host one million inhabitants (chapter 19).

Other private actors are extraordinary because of the innovative nature of their business models. In China, Wenxue Wang introduced the "industry first" approach to urban development and applied it to Gu'an. In his view, a new city without a clear economic rationale would run the risk of becoming a bedroom town. Over 3,700 of his company's employees work as a "corporate solicitation branch," focused on attracting investors to urban development projects. Another 300 employees help investors with local tax registration, patent applications, and legal support (chapter 11).

Not all significant private actors are individual entrepreneurs or companies though. Some are unusually cohesive collectives that managed to articulate a common vision, form an effective coalition, and discourage free riding. Places with strong social networks seem to have an edge in this respect.

In Pakistan, the government did not make Sialkot's development a priority, partly due to its proximity to the India-Pakistan border, a source of vulnerability in the event of a military conflict. By the 1980s, in the context of fast-growing global trade, this neglect put the city at a disadvantage. The Sialkot business community then decided to take matters into its own hands. Its ability to identify key urban development projects and mobilize resources to implement them is built on the *Biadari* system—a strong societal identification based on common ancestry and lineage (chapter 20).

Some of the unusually cohesive collectives behind successful private cities are civil society organizations, rather than businesses. In Bolivia, the city of El Alto was built by indigenous migrants with little government support on the inhospitable highlands overlooking the capital city. Influenced by a range of ideologies—from Trotskyism in the case of schoolteachers to socialism among former miners, indigenism for youth organizations, and even libertarianism for informal traders—they formed powerful neighborhood associations and resorted to mobilization and conflict to secure local infrastructure investments and service delivery (chapter 10).

Finally, some of the private actors derive their unusual effectiveness from their ability to influence government decisions, legally or otherwise. In Honduras, the emergence of San Pedro Sula was the result of the crudest form of influence by US entrepreneur Samuel Zemurray—namely, hiring mercenaries to stage a political coup. His involvement in the politics of the country did not stop there, as he lent money to the government on multiple occasions, he represented it four times in foreign debt negotiations, he bribed officials to ensure low taxes on banana exports, and he supported two rebellions on the terms of use of rivers and railroads (chapter 13).

Political connections have been used in more subtle forms in other cases. In India, Gurgaon could emerge thanks to clever ways to circumvent legal, political, and bureaucratic hurdles to assemble agricultural land and convert it to urban uses. K. P. Singh, a large developer, was the most significant private actor in this case. As a former army officer with close ties to its top brass, a leader of national-level business associations, and an acquaintance of former prime minister Rajiv Gandhi, K.P. Singh benefited greatly from these connections, with changes in government policies suiting his business interests (chapter 14).

An enabling institutional environment

Investment decisions are not made in a vacuum. When considering whether to commit the resources needed to build a city, the private actor may be understandably reluctant to proceed if transaction costs are too high, coordination among the relevant government agencies is too weak, and future policy directions are uncertain. An enabling institutional environment is therefore needed to reduce the regulatory and political risks faced by the private actor and to mitigate the time inconsistency challenges posed by a major sunk investment (Arezki et al. 2017). The review of outstanding private cities in developing countries reveals several ways in which this was accomplished.

In Pakistan, for example, urban development is under the purview of provincial authorities so that local governments have little autonomy and resources. However, in 2001 a devolution plan was adopted for five years. Although this time window was limited, the business community of Sialkot seized this opening to increase its participation in local affairs and champion major private-led infrastructure investments, including the international airport. The process also allowed the local business association to gain self-confidence on urban development issues (chapter 20).

An enabling institutional environment becomes even more important when local governments deliberately aim to crowd in private actors. In Indonesia, a development authority was established directly under the country's president to accelerate land acquisition and planning approvals in Batam. A regulation was also passed to allow foreign corporations to retain majority ownership of their facilities and to independently operate their industrial parks in Batam (chapter 16).

An enabling institutional environment is not necessarily static, however. Institutional fluidity is, in fact, one of the stylized facts from the review of experience with outstanding private cities worldwide. Similar transitions are underway in developing countries nowadays. Most often, private cities end up becoming conventional cities, run by a local government. But the speed of these institutional transitions varies considerably.

For example, Jamshedpur in India was declared a "notified area" in 1924, meaning that it was officially considered in transition from rural to urban. However, it has remained that way, despite a population of over 600,000. This is not for lack of trying. The first attempt to convert the area into a municipality was in 1967, but almost half a century later, the case is still pending before the Supreme Court. In the meantime, Jamshedpur is on a lease from the state government to the private actor, on the condition "to maintain the standard of Municipal Services and Civic amenities" (chapter 15).

On the other hand, the institutional transition was rapid in Gurgaon, also in India. In 2001—two decades after it had started developing—the private city was classified as urban. In 2008 a municipal corporation was established, and in 2011 the first local election was held. From 2016 onward, the municipal corporation started taking responsibility for public infrastructure and service provision. Further, a broader metropolitan authority was set up in 2017 with a mandate on urban planning and infrastructure development for the entire agglomeration (figure 4.3). This transition resulted in ever-expanding boundaries for the area under local government oversight (chapter 14).

There has also been institutional fluidity when deliberately crowding in private actors. For example, in Indonesia a municipal government was formally established for Batam in 1983. At the time, it was focused on public administration and public services,

FIGURE 4.3 **Institutional fluidity over time: Local government boundaries in Gurgaon, India**

░░░░ Gurgaon village
Municipal Corporation of Gurgaon (established in 2008)
▬▬▬ Gurugram Metropolitan Development Authority (established in 2017)

Source: Original figure for this book, based on chapter 14.

while a development authority under the nation's president was responsible for land management and investment promotion. But in 1998, following Indonesia's "big bang" decentralization reforms, the development authority handed over significant functions to the local government (chapter 16).

Remarkably, in the case of Gu'an, China, the timing and form of the institutional transition had been established in the contract between the local government and the private actor. The legal agreement signed between the two parties was for 50 years. Under its terms, the private actor assumed responsibility for urban planning, infrastructure development, city administration, and investment solicitation. In exchange for these services, it received the right to develop land and to accrue part of the revenue from the new city. During this period, the local government could only approve and supervise projects, but it is scheduled to acquire full ownership when the contract expires (chapter 11).

References

Arezki, Rabah, Patrick Bolton, Sanjay Peters, Frederic Samama, and Joseph Stiglitz. 2017. "From Global Savings Glut to Financing Infrastructure." *Economic Policy* 32 (90): 221–61.

LandScan Global. 2018. dataset, Oak Ridge National Laboratory. https://doi.org/10.48690/1524213.

World Population Review. 2021. dataset. https://worldpopulationreview.com/world-cities.

CHAPTER 5

Taking on local government functions ... and some more

In a private city, a significant private actor takes on roles usually performed by a local government. In terms of the proposed analytical framework, the private actor develops urban land, much the same as a local government would. On close inspection, however, this requires performing a range of diverse functions, such as assembling land, improving transport connectivity, or planning the use of land and delivering services. Private actors may take on some or all these functions to attain their goals, or they may even be compelled to do so by strategic local governments. But they may also go further and take on nontraditional roles, such as being an industrial champion to attract business to the city or a political actor to tilt policies and investments to the city's advantage (figure 5.1).

Land assembly

No urban agglomeration can emerge without successfully assembling a substantial amount of relatively unencumbered land. The review of empirical regularities at the global level presented previously shows that outstanding private cities in the developing world tend to occupy a strikingly high position in the ranking of cities in their own countries. This suggests that massive amounts of land were indeed assembled for their development. However, the extent to which private actors were involved in the land assembly process varied.

When land assembly was entirely conducted by significant private actors, the mechanisms used were most often unconventional. Local governments typically acquire land for urban development through eminent domain, which has an element of coercion,

FIGURE 5.1 **Local government functions performed by significant private actors in selected outstanding private cities**

Country	Private city	Traditional functions			Nontraditional functions	
		Land assembly	Connectivity enhancement	Land-use planning and service delivery	Business development	Political activism
Bangladesh	East Dhaka	●	○	◐	○	○
Bolivia	El Alto	●	○	◐	○	●
China	Gu'an	○	○	●	●	○
Egypt, Arab Rep.	Cairo Festival City	○	○	●	◐	○
Honduras	San Pedro Sula	◐	◐	◐	●	●
India	Gurgaon	◐	●	◐	●	◐
India	Jamshedpur	●	○	●	●	◐
Indonesia	Batam	○	◐	●	●	●
Indonesia	Kota Baru Maja	●	◐	●	○	○
Nigeria	Eko Atlantic	●	○	●	○	○
Pakistan	Bahria Town Karachi	●	○	●	○	○
Pakistan	Sialkot	○	●	○	●	◐
South Africa	Waterfall City	●	○	●	○	○
Vietnam	Phu My Hung	○	●	●	○	●

● Substantive involvement　◐ Partial involvement　○ No involvement

Source: Original figure for this book, based on chapters 9–22.

can be costly to implement, and is often met with resistance (Lozano-Gracia et al. 2013). But regardless of its merits, private actors are not vested with the legal authority to use this mechanism, which presents a significant challenge.

Legal constraints have not always been an effective deterrent, however. Forcible approaches to land assembly have often been reported in the development of private cities in developing countries. These efforts are more likely to succeed when land titling is partial, cadastres are incomplete, and land administration is weak, which are all quite common. Reports about land grabbing have thus been frequent in the media, especially in the South Asia region (Ohri 2017; chapter 14). In Pakistan, the methods used by Malik Riaz's company to acquire land for Bahria Town Karachi even led to a legal dispute that was settled by the Supreme Court only after the company paid US$3.1 billion as a compensation (chapter 19).

Given the difficulties of assembling land on a large scale near major urban agglomerations, a creative alternative has been to physically create new land. This is what

Gilbert Chagoury did in Nigeria for the development of Eko Atlantic. The city is indeed being built on land reclaimed from the ocean—an artificial peninsula the size of Manhattan on the shoreline of the country's most important economic hub. A Chinese company with expertise in dredging and sand-filling was mobilized to implement this innovative approach (chapter 18).

Other unconventional land assembly mechanisms have relied on financial rather than physical engineering. After the Asian financial crisis, many small developers went bankrupt in Indonesia. Several of them were active in Kota Baru Maja even before the government floated the idea of a new city. A bank restructuring agency formed to help rebuild the financial system seized and auctioned the failing developers' assets. Their purchase by a business partner allowed Pak Ciputra and other large developers to consolidate their grip on the urban development of the area (chapter 17).

However, given the difficulties for the private actor to assemble land on a large scale, in many cases the government has stepped in, directly allocating the area to be urbanized. For example, in the early development stages of Batam in Indonesia, land acquisition involved complex intergovernmental negotiations. Subsequently, a development authority, which was empowered to manage land issues without escalating them to the provincial government, was established under the country's presidency. This autonomy entitled the development authority to plan land use for the island as it deemed fit and to assign build and use rights to Singapore-based firms (chapter 16).

The process was similar in Vietnam, where the local authorities of Ho Chi Minh City were keen to develop its southern fringe, still mostly rural until the country's unification. This was to be done by experimenting with the new land-use rights legislation introduced as part of the country's economic reforms. Thus, the urbanization of this fringe, known as Saigon South, was to be partly in government hands, but strategically important sections would be under the responsibility of Lawrence Ting, the identified private actor. Once an agreement was reached on the areas each partner would develop, the local government of Ho Chi Minh City contributed the necessary land (figure 5.2).

Broader adjustments to the land regulatory regime—not on a case-by-case basis—have also been at play. In the Arab Republic of Egypt, the national government had decided in the 1970s to make large spans of the desert land it owned available for urban purposes. Initially, the development of new cities was tasked to a specialized government agency. Then, from the 1990s, desert land started being sold to private actors to get them involved in urban development. Majid Al Futtaim's company entered into one such agreement to build Cairo Festival City (chapter 12).

There are also cases in which governments did not formally modify the land regulatory regime but allowed for flexibility in its application. In India, for example, the legal framework for land acquisition, conversion, and resettlement stipulates that only government agencies and private actors authorized by the government can acquire land. This can be done only for defense, infrastructure development, industrial development,

FIGURE 5.2. **Land assembly: Public and private sections in the Phu My Hung area, Vietnam**

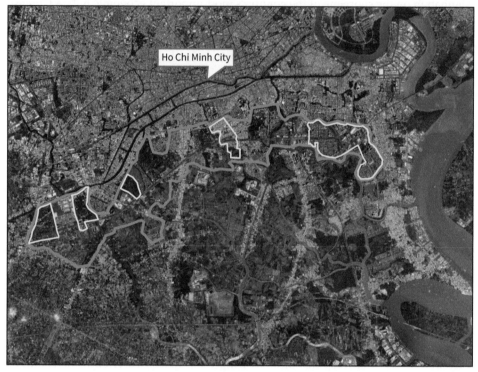

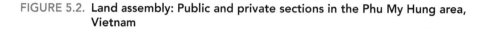

——— Overall land assembly ——— Phu My Hung

Source: Original figure for this book, based on chapter 22.

and public-private partnership (PPP) projects, and only provided that the occupants of the land get fair compensation.

In principle, the process is even more complex at the state level due to restrictions on the conversion of agricultural land. Yet, it is at the state level that flexibility was introduced. In the 1970s, to facilitate urban development and accommodate the needs of large developers, the state of Haryana made the entire Gurgaon district eligible for conversion to urban uses, thus circumventing the requirement that agricultural land be converted on a case-by-case basis.

Subsequently, the state of Haryana introduced a licensing system allowing private investors to directly acquire and assemble land from the market and to use the land for township development. This licensing system favored large developers, as it required a minimum threshold of 40 contiguous hectares of land (Balachandran, Joshi, and Li 2021). K. P. Singh's company alone accounted for 55 percent of all privately acquired land in the 1980s and nearly a third in the 1990s. As a result of this process, a vast majority of the urban land in Gurgaon has been developed by large investors (figure 5.3).

FIGURE 5.3. Land assembly: Urban land by type of developer in Gurgaon, India

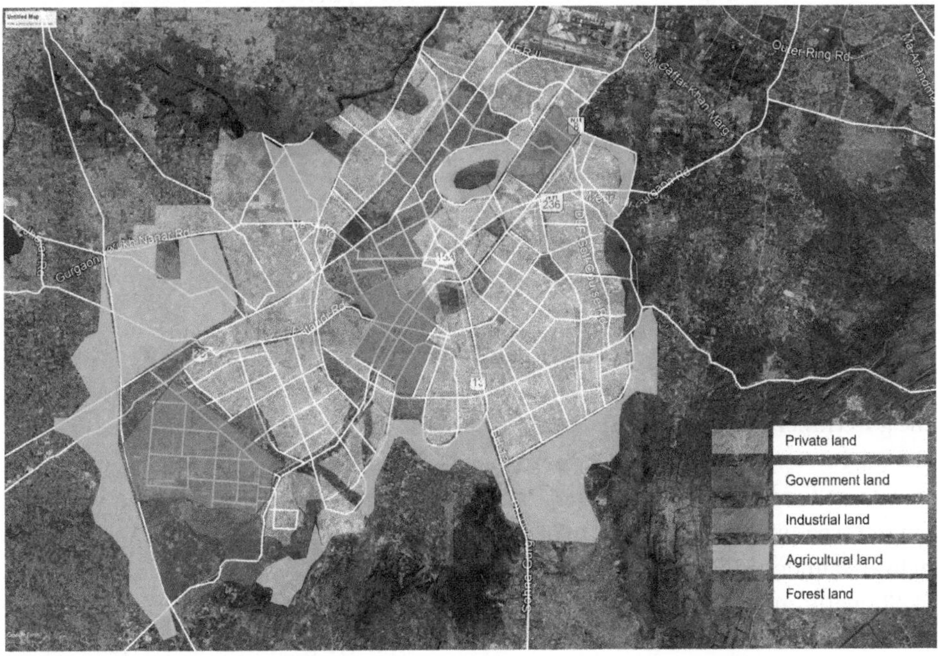

Legend:
- Private land
- Government land
- Industrial land
- Agricultural land
- Forest land

Source: Original figure for this book, based on Balachandran, Joshi, and Li 2021. Mapping and visualization using Google Earth © 2020 Maxar Technologies.

Connectivity enhancement

Large-scale infrastructure is generally provided by the government, with the private actor being opportunistic in tapping it to ensure access to markets for its project. Thus, most of the outstanding private cities reviewed emerged in the proximity of a highway, a port, or an airport that had been built for other purposes—from boosting economic activity in the surrounding region to supporting the connectivity of an existing urban agglomeration.

In Honduras, for example, Puerto Cortés existed as a port before banana companies started operations in nearby San Pedro Sula (chapter 13). In Vietnam, the main north-south highway had been built much earlier than when the development of Phu My Hung was conceived by the Ho Chi Minh City government (chapter 22). And in India, the construction of Terminal 3 in Delhi's international airport, one of the biggest in the world, was independent from efforts to develop Gurgaon (chapter 14).

However, governments have also been deliberate in building connecting infrastructure in support of private cities. In India, several expressways and a metro line linking Gurgaon to Delhi were delivered by the public sector (chapter 14). In Bolivia, similarly, the innovative cable car system of La Paz was designed by the national government in a way that would improve market access for El Alto, potentially redressing decades of neglect (chapter 10).

The focus on connecting infrastructure was particularly strong in Indonesia. There, all of the 1,679 kilometers of roads that existed in Batam as of 2019 had been built by the development authority under the president. This government agency had also built Batam's airport in 1996 and a network of six major bridges to the neighboring Rempang and Galang islands (figure 5.4, panel a). Similarly, in Kota Baru Maja, the public sector implemented several major infrastructure projects, including toll roads and a double-track commuter rail line connecting the new city to central Jakarta (figure 5.4, panel b).

However, in multiple instances, the private actor also became actively involved in enhancing connectivity and improving market access, sometimes in partnership with the government. In Pakistan, Sialkot's business association overhauled the internal arterial road system of the city, its dry port, and its international airport. The biggest investment was for a motorway to Lahore that is more than 90 kilometers long, with four lanes, seven interchanges, eight flyovers, 40 bridges, and 70 underpasses, and that was delivered under a PPP arrangement (chapter 20).

Similarly, in India, the public and private sectors came together to build an impressive 16-lane road spanning 8.3 kilometers to connect Gurgaon to Delhi. In parallel, the city benefited from the first privately financed light-rail system in India, a project that was jointly planned, financed, and executed by K. P. Singh's company and a major Indian infrastructure development and finance firm (chapter 14).

Land-use planning and service delivery

A functional city requires an efficient combination of commercial, residential, and recreational land; it also needs an adequate provision of basic services such as water, electricity, sewerage, and transportation. These two functions are traditionally in the hands of local governments. Allocating urban land to different uses and determining building heights by zone are typically handled by a planning unit, often with inputs from specialized firms and consultants. The provision of basic services, in turn, is generally in the hands of public utilities that recover some of their operating costs through user fees.

However, some or all of these functions can be taken over by significant private actors who want to increase productivity and improve the quality of life in the cities they develop and manage. Indeed, a well-planned city attracts more businesses and reduces congestion costs, whereas high-quality services are appreciated by households. If private actors internalize enough of the value created by these local public goods, it is in their interest to provide them (Engel, Fischer, and Galetovic 2005).

FIGURE 5.4. **Connectivity enhancement: Government led in Batam and Kota Baru Maja, Indonesia**

a. Bridges built by the government to connect Batam to neighboring islands

Name	Total span (m)	Vertical clearance (m)
 Tengku Fisabillilah	642	38
 Nara Singa II	420	15
 Raja Ali Haji	270	15
 Sultan Zainal Abidin	365	16.5
 Tuanku Tambusai	385	31
 Raja Kecil	180	9.5

(Figure continues on next page)

FIGURE 5.4. **Connectivity enhancement: Government led in Batam and Kota Baru Maja, Indonesia (continued)**

b. Commuter rail line built by the government to connect Kota Baru Maja to Jakarta

Name	Length (km)	Stations (number)
 KRL commuter line	55.6	17

Sources: Original figure for this book, based on information contained in chapter 16. Panel a (first row), © toffeespin from Singapore, licensed under CC BY 2.0, https://commons.wikimedia.org/wiki/File:Jembatan_Tengku _Fisabilillah_(jembatan_I).jpg. Panel a, second to sixth rows, © BP Batam. Used with permission. Further permission required for reuse. Panel b © Pilar Gusmao, licensed under CC BY-SA 4.0, https://commons.wikimedia.org/wiki /File:Combined_205_series_ex_Juanda_rail_crash-Palmerah.jpg.

Urban planning tends to be thorough in private cities associated with a major company or a large developer. In India, for example, the first blueprint for Jamshedpur was prepared by a US firm from Pittsburgh that was familiar with steel towns. As the local population grew, the plan was expanded by a British sanitary engineer influenced by the garden city principles, then by a British military engineer who was familiar with North American planning principles, and finally by a German architect who laid the groundwork for linear development along transport corridors (chapter 15). Decades later, the adherence of the city to an orderly layout is confirmed by satellite imagery (figure 5.5).

In South Africa, Waterfall City's master plan envisioned a compact urban layout that is at odds with the suburban sprawl prevailing in the area. Because local authorities expressed concern about the increased traffic congestion that such a large project could generate, the investor even financed a master plan that simulates traffic patterns up to 20 kilometers away from the private city (chapter 21).

In Vietnam, the master plan for Phu My Hung's central business district was chosen through an international competition. A high-profile jury was convened, and the pool of submissions was of exceptional quality. The final master plan received a Progressive Architecture Award in 1995, an honor award from the American Institute of Architects in 1997, and a Global Excellence Award for livability and sustainability from the Urban Land Institute in 2012 (chapter 22).

At the other end, when the main nongovernment actor is a business association or civil society, the growth of the private city is most often organic. One consequence of insufficient planning is the widespread presence of slums. For example, by the end of the 1980s, 37 percent of the dwellings in San Pedro Sula, in Honduras, were overcrowded and 53 percent of the population lived in informal settlements (chapter 13).

FIGURE 5.5. **Land-use planning: Thorough and properly implemented in Jamshedpur, India**

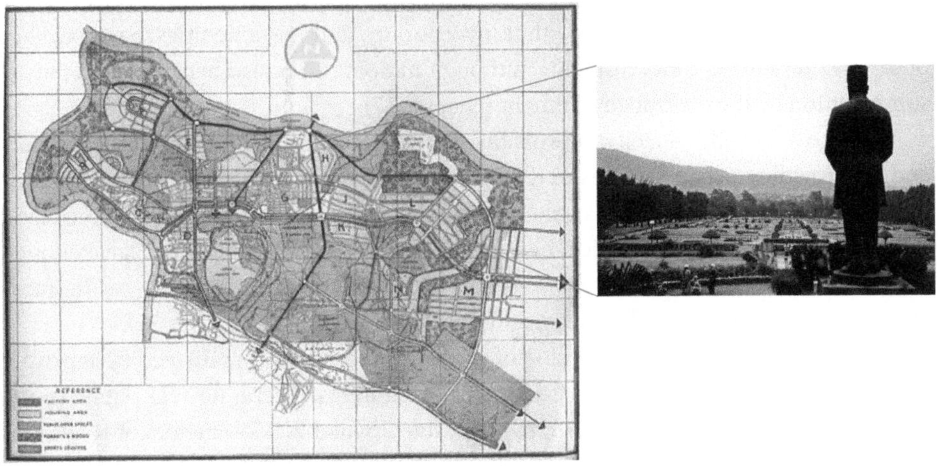

Source: ©TATA Central Archive. Reproduced with permission from TATA Central Archive; further permission required for reuse.

Planning is also partial in mixed cities where limited collaboration between public and private actors results in disconnected urban layouts. In Gurgaon, India, or in East Dhaka, Bangladesh, sizable portions of the urban agglomeration meet high planning standards. But others do not, and the whole would probably be more coherent had it been designed thoroughly rather than in a piecemeal fashion (chapters 14 and 9, respectively).

A similar diversity can be found in relation to service delivery. Private cities entirely built by large developers tend to fare better in this respect. There, the provision of amenities is often tailored to high- and middle-income groups, with a comprehensive package of services being one of the hooks allowing private actors to maximize their rent.

For example, uninterrupted electricity and water supply, efficient and timely solid waste management, good sanitation, a stable gas supply, reliable rescue and fire services, and 24-hour security are among the services that differentiate Bahria towns from other urban areas in Pakistan (chapter 19).

Similarly, Cairo Festival City in Egypt has an independent electricity station, a potable and irrigation water network, a sewerage system, natural gas network, and state-of-the-art telecommunications including two fiber-optic networks (chapter 12). And in Vietnam, Phu My Hung delivers services to its residents through a model that lumps all utility expenses together. In addition, it offers security, maintenance, street cleaning, and landscaping, and it has even established its own bus company to provide commuter service to downtown Ho Chi Minh City (chapter 22).

In some cases, the private actor had no other option than to take over service delivery, regardless of whether this was its preferred choice. In Indonesia, for example, the regional governance law mandates private investors to provide public services in the areas they develop. Kota Baru Maja thus incorporates multiple amenities in the package of services it delivers to its residents, although in doing so it also benefits from partial subsidization by the central government (chapter 17).

Weak government capacity is probably a more frequent reason why private actors end up providing urban services in the cities they develop. In India, a dedicated company was created to look after Jamshedpur's trunk infrastructure and service provision (chapter 15). And in South Africa, because the local government did not have enough resources to cover basic services, Waterfall City assumed responsibility for its road, water, sewerage, drainage, electricity, and fiber-optic networks (chapter 21).

It does not follow that the provision of urban services is always satisfactory in private cities. Gurgaon, India, illustrates frequent shortcomings. There, no real public transport system was in place until 2010; by then, the city had 200 kilometers of roads, but fewer than a quarter of them had sidewalks. Only two-thirds of the residents had access to piped water, and supply was intermittent. As of 2013, only half the residents were covered by the sewerage network. And power supply never stopped being an issue, as demand increased consistently faster than supply (chapter 14).

The provision of basic services in private cities is arguably the weakest when the relevant private actor is a business association or civil society. An extreme example is El Alto, Bolivia. Neighborhood associations tried to compensate for government neglect through approaches that amounted to community-driven development. However, half a century after the area had started urbanizing, 15 percent of El Alto's residents still had no access to electricity, only 25 percent had access to the sanitary network, and 65 percent to the potable water network (chapter 10).

Business development

The review of outstanding private cities in developing countries shows that significant private actors may also take on coordinating roles that go beyond the traditional functions of a local government. Being strategic in selecting the main economic sectors of their cities and actively supporting businesses, are two such nontraditional functions.

Significant private actors may not only mimic mayors who make decisions on intrinsically urban issues but may also behave as industrialists who run place-based policies to maximize the economic surplus of selected localities. Their actions are not sector-neutral but rather are aimed at championing specific drivers of local growth. In the spirit of an entrepreneurial state, they pick sectors and bet on winners.

A broad range of tools have been used to deliver this nontraditional function. A bold economic development vision can serve as a commitment device to coordinate with specific private businesses. It may also act as a signaling instrument to convince other stakeholders, mobilize resources, and mitigate the first-mover problem. Incentives can also be used to tilt the playing field—instead of leveling it—in favor of specific sectors of activity. And zoning, infrastructure, and services can be deliberately adjusted to accommodate the needs of the selected business partners, including foreign investors.

Nowhere is the link between private cities and business development more direct than in company towns. Almost by definition, these are urban agglomerations whose development inevitably centers around the activities of a large private firm.

This connection is obvious in the case of Jamshedpur, a private city founded in 1907 by Jamshedji Tata in one of India's poorest areas. By 1912, the steel plant anchoring the town was in full production. In 1945, Tata Motors was established as a manufacturer of locomotives, and in 1954 it entered automobile production. More recently, aviation steel started being produced in the city as part of the group's venture into the aerospace industry. This dynamism helped attract major international investors, making Jamshedpur one of the largest manufacturing hubs in eastern India (chapter 15).

A similar rags-to-riches story took place halfway around the globe in San Pedro Sula, Honduras. The area became the center of the global banana trade after Samuel Zemurray secured generous tax, land, and infrastructure concessions for his company. But his and other banana companies also became importers of basic goods (their cargo ships would have returned empty otherwise) and partnered with immigrants from Europe and the Middle East to produce goods locally. As the profitability of the banana business declined, the manufacturing side took off. Today, San Pedro Sula accounts for half of the country's exports and almost two-thirds of its GDP (chapter 13).

In other cases, the private actor developing the city is not directly related to the private firms making it thrive but is instrumental in attracting them. In the case of Batam, Indonesia, the government of Singapore is generally credited with articulating a vision for the city that was centered on boosting the competitiveness of its export-oriented firms. Large developers associated with the Singaporean government took care of planning and building the city, while Singapore-based firms moved there to take advantage of cheap urban land, reliable infrastructure services, and a supportive business environment. Electrical and electronic firms were heavily represented at the beginning; over time, Batam's economic activity expanded into shipbuilding and then tourism and the digital economy (chapter 16).

Gurgaon, India, is another illustration of this more detached form of business partnership. There, the main large developer shifted from residential to commercial property development to capitalize on growing foreign direct investment. Thanks to his extensive business network and political influence, K. P. Singh convinced the CEO of

General Electric to outsource business operations to India and more specifically to the facilities he offered in Gurgaon. Many other multinationals followed. By 2015, Gurgaon hosted more than half of the Fortune 500 companies, had gained a reputation as the startup capital of India, and had become an iconic image of the country's economic ascent (chapter 14).

Among the outstanding private cities in developing countries reviewed in this book, the most proactive approach to business development is probably that of Wenxue Wang, the private actor behind China's Gu'an. Aware that he would not be able to compete with large developers on volume, he adopted a strategy that bears similarities to Michael Porter's "business cluster" notion (Delgado, Porter, and Stern 2010). The motto of his company became "industry first," meaning that for urbanization projects to be successful they needed a clear economic rationale, otherwise running the risk of becoming bedroom towns.

In 2002, Gu'an was a poor agricultural county, with almost no industrial presence. Yet, based on its research, Wenxue Wang's company concluded that it should focus on advanced display manufacturing, aviation and aerospace, and biomedical research and development.

To attain this goal, it established industry-specific venture funds, partnerships with dozens of prestigious universities and research institutes, and an incubator to aid high-growth firms. Whereas competing localities offered land and tax subsidies, his company brought in clean room manufacturing experts from its aerospace clients to secure key investments. With suppliers and partners following, momentum built. Gu'an was dramatically transformed in barely two decades (figure 5.6). With over 520 companies attracted to the locality and 30,000 new jobs created, it now ranks as one of the top 100 counties in which to invest in China (chapter 11).

Political activism

Every local government tries to get support for its locality from authorities higher up. In addition to their more traditional functions, mayors are most often politicians too, and their daily work involves influencing public opinion and lobbying decision-makers. However, the review of outstanding private cities in developing countries suggests that such political activities are more prominent in some of them. Depending on the case, significant private actors have not only secured public funding for their urban endeavors—much the same as local governments would do—but have also managed to successfully tilt national policies in ways that benefit their urban projects. On a couple of occasions, significant private actors have also fought with authorities higher up and even seized power at the national level.

Moreover, there is a thin line between visionary undertakings and state capture. Private actors often bring new ideas and greater capacity, all of which are reflected in their usually oversized "clout." But there are many roads to success. In some cases,

FIGURE 5.6. Business development: The technology parks of Gu'an, China

a. Aerospace industry park

b. Pilot trial incubation base for major technology of Tsinghua University

clout can become shorthand for greased palms and graft. In others, it may even be more direct than that.

The most extreme example is of course that of San Pedro Sula. Samuel Zemurray, a successful entrepreneur in the global banana trade, took indirect control of the government of Honduras to secure favorable conditions for his business. To do this, he recruited mercenaries who overthrew the president of the country, and in 1912 he installed an exiled politician in the ousted president's place. In exchange, he was rewarded with generous tax, land, and infrastructure concessions. This is how the term "banana republic" came to be.

Samuel Zemurray's political engagement in Honduras lasted decades. He lent money to the government on several occasions, he represented it four times in foreign debt negotiations, he bribed officials to ensure low taxes on banana exports, and he supported two rebellions on the terms of use of rivers and railroads. His and other fruit companies also shaped the development of San Pedro Sula by advising its weak municipal government on local development policies (chapter 13).

Also in the Latin American region, the emergence and development of Bolivia's El Alto were associated with intense political infighting along ethnic lines. In the eighteenth century, the area was the starting place of a major rebellion against colonial power. The movement was led by indigenous leader Julián Apasa, who took the name Túpac Katari to honor illustrious predecessors in the fight against the Spaniards. The city of La Paz was sieged for over six months, and while the rebels were eventually defeated, the episode left a lasting imprint.

The area's urbanization process started two centuries later, driven by the influx of mostly indigenous rural migrants and retrenched miners. It was shaped by an unusually strong civil society movement that brought thousands of people together to mobilize for better urban services and economic opportunities in a context of neglect by the authorities. To achieve these goals, a myriad of neighborhood associations regrouped under powerful federations with names as suggestive as FURIA, meaning "fury" in Spanish.

Confronted with limited receptiveness by the authorities, civil society organizations actively participated in movements against the country's recurrent military dictatorships. They eventually contributed to the election of Evo Morales as Bolivia's first indigenous president in 2006. Over time, the relationship between civil society and the government became increasingly clientelist (Villegas Limas 2021).

In other cases, significant private actors indirectly influenced national policies in favor of their urban projects, without seizing political power. In Sialkot, Pakistan, the main problem faced by the local business community was the reluctance of the national government to invest in a city so close to the border with India, hence so vulnerable in the event of military conflict. To offset this neglect, the local business association closely interacted with a series of central government entities to secure support for key investments in the city.

The main vehicle for the local business community to influence policies toward the city was not so much to participate in local government bodies as it was to lobby the central government at the highest level, even bypassing local counterparts. The interaction with national authorities also relied on creative arrangements such as trust funds, PPPs, and matching grants. There is arguably a "shared governance" of the city, but in an entrepreneurial rather than institutional way (chapter 20).

A similar type of informal interaction with government authorities at the highest level can be found in the case of Gurgaon, India. There, key changes to the legal framework made by the government of the state of Haryana, facilitating the assembly of land and its conversion to urban uses, clearly suited K.P. Singh's business interests (chapter 14).

Finally, it is interesting to note that national policies relevant to urban development have also been influenced by significant private actors from foreign countries. In Indonesia, the vision behind the emergence of Batam was articulated in 1989 by the Singaporean Deputy Prime Minister of the time, Goh Chok Tong. Just across the straits from the land-constrained city-state, Batam island was ideally suited to accommodate sprawling industrial plants. The main goal was to relocate production facilities from Singapore and, by the same token, attract other investors.

Shortly after, the governments of Indonesia and Singapore signed a cooperation agreement building on this vision (figure 5.7). Not only did the government of Singapore

FIGURE 5.7. **Political activism: Indonesian president and Singaporean prime minister at the ceremony for a gas transmission line for Batam, Indonesia**

Source: © Ministry of Information, Communications and the Arts Collection, courtesy of National Archives of Singapore. Used with permission of National Archives of Singapore. Further permission required for reuse.
Note: The Indonesian president is third from left; the Singaporean prime minister is third from right.

negotiate protection by the government of Indonesia for the planned industrial parks, but it also participated in the selection of the consortia that would develop such parks. It has even been argued that the government of Singapore provided inputs to the policy agenda of the authorities of Batam, using to that effect both diplomatic channels and Indonesian conglomerates that had good access to policy makers (chapter 16).

References

Balachandran, Balakrishnan, Arjun Joshi, and Yue Li. 2021. "Gurgaon: A Case Study of Private Cities in India." Background paper, *Private Cities: Outstanding Examples from Developing Countries and Their Implications for Urban Policy*, World Bank, Washington, DC.

Delgado, Mercedes, Michael E. Porter, and Scott Stern. 2010. "Clusters and Entrepreneurship." *Journal of Economic Geography* 10 (4): 495–518.

Engel, Eduardo, Ronald Fischer, and Alexander Galetovic. 2005. "Highway Franchising and Real Estate Values." *Journal of Urban Economics* 57 (3): 432–48.

Lozano-Gracia, Nancy, Cheryl Young, Somik V. Lall, and Tara Vishwanath. 2013. "Leveraging Land to Enable Urban Transformation: Lessons from Global Experience." Policy Research Working Paper 6312, World Bank, Washington, DC.

Ohri, Raghav. 2017. "Land Deal: Robert Vadra Made Gains of Rs 50 Crore from a Land Deal in Haryana in 2008: Dhingra Panel." *Economic Times*, April 28, 2017. https://economictimes .indiatimes.com/news/politics-and-nation/robert-vadra-made-gains-of-rs-50-crore-from-a -land-deal-in-haryana-in-2008-dhingra-panel/articleshow/58407295.cms.

Villegas Limas, Arturo. 2021. "Case Study: El Alto, Bolivia." Background paper, *Private Cities: Outstanding Examples from Developing Countries and Their Implications for Urban Policy*, World Bank, Washington, DC.

CHAPTER 6

Land value capture: By whom and how

The economic surplus a locality generates increases significantly with urbanization. While the locality remains rural, most of the surplus is associated with agricultural activities. But after it urbanizes, its better connectivity to markets, together with land development, and with service provision, typically results in diversified economic activity and much higher income levels (figure 6.1).

Who captures this gain over time is critically important for the viability of a private city. Viability depends on financial considerations, as the returns of the private actor must at least compensate for the investments it made to develop the city. But it also depends on political considerations, as some stakeholders may lose, while others may consider that they did not get their fair share.

For example, it could well be that most of the gain accrues to the private actor, whereas the original residents of the locality and the taxpayers whose resources were mobilized to incentivize private participation end up being worse off. This possibility was highlighted in the proposed analytical framework, which showed that urban outsourcing allows maximizing the surplus of the locality but benefits all stakeholders only if accompanied by significant redistribution. A key question, therefore, is whether that kind of redistribution is feasible.

Taxing the income of the locality

The most important mechanisms to tilt the allocation of the surplus of the locality in a socially acceptable direction involve the government and are typically enshrined in laws, regulations, and contracts. Taxes are one such explicit surplus-sharing arrangement. In the spirit of the welfare economics approach to policy making, raising tax

FIGURE 6.1. **The surplus of the locality before and after urbanization**

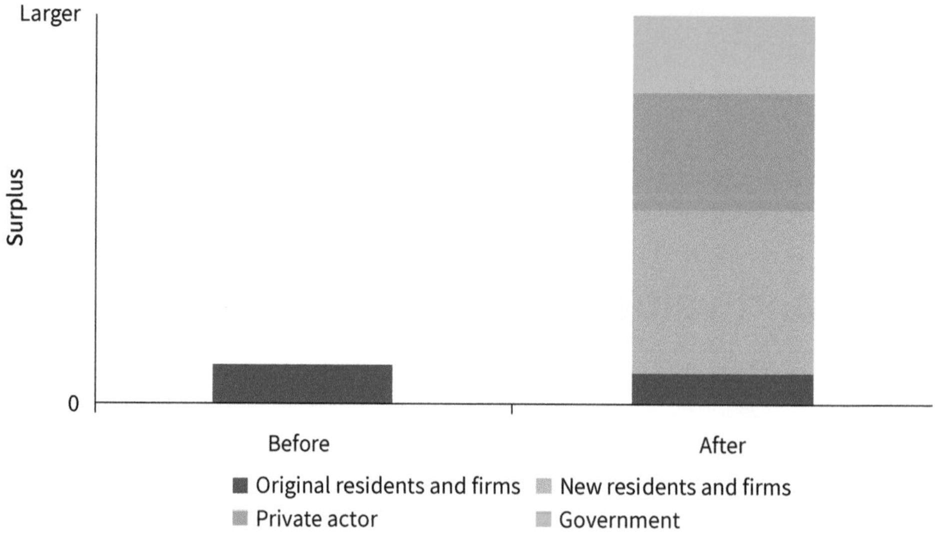

Source: Original figure for this book.

revenue allows the government to capture some of the surplus of the locality and to redistribute it to others who may have lost from its transformation into a private city.

With sufficient administrative capacity, property taxes would be the most effective tool available to the government. Indeed, if capital and labor are geographically mobile, much of the surplus of the locality is reflected in a higher price for land, the production factor that is inherently not mobile. In theory, the price of a plot of land in the city should be close to the discounted value of the income stream that can be derived from living or producing on it. Taxing land and taxing income would thus be close substitutes. And because land is not mobile, the distortions created by taxation would be much lower.

However, in many developing countries, the land administration system is unable to support a significant revenue collection from property tax. Land titling is most often partial, cadastral records are incomplete, land transactions are registered with a significant lag, land valuation for tax purposes is well below market prices, and the adjudication of land-related disputes is challenging. A detailed analysis of land records in East Dhaka, Bangladesh, illustrates some of these frequent weaknesses (Bird et al. 2018, 70–72).

How much revenue can be derived from a private city was quantified in East Dhaka's case, relying on a spatial general equilibrium model of the broader Greater Dhaka agglomeration. The analysis considered three increasingly ambitious urban development scenarios eastward, ranging from the construction of a major river embankment to a more comprehensive approach including new urban transport infrastructure to a strategic approach also involving the establishment of a new central business district in the area.

Simulation results showed that after 20 years of urban development eastward, the GDP of the Greater Dhaka agglomeration would increase significantly, with land value appreciating throughout the city and not only in East Dhaka. The more ambitious the scenario considered, the larger the increase is. Applying the current tax-to-GDP ratio of Bangladesh, the simulation confirmed that general tax revenue from the city would increase substantially as well. And it would increase much more than the proceeds from the existing property tax regime, even under the unrealistic assumption that all land plots in Greater Dhaka are duly taxed, with their tax valuation based on market price (figure 6.2).

However, despite this significant potential, the actual amount of tax revenue collected from the outstanding private cities reviewed varies widely. Outcomes in South Asia are among the most encouraging. In India, for example, about 45 percent of the revenue of the state of Haryana stems from collecting excise duty, sales tax, stamp duty, and registration fees in Gurgaon. Under plausible assumptions about Gurgaon's GDP, the general tax revenue the government of India derived from the city can be estimated at around US\$4.7 billion in 2011 and about US\$9 billion in 2019, nearly doubling in less than a decade (Balachandran, Joshi, and Li 2021).

FIGURE 6.2. **General taxes versus property taxes in Greater Dhaka, Bangladesh**

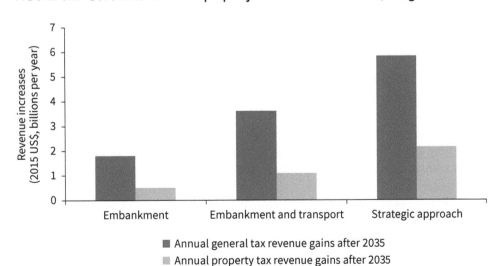

Source: Bird et al. 2018.

The outcome is similar in Sialkot, which is by now the third-largest economic hub in Pakistan and its second-largest source of foreign exchange after Karachi. The city's income per capita is among the highest in the country, and the city yields US$1,200 in annual tax revenue per person, more than any other administrative jurisdiction in Pakistan (chapter 20).

At the other end of the spectrum, tax revenue collection from private cities has been modest in Latin America. In Honduras, an analysis of eight years of San Pedro Sula's budgets between 1901 and 1935 shows only two occasions when tax revenue was collected from the local banana businesses. Most of the city's income came from other local commercial activities (chapter 13).

In Bolivia, the population of El Alto is similar to that of La Paz, but its tax revenue is six times lower. High poverty and informality levels, together with weak local government capacity, underlie this result. The municipality has also had difficulties updating its cadastral records and, as a result, revenue from property tax is almost nil. More fundamentally, there is strong resistance to taxation by the local community. In 2003, violent protests erupted after an attempt to impose a 12.5 percent income tax (chapter 10). Neighborhood associations argued that the proposed tax aimed to "get more money from the poor" (Arbona 2007).

Selling the rights to the city

To claw back some of the surplus generated by the locality after urbanization, the government can also choose to totally or partially "sell" the rights to the city. This other way to affect the distribution of the gains from urbanization is in the spirit of the law and economics approach to policy making. In this case, it is the proceeds from the sale—rather than tax revenue—that can be used to compensate those who would otherwise lose from the development of the private city.

The most straightforward way to sell rights to the city is through the licensing of land concessions for urban development. The approach bears similarities with more traditional instruments for land value capture, such as selling "water lots" to finance the early development of New York City or using the land around major avenues as collateral in the rebuilding of Paris by Baron Haussmann (Ingram and Hong 2012; Peterson 2009). However, in the land concessions considered here, investments for urban development are undertaken by the private actor, not by the local government.

In India, land licensing proceeds, external development charges, and user fees paid by large developers became important sources of revenue for the government authorities overseeing Gurgaon. The large gap between the revenue the state of Haryana derived from the city and the resources it spent on developing its infrastructure even caught media attention, nurturing the long-held contention by Gurgaon residents that the government had been profiting from the city but not investing in it. On the positive side, the gap indicates that there was a net transfer to less prosperous areas in the state (Balachandran, Joshi, and Li 2021).

However, deciding on the terms of land concessions is not a trivial matter. In the Arab Republic of Egypt, those concerning Cairo Festival City were initially done through direct purchase agreements. The terms were reached through private negotiations, with considerable variation regarding land price, payment process, and land title transfer conditions. A decade later these transactions led to court cases, which concluded with land price reassessments and price adjustment fees to be paid by private developers (chapter 12).

Another way to sell the rights to the city is to create joint ventures for urban development that bring together the local government and the private actor. An important difference between selling a land concession and entering a joint venture concerns the distribution of risk. In the early stages of urbanization, it is difficult to accurately predict how much surplus a city will generate. When selling a land concession, the government does not bear any risk, with any unexpected windfalls or losses accruing to other stakeholders, including the private actor (figure 6.3, panel a). But when entering a joint venture with the private actor, the local government takes on some of the risk (figure 6.3, panel b).

In some cases, the joint venture with the private actor concerns specific urban development components. For example, in Pakistan, the construction of Sialkot International Airport was financed under a public-private partnership (PPP) arrangement, with the government contributing the land, and the business association contributing the resources required to build and manage the airport (Qureshi and Li 2021).

However, when the government acts strategically, the joint venture may be set up for the development of the entire private city, rather than for specific investments. This is what happened in Vietnam, through the creation of a corporation bringing together the local government and the private actor. Under the agreed-upon terms, the development

FIGURE 6.3. Risk is shared differently depending on how the rights to the city are sold

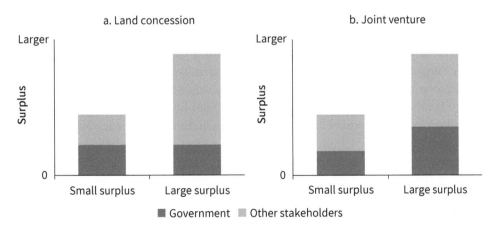

Source: Original figure for this book.

of Phu My Hung was to be funded and managed by the latter, whereas the former would contribute the land, exercise oversight, and serve as facilitator. Revenue from land sales as urbanization proceeded was to be split on a 70–30 percent basis between the private and public partners, respectively (chapter 22).

A different way to split the surplus is over time rather than on a recurrent basis. In the case of Batam, Indonesia, the urban development authority allocated rights to large joint venture manufacturing companies and industrial estate companies for 30 years, with the possibility to extend them for 20 more and then for an additional 30. The private beneficiaries of the concessions could in turn sell those rights to others as deemed appropriate (Amri et al. 2021).

Time-based agreements to share the surplus of the locality can also be citywide. In China's case, a PPP agreement for the development of Gu'an was signed by the local government and the private actor, with terms similar to those used in Phu My Hung's case. However, instead of splitting the surplus of the locality on a 70–30 basis, the private actor retained full rights to the city for 50 years. During this period, the local government needs to compensate the private actor for 115 percent of the investments it had made in the locality in the previous year, 110 percent of the planning and design costs it had incurred, and 45 percent of the value of fixed investments made by the companies it attracted to the locality. But once the 50 years elapse, the private actor needs to transfer the rights to the city back to the local government, in full (chapter 11).

Sharing the surplus with key stakeholders

The development of a private city may benefit key stakeholders in ways that do not require government intervention or even monetary transactions. Chief among these stakeholders are households who own or occupy land in the right place at the right time. But their gains can be amplified by private actors keen to get support for their urban development projects. Rather than confronting valuation disputes, corruption accusations, and bad press, some private actors have chosen innovative mechanisms to share the surplus of the locality more broadly, thus avoiding social and political turmoil.

In Gurgaon, India, large developers eager to assemble land at a fast pace paid some landholders more than what government agencies would have offered as compensation. Other landholders were given more fertile land elsewhere through swaps. And some were even invited to convert their land into shares in the new urban development projects (chapter 14).

Another innovative practice in Gurgaon was to keep existing villages as residential areas in the new urban development projects. According to Haryana state's regulatory framework, residential settlements that are demarcated from agricultural land are excluded from direct public land acquisition and urban planning. While large developers were purchasing land parcels on a massive scale, they left these villages untouched. And these were not just a few standalone exceptions, as 94 urban villages could be counted in the Gurgaon metropolitan area in 2011 (figure 6.4, panel a).

FIGURE 6.4. **The urban villages of Gurgaon, India**

a. Spatial distribution of urban villages

___ Gurugram Metropolitan   ___ Main roads   ___ Metro rail
     Development Authority   ○ Urban villages   ┼─┼ Railway network

b. An urban village example: Garhi

___ Urban village

c. An urban village example: Dhanwapur

___ Urban village

Source: Original figure for this book, based on chapter 14.

Original residents have benefited from the densification of the surrounding areas. Their villages now sit in urban neighborhoods that are better planned, with a clear grid system and high-rise buildings (figure 6.4, panel b and panel c, respectively). Along the way, these villages have become denser, now consisting mostly of three- to five-floor small apartment structures of low quality. Protected legally and politically from the building regulations applicable to the surrounding urban areas, they effectively provide affordable housing for low-income groups, including many of the low-skilled workers employed in the city.

Innovative practices such as relatively high monetary compensation, swaps with more fertile land elsewhere, conversion into shares in the new urban development projects, and the preservation of old urban villages, have been credited for a more muted opposition to land acquisitions in Gurgaon than in other Indian localities (Balachandran, Joshi, and Li 2021).

Often, stakeholders from outside the private city have gained from its dynamism. Indeed, greater economic vibrancy within the boundaries of the urban development may foster urbanization around it, with higher prices of land in the surrounding areas benefiting the households and firms that owned it or occupied it. This possibility was already apparent in the simulations of the development of Greater Dhaka as East Dhaka urbanizes, as previously mentioned. But spatial spillovers of this sort have been at play in several of the outstanding cities from developing countries reviewed.

In India, Jamshedpur's prosperity attracted substantial internal migration, and over time the surroundings densified in an organic manner (chapter 15). In Egypt, delays in the construction of Cairo Festival City failed to deter small-scale private developers, whose frantic activity in the areas around it strongly stimulated the local property market (Ibrahim, Elshayal, and Athar. 2021). And in Vietnam, the partial implementation of public master plans around Phu My Hung resulted in a population density 10 times higher than in the private city itself (chapter 22).

Battling through courts and in streets

The way the surplus of the locality is distributed among stakeholders may be altered in unexpected ways—sometimes dramatically—as a private city develops. The very success of the undertaking may create openings for redress, invite opportunistic behavior, or become a source of market power.

The review of outstanding private cities in developing countries reveals instances in which stakeholders that felt aggrieved by the distribution of the surplus sought compensation through the legal system. In Egypt, land concessions such as those involving Cairo Festival City became the subject of a heated public debate, with allegations made about irregularities and corruption. Court cases concluded with land price reassessments, leading to adjustment fees to be paid by private developers (chapter 12).

Courts were also central to the settlement of disputes in Bahria Town Karachi, Pakistan. There, the process through which some of the land had been assembled was the subject of much controversy. There were farmers' demonstrations against alleged land evictions, media reports on suspected corruption, and court litigation on some of the permissions. In 2019, the Supreme Court confirmed the legality of the disputed land acquisition, but only after the large developer paid US$3.1 billion as a compensation (chapter 19).

Defaults on agreed-upon obligations have been another mechanism to unexpectedly shift the distribution of the surplus of the locality. In China, the large developer behind Gu'an had financed its construction by issuing bonds. Perhaps the result of having stretched itself too far, in 2021 it failed to repay its bondholders, triggering its downgrade to a restricted default rating. With US$9.8 billion of bonds outstanding—US$4.6 billion of them offshore—investors in China and abroad could end up footing part of the bill for the extraordinary development of the city (chapter 11).

In other occasions, it is the local government who defaults on its side of the bargain. This is typically the case with infrastructure development and service delivery. For example, the public water supply system met only 30 percent of Gurgaon's water needs as of 2017. The gap in supply is filled by private tanker deliveries and groundwater withdrawal by users. Private developers have also been trying to compensate for deficient service delivery through the private provision of water, backup generators for electricity, and even private sewage lines and treatment plants (Balachandran, Joshi, and Li 2021).

Cases where costs are abruptly shifted back to the private actor can also be found elsewhere. In South Africa, because the local government did not have enough resources to cover basic services in Waterfall City, the large developer had to step in and assume responsibility for roads, water, sewerage, drainage, electricity, and 130 kilometers of optical fiber (chapter 21). In Vietnam, Phu My Hung's utility infrastructure is most often under a licensing agreement with a public operator. However, proprietary infrastructure for water treatment had to be built once it became clear that the government would not be able to provide it as planned (chapter 22).

Finally, San Pedro Sula in Honduras provides a rare example of open social conflict triggering a dramatic change in the trajectory of the city. There, banana plantation workers repeatedly tried to raise their share of the surplus of the locality by mobilizing for higher wages. Labor unrest was swiftly contained in the 1920s and 1930s, but the landmark 1954 strike lasted for more than two months and spread into other regions (figure 6.5). While defeated, it prompted the banana companies to drastically reduce their workforce and eventually move out of the country (chapter 13).

FIGURE 6.5. **The 1954 "banana strike" in San Pedro Sula, Honduras**

Source: Photo by Rafael Platero Paz, 1954. Used with permission of Kevin Coleman. Further permission required for reuse.

References

Amri, Mulya, Tony Hartanto Widjarnarso, Mark Roberts, and Yue Li. 2021. "Batam: A Case Study of Private City Development in Indonesia." Background paper, *Private Cities: Outstanding Examples from Developing Countries and Their Implications for Urban Policy.* World Bank, Washington, DC.

Arbona, Juan M. 2007. "Neo-liberal Ruptures: Local Political Entities and Neighbourhood Networks in El Alto, Bolivia." *Geoforum* 38 (1): 127–37.

Balachandran, Balakrishnan, Arjun Joshi, and Yue Li. 2021. "Gurgaon: A Case Study of Private Cities in India." Background paper, *Private Cities: Outstanding Examples from Developing Countries and Their Implications for Urban Policy,* World Bank, Washington, DC.

Bird, Julia, Yue Li, Hossain Zillur Rahman, Martin Rama, and Anthony J. Venables. 2018. *Toward Great Dhaka: A New Urban Development Paradigm Eastward.* Washington, DC: World Bank.

Ibrahim, Kareem, Tamer Elshayal, and Sohaib Athar. 2021. "Private Cities in Egypt." Background paper, *Private Cities: Outstanding Examples from Developing Countries and Their Implications for Urban Policy,* World Bank, Washington, DC.

Ingram, Gregory K., and Yu-hung Hong, eds. 2012. *Value Capture and Land Policies.* Cambridge, MA: Lincoln Institute of Land Policy.

Peterson, George. 2009. *Unlocking Land Values to Finance Urban Infrastructure.* Washington, DC: World Bank.

Qureshi, Nadia, and Yue Li. 2021. "Sialkot: A Case Study of Private Cities in Pakistan." Background paper, *Private Cities: Outstanding Examples from Developing Countries and Their Implications for Urban Policy,* World Bank, Washington, DC.

CHAPTER 7

Main shortcomings of private cities

P rivate cities help tap urbanization opportunities in places where local governments are weak, and they may support considerable economic dynamism, but they also have important limitations. Several of them are nonmonetary in nature, hence beyond the scope of the proposed analytical framework. Environmental sustainability was far from assured in many of the outstanding private cities reviewed, with uncoordinated profit-seeking even creating significant disaster risk. The review also exposed the social tension created by well-functioning private cities that cater to higher-income groups but are segregated from the messier and poorer urban environment around them. In some cases, it also appears that private cities eschew democratic governance, violating individual rights and freedoms. And this is for private cities that managed to emerge and thrive; others might have burned considerable resources without leading to significant urbanization. Such shortcomings need to be documented, and a judgment made on whether they are unavoidable or rather the hallmark of specific subsets of private cities.

White elephants

The outstanding private cities from developing countries reviewed in detail for this book represent a biased sample. These are cities that not only managed to emerge but also were successful enough to accommodate a sizable population and deliver a strong economic performance. Private cities that did not attain such remarkable outcomes are not among those covered. And a relevant question is whether outright failures were common as well.

Not surprisingly, even promising undertakings failed in practice. In Kenya, for example, Konza Techno City was launched in 2009 as a flagship project by the Ministry of

Information and Communication. Foreign and domestic companies with expertise in architecture, engineering, and real estate were competitively hired to plan the city and manage its construction. By relying on cutting-edge green technology, the project was expected to attract major multinational firms in the information technology sector.

However, Konza Techno City was stalled from the onset. A development authority was established, but no clarity was provided on its functions. Tensions between the Ministry of Information and Communication and the Ministry of Land, Housing and Urban Development further undermined the process. And the decentralization process launched in 2013 stimulated the emergence of competing urban development initiatives, some of them just a few kilometers away. More than a decade later, this private city has failed to take off (Splinter and Van Leynseele 2019).

Once labeled a private utopia in India, Lavasa suffered a similar fate. This private city was intended to combine a multiplicity of prestigious international models. It would be inspired by the American New Urbanism for its physical plan, by the seaside town of Portofino in Italy for its architectural style, and by a combination of Davos in Switzerland and Cambridge in Massachusetts for its business model (Kennard and Provost 2015).

Design awards and global news coverage made Lavasa famous worldwide. Its parent company, Hindustan Construction Ltd., had a strong reputation from a trajectory of nearly 100 years in infrastructure, having built roads, power plants, tunnels, and more than 300 bridges around the country. With such a strong background, Lavasa was supposed to become a "replicable model for the development of future Asian cities" and to bring "world-class standards to Indian urban life" (figure 7.1).

However, the project fell from grace as its private investor, Lavasa Corporation Limited, filed for bankruptcy in 2018. By then, almost two decades after its inception, the city was an incomplete shell housing some 10,000 people rather than the 200,000–300,000 originally expected. And the investor struggled to repay US$610 million of debt.

One possible reason for this failure is location, one of the necessary conditions for private cities to emerge. Lavasa is situated in the Sahyadri Mountain range, along the picturesque Warsagaon Lake. This area is near the Pune-Mumbai economic corridor but lacks good transportation infrastructure. Perhaps not coincidentally, Amby Valley, a smaller private city following the same business model and located on the same corridor, became deserted as well (Antony and Pandya 2018; Nallathiga et al. 2015; Parikh 2015).

Regardless of the reasons for the failure, the examples of Konza Techno City and Lavasa prove that private cities indeed face the risk of becoming white elephants, a term often used to describe a project that does not take off despite spending considerable resources on it.

While this prospect could be seen as an important shortcoming of private cities, conventional cities do not necessarily do better. From Yamoussoukro in Côte d'Ivoire to Naypyidaw in Myanmar, several developing countries have been in the process of relocating their capital cities for decades. But the new cities they developed have often failed to provide adequate housing and infrastructure and have proven very expensive to build, so they hardly qualify as urban successes (Abubakar and Doan 2017).

FIGURE 7.1. Lavasa, India: A playground for the rich, gone bankrupt

a. An appealing natural setting

—— City boundary

b. A well-planned city

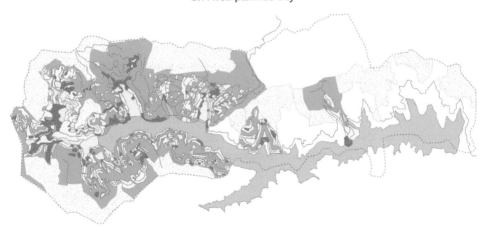

(Figure continues on next page)

FIGURE 7.1. Lavasa, India: A playground for the rich, gone bankrupt *(continued)*

c. A failure to take off

Sources: Panels a and b: original figures for this book based on master plan information. Panel c: © Cryongen, licensed under CC BY-SA 3.0, https://commons.wikimedia.org/wiki/File:Lakeside_View_at_Dasve_-_Lavasa.JPG.

There may not be enough white elephants of this sort to conduct a rigorous comparison of failure rates between conventional and private cities. But there are economic reasons to believe that failure could be less frequent in the latter case. Significant private actors are risking their own resources, and they may want to retrieve their investment. Governments, on the other hand, may be driven by prestige motives or geopolitical considerations, paying less attention to economic dynamism.

Environmental degradation and disaster risk

Private cities could also be characterized by worse environmental outcomes than their government-led counterparts. This time, economic reasoning would tend to support this proposition. After all, significant private actors only care about the monetary returns they can derive from their investments in private cities. Nonmonetary outcomes, such as increased pollution or greater environmental risk, may be less of a concern for them than for governments that care about the population's well-being—unless monetary incentives are provided.

The example of East Dhaka, Bangladesh, gives support to this hypothesis. As a result of organic urbanization eastward, canals and water storage areas that help absorb excess water in times of heavy rainfall have been encroached on by housing construction, clogged by solid waste, or filled with sand. By now only about 2 square kilometers of permanent wetlands remain in the area, further reducing the area's ability to cope with floods, and threatening its biodiversity.

Seismic risk has increased as well. Major earthquakes cannot be ruled out in areas outside the Madhupur Tract, the relatively firm surface above flood levels on which the older parts of Dhaka had developed. Seismic impacts could be amplified by the large-scale sand-filling undertaken by large developers, as it leads to a loose and segregated soil structure. Ground vibration can indeed make the properties of this kind of soil change rapidly—a process known as liquefaction—destroying urban infrastructure and making buildings sink or fall over (chapter 9).

Private cities have also had other adverse environmental impacts. In India, the depletion of groundwater has been a concern in Gurgaon for many years. The water level was about 19 meters below the surface in 2005, but it went down to about 35 meters by 2014 and to 38 meters more recently. Groundwater is supplied through private borewells, but the rate of extraction is much higher than the rate of aquifer recharge from rainwater. And because sufficient drainage has not been built and traditional water bodies have disappeared in the course of development, many locations in Gurgaon are consistently flooded during the monsoon season. Surface water is also increasingly polluted due to industrial effluents, disposal of untreated sewage, and unscientific disposal of solid waste. It is not by chance that Gurgaon had the dubious distinction of being considered the world's most polluted city in 2018.

However, Gurgaon's shortcomings need to be put in context. Urbanization has outpaced planning and implementation across developing countries, which has resulted in consistent environmental stress. And it is not clear that Gurgaon fares worse than conventional cities in India in this respect. Ranking 31st among 62 cities of similar size in the country's latest Ease of Living Index, it seems to be an average performer. In other words, Gurgaon may look like Singapore on private sector development but still resembles many other Indian cities in urban services provision (chapter 14).

Several of the private cities reviewed have excelled on environmental grounds. Also in India, Jamshedpur is arguably a model city in this respect. "Be sure to lay wide streets planted with shady trees," wrote its founder Jamsetji Tata in 1902. "Be sure that there is plenty of space for lawns and gardens. Reserve large areas for football, hockey, and parks" (Tata Steel, n.d., 1).

The city was planned and built following this guidance. Nowadays, its notified area has 37 percent green cover, and its more than 45 community parks have a total surface greater than 160 hectares. Jubilee Park and the Tata Steel Zoological Park are popular recreation spaces. Despite having been designed more than a century ago, Jamshedpur also stands out for its relatively low carbon footprint. While green areas are prevalent, its population density exceeds 10,000 inhabitants per square kilometer (chapter 15).

In Vietnam, the environmental performance of Phu My Hung is also widely recognized as solid. The city is organized as a set of walkable islands separated by canals that continue to support waterway transportation and trade. The regular dredging of these canals facilitates their flushing by the region's often heavy rains. It also provided the sand-fill to raise the ground 1.5 meters above the highest tide level in preparation for sea-level rise. In recognition of these accomplishments, the city received a Global Excellence Award for livability and sustainability from the Urban Land Institute in 2012 (chapter 22).

Other outstanding private cities from developing countries have been commended for their green promise. In 2009 Eko Atlantic, Nigeria, received the Clinton Global Initiative Commitment Certificate. And in 2018 one of the international financial institutions funding the project concluded that "its new infrastructure will reduce the level of carbon emissions and improve sustainability." How the city's oceanic wall may reshape coastal Lagos in the longer term is less understood, however (chapter 18).

These examples suggest that proper attention to environmental issues can be perceived by the private actor as a plus, potentially outweighing its cost. This is more likely to happen when green spaces, low levels of pollution, and a visible concern for the planet are seen as part of the private city's value proposition.

Social segregation

Private cities in developing countries often become cocooned enclaves for the rich. With their higher overall efficiency and generally better amenities, they drive an elitist selection of residents—be they higher-income households or more productive firms. Their pricier urban land generates a cream-skimming effect, leading to islands of wealth and efficiency and exacerbating spatial segregation (figure 7.2).

In Vietnam, for example, Phu My Hung received an honor award from the American Institute of Architects as the best urban design in 1997, the first ever given to an Asian city. By 2006, however, the price of an apartment was US$62,000 or higher (85 times the per capita GDP of the country), making the place too expensive for the country's middle class. Not surprisingly, many of its current residents are expatriates working in Ho Chi Minh City; the rest are affluent Vietnamese (chapter 22).

Social segregation is at times a deliberate outcome of private cities. In the Arab Republic of Egypt, Cairo Festival City purposely caters to high-income population segments. Its residential offerings are gated, with private accesses separating its living community from general visitors. When asked whether the existing business model could incorporate middle-income residents to increase inclusiveness, the management of the city noted that socioeconomic diversity is not an urban feature desired by its current

FIGURE 7.2. **Eko Atlantic versus downtown Lagos, Nigeria**

a. Design for Eko Atlantic

b. Downtown Lagos

Sources: Panel a, © MZ-Architects. Used with permission of MZ-Architects. Further permission required for reuse. Panel b, © Robert Prather, licensed under CC BY 2.0, https://www.flickr.com/photos/25653865@N00/2363479089.

population. Mixedness could in fact deter potential clients who are willing to pay a premium for an exclusive residential environment (chapter 12).

In South Africa, sharply rising crime rates, together with significant infrastructure investments to enhance employment opportunities for peripheral Black populations following the end of Apartheid, made Johannesburg evolve into a polycentric metropolis. Most of the urban poor now live in the south of the agglomeration, around townships that had been reserved for the Black population under Apartheid. Meanwhile, the incorporation of new urban areas in the north launched the drift of wealthier population groups toward new private developments, of which Waterfall City is the biggest. With its high-quality services, including a thick surrounding wall and strict security measures, this private city embodies spatial segregation to an extent that may seem paradoxical in the post-Apartheid era (chapter 21).

In some cases, segregated living conditions for the poor can be found within the private cities themselves. In India, the middle- and high-income residents of Gurgaon live in gated enclaves with high-quality services, while large numbers of migrant workers stay in crowded housing, with minimal access to basic amenities like electricity and water. Indian regulations require that one-fifth of the housing built by large developers be reserved for disadvantaged population groups. However, as property prices skyrocketed, the affordable housing plots were resold and reregistered illegally, then developed in violation of the regulation (chapter 14).

However, not all the outstanding private cities reviewed follow this pattern. In Indonesia, flexible urban policies that created opportunities for large developers also mandated local service provision and helped keep land and housing affordable. Partly as a result of these policies, Kota Baru Maja does not suffer from disproportionate market segregation relative to other urban areas in the country. Almost 90 percent of the dwellings in its biggest development actually fall into the category of affordable housing (chapter 17).

Some private cities in the developing world have been an avenue for upward social mobility, especially in the context of neglect or even outright discrimination. In Bolivia, El Alto emerged as the urban agglomeration of impoverished indigenous communities displaced by the scarcity of agricultural land and the closing of tin mines. Its pugnacious neighborhood associations exerted pressure on authorities to boost local investments, focusing on the construction of markets and schools. The area remains disproportionately poor and crime-ridden, but nowadays it contributes about 6 percent to Bolivia's GDP, 12 percent to its exports, 16 percent to its industrial employment, and 22 percent to its manufacturing output (chapter 10).

More generally, the outstanding private cities reviewed have supported urbanization in places where local governments were failing to deliver. And they have often done so with better standards in terms of spatial planning, connecting infrastructure, and service delivery. As a result, these private cities have been able to deliver high levels of economic activity and boost local labor demand. Their messy outgrowths may be shockingly poor and underserviced compared with the private cities themselves, but the very existence of these outgrowths is a manifestation of economic opportunity.

Institutional secession

Perhaps the greater concern raised by private cities around the world is their potential undermining of democratic governance. Modern political institutions are anchored in voice and accountability, and nowhere do these two concepts manifest themselves more directly than in the way cities are run.

The notion of citizenship may be applied to national political entities, but the name itself evokes participation in the matters of the city. Mayors are central figures in the political life of many countries, and several of them—from Jacques Chirac in France to Joko Widodo in Indonesia—leveraged their city experience to become leaders at the national level. By contrast, private cities are run as corporations by unelected managers. And they often enforce rules of social interaction that differ—at times dramatically—from those of the countries in which they sit.

This concern had been repeatedly evoked in advanced economies. In his historical account of the Pullman company town in the US, Ely (1885) compared the power of its management over the city to that of Bismarck over Germany. He quoted a resident as saying, "whether the power be exercised rightfully or wrongfully, it is there all the same, and every man, woman, and child in the town is completely at its mercy, and it can be avoided only by emigration."

More recently, Garreau (1992) saw the large developers behind edge cities in the US as "shadow governments," arguing that they were undemocratic and discriminatory, and operated outside the constitutional restrictions that public governments face.

Some of the departures from the national institutional environment characterizing outstanding private cities in developing countries may seem relatively innocuous, as they can also be found elsewhere in the same countries. Such is the case with more favorable conditions to do business, which are more in the spirit of special economic zones than of institutional secession.

Thus, El Alto became one of the three free trade zones under a new regime established by the Bolivian government in the late 1990s (Villegas Limas 2021). San Pedro Sula in Honduras also benefited from several special regimes for doing business, including the creation of the Puerto Cortés free trade zone in 1977 and the tax incentives to industrial parks granted by the Export Processing Zone Law of 1987 (chapter 13). And the development of Batam in Indonesia owes much to a 1978 presidential decree that converted the entire island into a bonded area, followed by a 1989 authorization for foreign corporations to independently operate industrial parks there and to retain majority ownership of their facilities (chapter 16).

From an institutional point of view, idiosyncratic rules that infringe upon individual freedoms are a much greater concern. Many such rules are security-related. Private cities that aim to attract higher-income residents tend to have low crime rates as one of their strongest selling points. In line with this focus, many have their own security forces, and their relationship with law-and-order authorities is often controversial. For example, in India, the city of Gurgaon was reported to have some 35,000 private security guards in 2010 compared with only 3,100 public police officers (Balachandran, Joshi, and Li 2021).

Rules are even more constraining in East Dhaka, Bangladesh. There, the residents and visitors of the large Bashundhara real estate development project receive car stickers only upon approval by its local "welfare society office." It is even reported that local security guards do not allow the police to enter the area without their explicit permission, even when there is a reported case of violence (chapter 9). In South Africa, meanwhile, the residential zones of Waterfall City are surrounded by 4-meter-high reinforced concrete walls, topped with an electric fence and mounted with closed-circuit television cameras. Thermal detection and fingerprint recognition provide additional protection against intruders, with armed-response vehicles ready to intervene (Herbert and Murray 2015).

Not only does the balance between private security and public policing differ between some private cities and conventional cities in the same country, but also in some cases the rules being enforced are different as well. In Nigeria, for example, the managing director of Eko Atlantic declared that "any vehicle seen on the street will be termed abnormal either that it was stolen or to be used for criminal purposes. In that way such vehicles will be towed away and never to get back to the owner" (Adeoti, Nweke, and Obienyi 2020). This statement suggests an idiosyncratic take on the presumption of innocence in the private city.

Individual freedoms related to worshipping and lifestyle may also be at stake. In South Africa's Waterfall City, the strict devotion of the private actor behind it to an austere version of Islam has resulted in restrictive codes that businesses and households need to abide by. Alcoholic beverages are available in restaurants, but there is a strict prohibition on establishing liquor stores anywhere else in the city. And while there is a mosque in the development, the establishment of Christian churches is banned, as is the public display of religious signs (Herbert and Murray 2015).

It must be noted, however, that not all the outstanding private cities reviewed display signs of institutional secession. Overall, those run by business associations or civil society organizations seem less concerned about individual freedoms and rights than about a conducive business environment and the provision of services. And in other cases, national urban policies do not seem to allow private cities to depart from the legal framework regulating urban life in other parts of the respective countries.

References

Abubakar, Ismaila Rimi, and Petra Leisenring Doan. 2017. "Building New Capital Cities in Africa: Lessons for New Satellite Towns in Developing Countries." *African Studies* 76 (4): 546–65.

Adeoti, Femi, Maduka Nweke, and Chinwendu Obienyi. 2020. "Eko Atlantic City to Put Nigeria among 20 Economic Power—Frame." *Sun News Online*, January 10, 2020.

Antony, Anto, and Dhwani Pandya. 2018. "Billionaire's Folly Becomes Bankers' Nightmare." *Bloomberg*, June 19, 2018.

Balachandran, Balakrishnan, Arjun Joshi, and Yue Li. 2021. "Gurgaon: A Case Study of Private Cities in India." Background paper, *Private Cities: Outstanding Examples from Developing Countries and Their Implications for Urban Policy*, World Bank, Washington, DC.

Ely, Richard Theodore. 1885. "Pullman: A Social Study." *Harper's Magazine* 70: 452–66.

Garreau, Joel. 1992. *Edge City: Life on the New Frontier*. New York City: Anchor.

Herbert, Claire W., and Martin J. Murray. 2015. "Building from Scratch: New Cities, Privatized Urbanism and the Spatial Restructuring of Johannesburg after Apartheid." *International Journal of Urban and Regional Research* 39, no. 3: 471–94.

Kennard, Matt, and Claire Provost. 2015. "Inside Lavasa, India's First Entirely Private City Built from Scratch." the *Guardian*. November 19, 2015.

Nallathiga, R., K. Tewari, A. Saboo, and S. Varghese. 2015. "Evolution of Satellite Township Development in Pune: A Case Study." 63rd National Town and Country Planning Conference, Chennai. January 9–11, 2015. https://www.researchgate.net/publication/270894930_Evolution _of_Satellite_township_development_in_Pune_A_Case_Study.

Parikh, Anokhi. 2015. "The Private City: Planning, Property, and Protest in the Making of Lavasa New Town, India." thesis, Department of International Development of the London School of Economics and Political Science.

Splinter, Eline, and Yves Van Leynseele. 2019. "The Conditional City: Emerging Properties of Kenya's Satellite Cities." *International Planning Studies* 24 (3–4): 308–24.

Tata Steel. n.d. "Jamshedpur: A City Guide." https://www.tatasteel.com/media/7155/jamshedpur -brochure_revised_final.pdf. Accessed November 2022.

Villegas Limas, Arturo. 2021. "Case Study: El Alto, Bolivia." Background paper, *Private Cities: Outstanding Examples from Developing Countries and Their Implications for Urban Policy*, World Bank, Washington, DC.

CHAPTER 8

Implications for urban policy

Large urban agglomerations whose development has been shaped by a significant private actor have become a fact of life in developing countries. And this is regardless of the countries' development level, cultural tradition, or political system. While these private cities have generally been successful on economic grounds, their record is mixed on the environmental, social, and institutional fronts. From a public policy perspective, the key question is what should be done about them.

Just ignoring them amounts to accepting the status quo as the best conceivable situation, which would be hard to defend. Moreover, in the presence of significant private actors, some of the standard urban policy recommendations could fail to yield the expected outcomes.

This book can be read as an attempt to address this important issue, building on the findings from a simple but novel analytical framework, on thorough inventories of private cities in four developing countries, and on detailed reviews of outstanding private cities from around the developing world. None of these perspectives is sufficient on its own to derive robust recommendations. But taken together they yield new insights into urban policy in developing countries.

The cost of ignoring private cities

The outstanding private cities of developing countries reviewed are diverse in many ways. Some serve as the operating platform of a powerful firm, similar to the company towns of advanced economies during the industrial revolution. Others are run by business associations, or even civil society organizations, to serve their collective goals. Many are associated with one or several large developers catering to firms that seek plug-and-play infrastructure or world-class commercial space and to higher-income households that look for residential areas with reliable services and adequate security.

There is also diversity in the roles played by the significant private actor and the corresponding local government. In some cases, the latter is essentially passive, with most of the initiative related to the city being in the hands of the former. In others, the local government is strategic in crowding-in a private actor—domestic or foreign—with greater capacity for spatial planning, infrastructure development, and service delivery. In many cases, actions undertaken by the two players are uncoordinated, which tends to result in a mixed city.

Despite the diversity of private actors and the various ways in which they interact with local governments, there are also important commonalities. Strikingly, private cities can be found across countries with different income levels, economic structures, and political systems, which suggests that their existence is related to untapped urbanization opportunities more than country specifics.

The review of outstanding private cities in the developing world showed that they tend to be successful on economic grounds. Most of them are large, in terms of both their population and their ranking in the national hierarchy of cities. Many account for a significant share of their country's employment, economic activity, or exports. High-quality amenities are also common, suggesting that their overall economic performance is strong.

And yet, the proposed analytical framework concluded that both the population size and the economic surplus of private cities are likely to fall below what would be socially optimal. This analytical result holds regardless of the nature of the game between the private actor and the local government. Company towns, mixed cities, and strategic cities are all smaller than they should ideally be, in terms of both population and economic activity.

The main reason for this suboptimality is that the private actor does not internalize all the benefits from urban land development. It values the urban land it develops at the price it can sell it to firms and households, which in a well-functioning market should be equal to the output that the marginal plot of urban land can generate. Therefore, if the private actor were to build a bigger city, the output of the marginal plot of land would fall and with it, the value of all the other plots it had previously developed.

In the same way as a monopolist maximizes its profit by generating less output than is socially optimal, the private actor maximizes its rent by developing less urban land than would be desirable. Weak government capacity and the noncooperative nature of its interaction with the private actor only amplify this fundamental inefficiency.

Private cities may also be suboptimal in other ways. The review of outstanding private cities in developing countries reveals a mixed performance on nonmonetary outcomes. Environmental degradation and disaster risk can be significant. A wide social gap often emerges between better-off groups living in functional private cities and the broader population struggling with chaotic urbanization. And private cities have also been associated with idiosyncratic regulations that impinge upon the individual freedoms and rights all citizens are supposed to enjoy.

Yet, the standard advice on urban policy for developing countries is silent in relation to significant private actors with significant capacity and disproportionate clout. The standard urban policy recommendation to developing countries has been to improve the capacity of their local governments to plan cities, build infrastructure, and deliver services. Advice on what to do or not to do in relation to private cities is conspicuously absent from the toolkit being offered.

This is problematic, as building capacity takes time and empowering local governments may require constitutional changes that enjoy little political support among existing elites. Meanwhile, developing countries are urbanizing, consolidating inefficient city structures that could be costly to retrofit in the future.

Moreover, in the presence of significant private actors, greater capacity alone may not lead to better outcomes. A more capable local government may be able to develop more urban land and do it better than before. But the proposed analytical framework shows that as long as the quality of the urban land developed by the local government is lower than that of the land developed by the private actor, the net outcome could be a lower economic surplus of the locality—despite a potentially bigger city. The risk is more significant when the initial capacity of the local government is very low (Li and Rama 2022).

An illustration of the crowding-out risk is provided by Purbachal, an urban development led by the local government in East Dhaka, Bangladesh. This project sits on the best land available outside the historic core of Dhaka, in an area on top of the Madhupur geological tract, hence less vulnerable to flooding and earthquakes. Formally inaugurated in 1995 and initially scheduled for completion in the early 2010s, Purbachal's progress on the ground has been modest at best. Meanwhile, large developers are rapidly taking over the much more vulnerable areas around it. Their actions have led to rapid urbanization but also to a much greater disaster risk than if land on the Madhupur tract had been available to them (Bird et al. 2018).

Banning significant private actors from participating in the urbanization process could be counterproductive as well, especially in localities where local government capacity is very low. In such cases, there is a real risk that localities with a significant urbanization potential may remain rural. Private cities may have significant shortcomings, but no urbanization at all is arguably an even worse outcome—and this is what may happen if significant private actors are kept at bay.

Public-private partnerships for urbanization

The reality of private cities calls for reconsidering urban policy in developing countries. If local governments lack the capacity to deliver functional cities on their own and significant private actors lack the incentives to do so in a socially optimal way, a different approach is needed.

The role of urban authorities needs to be broadened, from planning, building, and servicing cities to also regulating, incentivizing, and overseeing large private actors that have the necessary technical expertise, coordination capacity, and business integrity. This other way of steering the urbanization process is more aligned with the division of responsibilities between the government and the private sector envisioned by welfare economics, a division not often considered in urban economics.

In some cases, local governments may lead the urban development process while, in others, they may totally or partially outsource it. The mix of roles may vary depending on the circumstances, but it should not be assumed that conventional cities are always the best response to an urbanization challenge. However, if a private actor is to be involved, a key role of urban policy would be to align its incentives with the objectives of society at large. This requires understanding the ways a private city may be suboptimal and designing the interventions that can correct the inefficiencies.

The review of outstanding private cities in developing countries suggests that four conditions must be met for them to emerge. The location must be especially advantageous. The local government must be willing to allow more capable private counterparts to actively participate in urban development. The private actor must be exceptional in terms of its ability to implement at scale its innovative business model, its cohesive nature, or its clout to secure the public policies needed for the project to succeed. And the institutional environment must enable the emergence of private cities.

In the absence of any of these four conditions, some private cities may simply become white elephants, a term used to describe projects that absorb substantial resources but fail to deliver. This would not be a major issue if all the associated losses were borne by the private actor. However, through bankruptcies or other mechanisms to default on obligations, the cost of a doomed private city project could end up falling on the government's budget, and hence on taxpayers.

Assuming these four conditions are met, the possible deal between a local government and a significant private actor to urbanize a locality can be thought of as a public-private partnership (PPP) for urban development. As in other agreements of this sort, it is essential to agree on the responsibilities of the two parties. In a conventional city, the local government assembles land, builds the connecting infrastructure, plans the use of land, and delivers urban services. But the review of outstanding private cities shows that some of these functions may be taken over by the private actor. Understanding where the comparative advantages of the two players lie may help determine who should be responsible for what.

The review of outstanding private cities also shows that significant private actors may take on nontraditional functions, such as embracing specific economic sectors, or tilting policies in favor of the city by influencing the national government. Whether these activities should be welcome—or even at all tolerated—is an issue that local authorities need to consider. While the government should not be in the business of picking winners, an industrial policy approach to urban development may be acceptable if it is undertaken by a private investor. On the other hand, political activism by the significant private actor seems problematic under most circumstances.

A sensible PPP design must consider returns as well. The way the economic surplus generated by the locality is distributed among key stakeholders is critically important in this respect. In particular, the distribution of the surplus should ensure that the private actor finds it profitable to build a city with the right size and characteristics.

The review of outstanding private cities reveals multiple ways in which additional incentives for a locality to attain its full potential have been provided in practice. Typically, the government builds the transport infrastructure needed to connect the location to markets. It may also contribute large tracts of land for urban development, or it may take care of delivering basic services for the city.

In some cases, rules on the returns to each of the two partners have been explicitly established. In Gu'an, China, the local government compensates the private actor for planning and investment costs, and even provides a bonus for each significant firm attracted to the city. The deal is for a period of 50 years, after which the private actor must transfer all its urban assets to the local government (chapter 11).

Providing appropriate incentives for the private actor to build the city is not all, however. The other top objective of urban policy should be to ensure a fair distribution of the surplus of the locality. This is especially important when the private actor had to be incentivized to support the emergence of a city with the desired characteristics. The proposed analytical framework shows that in such situations the windfall for the rest of society—from the original residents of the locality to taxpayers elsewhere—could be nil or even negative. Achieving economic efficiency in such an inequitable way would not only be morally wrong: it could also be politically explosive.

The review of outstanding private cities in developing countries shows multiple ways in which governments have managed to capture back part of the surplus of the locality—or equivalently, part of the land value appreciation. They have done so by raising tax revenue from the private city, by selling land development licenses to the private actor, or by entering into a joint venture with it for the development of the city. In the case of Vietnam's Phu My Hung, for example, the joint venture was structured in such a way that 70 percent of the profits accrue to the private actor and 30 percent to the local government (chapter 22).

Private actors have also established creative deals with key stakeholders to ensure that there is buy-in for their projects. In India, the large developers behind the emergence of Gurgaon left the traditional villages of the area untouched so that their homeowners could benefit from land appreciation. They also offered swaps in which original residents would exchange their land for shares in the urban development projects (chapter 14). Urban policy should include legal provisions that make fair compensatory deals easier to happen, and to be enforced.

An adequate distribution of the surplus of the locality, desirable as it is, would not address some of the main shortcomings of private cities. Potential risks in relation to environmental degradation, social segregation, and institutional secession need to be assessed and tackled. The first step in this respect is to identify where the problems lie. Indeed, not all the outstanding private cities reviewed face these challenges. For example, some have made high environmental standards part of their value proposition.

Once the shortcomings are identified, urban policies can be adjusted to address them. In Indonesia, for example, the same legal framework that created the space for large developers to participate in the urbanization process also mandated them to ensure the delivery of basic services in the cities they build. Together with the facilitation of land assembly and the provision of connecting transport infrastructure, this approach has ensured the ample availability of affordable housing in a city like Kota Baru Maja (chapter 17).

Similar approaches can be used to contain institutional secession. Having the private actor make important decisions on urban development in the spirit of a CEO may be unavoidable in the initial development stages of a private city. But urban policy can set clear limits on the issues the private actor can decide upon, especially ensuring that all individual freedoms and constitutional rights available to citizens are upheld in the city.

Some of the biggest challenges in designing a PPP for urban development stem from the time inconsistency of decisions by the two players. Contracts may be written, but not all issues may be covered, not all contingencies may be foreseen, and strict enforcement may not be feasible.

Over the long course of city development, the private actor faces various regulatory and political risks, including the government not delivering on its commitments, withdrawing its institutional support for the private city approach, or directly seizing urban assets. Conversely, the private actor may free ride on public goods provided by the government or underinvest in public goods needed for an efficient city to emerge, knowing that the government may have no choice but to step up.

The magnitude of the sunk investments associated with a large city, and the uncertainty of whether it will be successful, amplify the time-inconsistency challenges associated with PPPs. This may explain why there are not more private cities in the developing world. The review of outstanding private cities conducted for this book shows that they are unusually large relative to their more conventional urban counterparts, and they also tend to be more productive, or more livable. But their number remains surprisingly small when considering the untapped urbanization potential of the developing world and the limited capacity of many local governments to handle the task.

Identifying effective mechanisms to align the decisions of local governments and the significant private actors would be critically important to boost urbanization in developing countries. But savvy contract design alone may not be sufficient. Urban policy in relation to private cities may need to consider alternative, second-best arrangements for these unusual PPPs to succeed.

One of those arrangements is to deal only with highly reputable private actors, whose image—hence long-term success—would be tainted by a failure to deliver. Such actors face a bigger cost if they default on their commitments than smaller, untested private investors do. In selecting the United Arab Emirates–based Al Futtaim group for the development of Cairo Festival City, the Egyptian government might have considered not only its high technical and financial capacity but also its sheer scale and track record (chapter 12).

Another possible arrangement is to rely on international agreements as the enforcement mechanism for the urban development deal. Such is the approach followed by the government of Indonesia in relation to Batam. The government of Singapore had a keen interest in the private city's development, to keep its manufacturing companies competitive at a time when its domestic land prices were increasing rapidly. Its affiliated companies undoubtedly had the capacity to undertake such development. A bilateral deal between the two governments was in this case tantamount to a viable PPP arrangement (chapter 16).

This logic can be pushed further by envisioning agreements involving international financial institutions, such as multilateral development banks. Their participation would provide guarantees to private actors that commitments by the local government would be honored. At the same time, their higher procurement standards would ensure that only reputable private actors with the necessary technical expertise and financial strength would be eligible to bid for urban development projects. In this way, international financial institutions could be helping to create an international market for urbanization services.

A tentative protocol

Private cities are not the solution to the urbanization challenges of the developing world. They are only one more instrument in the urban policy toolkit. This instrument is more likely to be useful when the capacity of the local government to steer the urbanization process is low, and when significant private actors with sufficient expertise and integrity can be mobilized for the task. Even so, private cities are bound to have downsides and not only upsides. Minimizing the former and maximizing the latter should be a central objective of a local government that considers using this alternative instrument.

It is still too early to come up with conclusive recommendations on how to do so. More research is needed in at least three areas.

The first matter is analytics. The framework proposed in this book is deliberately simple. Its goal is to provide new perspectives on how weak capacity by local governments affects the type of city that emerges and potentially modifies standard urban policy recommendations. More thorough research, based on richer analytical models with strong microeconomic foundations, is needed before the insights from this simple model can be considered robust guidance in practice.

The second area is empirics. Perhaps as a result of local governments being the natural counterpart of urban practitioners, or maybe because of more limited access to data from significant private actors, the empirical evidence on private cities is shallow. This book built comprehensive inventories for four developing countries, but the effort should be expanded. It also reviewed the experience of 14 outstanding private cities in the developing world, but more is needed to understand in which ways they can improve urbanization outcomes, how they affect distribution across populations and across space, and what kinds of environmental and social risks they may pose.

Last, but not least, is mechanism design. Most of the literature on PPPs refers to sectors such as transport infrastructure, energy generation, or service delivery. Very little is known about the much bigger deals underlying the emergence of some outstanding private cities in the developing world. With weak local governments and significant private actors, there could be a substantial power imbalance. And the magnitude of the sunk investments involved amplifies the risk of opportunistic behavior. Given the mixed record of PPPs so far, fully understanding how they work—or fail—in the context of urban development is a key research priority.

With these caveats in mind, this book's main implications for urban policy in developing countries can be summarized under the form of a tentative protocol (box 8.1). The steps in it will certainly need to be refined as more research becomes available. For now, however, making this tentative protocol available to decision-makers in developing countries may hopefully stimulate their thinking and promote sounder urban policies, regardless of whether they involve private cities or not.

BOX 8.1 A tentative protocol for urban policy in relation to private cities

The implications of the analyses in this book can be organized under the form of a series of sequential questions, as follows:

1. *LOCATION POTENTIAL. Does the area or jurisdiction considered have characteristics that make it especially well suited for urban development?*

   Such characteristics may include the availability of natural resources of particular interest for some sectors of activity or natural scenery that makes it a touristic asset. Most importantly, the location needs to be well connected to a major urban agglomeration. If such is not the case, there is a risk that a private city in that area or jurisdiction will become a white elephant.

2. *PRIVATE ACTORS. Are there firms or associations with the technical expertise, coordination capacity, and business integrity to be entrusted with the development of the locality?*

   The capacity of the private actors who could conduct spatial planning, build connecting infrastructure, and deliver urban services should be substantially higher than that of the local government. They should also have a track record of delivering at scale and not be suspected of corrupt practices or political tinkering. Actors not meeting these criteria should be ruled out.

3. *GOVERNMENT FUNCTIONS. Where does the comparative advantage of the identified private actor lie relative to the local government?*

(Box continues on next page)

BOX 8.1 **A tentative protocol for urban policy in relation to private cities** (continued)

To develop a city, it is necessary to assemble land, build connecting infrastructure, and deliver urban services. Technical and institutional constraints may result in one of the two players being better placed than the other to take on each of these functions. This comparative advantage should guide the allocation of responsibilities for urban development.

4. *LAND VALUE CAPTURE. How will the economic surplus generated by the city be distributed among key stakeholders?*

Building the right type of city must be profitable for the private actor, and the local government may have to provide additional incentives to that effect. But the surplus generated by urbanization must benefit society at large. General taxation, land concessions, or a joint venture with the private actor can be used as tools for land value capture and redistribution.

5. *INCENTIVES AND REGULATION. Could the allocation of key functions to the private actor result in environmental damage, social exclusion, or institutional secession?*

If so, mechanisms should be found to align the incentives of the private actor with those of society at large. Such mechanisms may take the form of mandates, for example in relation to environmental protection or individual freedoms. They could also take the form of economic incentives such as subsidies for affordable housing.

6. *CONTRACT ENFORCEMENT. Could the private actor default on its commitments or be reluctant to engage because the local government cannot credibly commit?*

Even well-specified contracts may not foresee all the uncertainties related to urban development or be robust enough to deter opportunistic behavior by the signing parties. Specifying credible mechanisms for the settlement of disputes and possibly involving reputable foreign partners—such as cities from more advanced economies or international financial institutions—may help.

References

Bird, Julia, Yue Li, Hossain Zillur Rahman, Martin Rama, and Anthony J. Venables. 2018. *Toward Great Dhaka: A New Urban Development Paradigm Eastward*. Washington, DC: World Bank.

Li, Yue, and Martin Rama. 2022. "Private Cities: Implications for Urban Policy in Developing Countries." Policy Research Working Paper 9936, World Bank, Washington, DC.

Part II: Outstanding private cities from developing countries

CHAPTER 9

Bangladesh | EAST DHAKA

Julia Bird, Yue Li, Hossain Zillur Rahman, Martin Rama,
and Anthony J. Venables*

A vast flood-prone area next to the densest parts of Dhaka is rapidly urbanizing as large developers rely on sand-filling for their projects, one of which has become a city within a city. The economic potential of this organic urbanization is significant, but so are the environmental risks.

Private actor

The Bashundhara Group is one of largest private conglomerates in Bangladesh. Founded in 1987 by Ahmed Akbar Sobhan—its current chair—its affiliated companies operate in a broad range of sectors, from shipping to cement, and from textiles to oil and gas (Bashundhara Group 2022). However, real estate remains its core business, with Ahmed Akbar Sobhan also serving as president of the influential Bangladesh Land Developers Association.

One of the most significant undertakings of the group is the Bashundhara Residential Area, the largest real estate project in Bangladesh. Launched in 1988, it seeks to satisfy the rapidly growing demand for urban space with modern amenities, good connectivity, and high-end services. The development sits in East Dhaka, a largely rural plain that is prone to floods but stands very near the central business district of the capital city (Rahman 2017).

The Bashundhara Residential Area is not the only large urban development initiative in that zone. By 2018, there were at least 19 large real estate projects,

---

*This private city snapshot is based on Bird et al. (2018).

by 18 private investors. However, the scale and success of its undertaking make the Bashundhara Group the leader of the spatial transformation currently under way in East Dhaka (Bird et al. 2018).

Interaction with government

The Greater Dhaka area encompasses an urban core, satellite cities, and towns and villages, with almost 40 percent of its surface still devoted to agriculture (RAJUK 2015). Four city corporations (CCs) are responsible for its more urbanized jurisdictions, while more than 70 union councils deal with its rural communes. Two of the four CCs, formally in charge of different parts of the urban core—the west of the city—now divide responsibilities over East Dhaka (BBS 2011).

The authority of these two CCs remains limited despite recent moves toward greater decentralization. Meanwhile, large numbers of central government units are mandated to work on almost every key functional area within the CCs' jurisdiction. As of 1998, over 50 agencies were involved in urban development and the provision of services to the city (ADB 1998).

No effective coordination mechanisms between functional areas have been put in place since then, nor does each area work well by itself. Urban development plans have been designed largely in isolation, often by external consultants, with little input from the relevant stakeholders. There is weak ownership of these plans by local authorities, defuse accountability for their implementation, and a limited capacity to act on them (Rahman 2017). Local authorities also face severe budget constraints, as revenue from property-related taxes and fees is barely sufficient to finance the day-to-day operations of the two Dhaka CCs (Bird et al. 2018).

Location and connectivity

Dhaka stands on a vast deltaic plain near the confluence of three grand rivers: Jamuna, Padma, and Meghna. Twice a day, the tide pushes a substantial portion of this plain below sea level, and only a vast network of dikes and embankments keeps water out of inhabited areas. Staying dry is especially challenging in the monsoon season.

Historically, the urban core of Dhaka developed atop the Madhupur tract, a relatively firm surface above flood levels. However, as population grew, the city expanded into the surrounding plain. Its western part is largely shielded by a river embankment built in response to the massive 1988 floods. But no similar embankment has been developed on the river bordering its urban core toward the east (Alam 2014; Hasan 2008; Talukder 2006).

Two major transport corridors intersect near that missing embankment. In the east–west direction, an expressway passing through the recently completed Padma Bridge connects Dhaka to Kolkata, India, the region's wealthiest city. In the north–south direction, the Sylhet-Chittagong highway links Bangladesh with major East Asian cities including Bangkok, Yangon, and Kunming (ADB et al. 2018).

Development time line

In 2011, the western part of the two Dhaka CCs was home to about 8 million residents, with an average density of 41,000 persons per square kilometer. But the eastern part, with an area comparable to that of a major European city, had only 900,000 inhabitants—many of them farmers. Even parts of East Dhaka that lie within walking distance from the city's central business district had a very low population density barely one decade ago (BBS 2011).

The most significant government initiative to develop Dhaka eastward is Purbachal New Town, a large real estate project spanning 25 square kilometers. Formally inaugurated in 2002 and originally scheduled for completion in 2018, the project, and its progress on the ground, has been modest. As of 2017, few of the 30 sectors originally foreseen had basic infrastructure, 29 of them lacked electric substations, and the feasibility study of sewage treatment and solid waste management remained incomplete (Rahman 2017; RAJUK 2022). By contrast, in just two decades the Bashundhara Residential Area became a coveted city within a city, home to primarily upper-middle-class and high-income residents (Bird et al. 2018).

The other major development in East Dhaka during this period was the completion of the 300-Feet Road, a highway linking Dhaka's central business district to Purbachal New Town. The availability of this new trunk infrastructure, together with the evident success of the Bashundhara Residential Area, made other private investors see the potential of the flood-prone areas toward the east, triggering many other real estate projects (Rahman 2017; RAJUK 2022).

Without the protection of a major river embankment, these real estate projects must first fill their sites with sand, so that they stand above high-water levels. Satellite images of East Dhaka show how private initiative led to the rapid conversion of much of its flood-prone agricultural area into areas for urban development. Sand-filled sites were still scattered in 2003, occupying less than 1 square kilometer altogether. By 2016, however, their aggregate surface—including Purbachal New Town—had increased to almost 40 square kilometers (Bird et al. 2018).

Institutional status

The two Dhaka CCs were established in 2011 as part of a reorganization of local governance. Their first mayors were elected in 2015, but both their CEOs and their secretaries must belong to the senior pool of the Bangladesh civil service cadre.

These two CCs did not cover the eastern part of the urban core, as defined by the metropolitan development plan of 2015 (RAJUK 2015). To a large extent, the area identified here as East Dhaka remained under the purview of union councils, like any other rural area in the country. Only in 2016 were 12 of these union councils brought under the two urban jurisdictions. That move also encompassed four union councils to the north of the city, so eight councils were added to each of the two Dhaka CCs. This administrative reform increased the official area of the urban core from 127 to 307 square kilometers.

Despite the more than doubling of the area they were responsible for, the two Dhaka CCs remained focused on the perennial challenges of the western part: growing congestion, recurrent flooding, and overall messiness. Ongoing initiatives to address those challenges include revitalizing old Dhaka, retrofitting the urban core of the city, and building satellite towns toward the north (Bird et al. 2018). No strategy to tap into the potential offered by the vast and still relatively empty East Dhaka area has been articulated so far.

Land assembly

By 2016, large private sector investors had purchased or developed about 28 square kilometers of land within East Dhaka, amounting to about one-quarter of its total area. Among the 19 real estate development projects identified, the Bashundhara Group is the dominant player, occupying 7 square kilometers of land immediately to the south of 300-Feet Road. The land was acquired mostly from farmers and individual owners, through both market purchases and negotiations (Bird et al. 2018).

Economic activity

The Bashundhara Residential Area has become a hub for high-end businesses, including a state-of-the-art hospital and two major universities. The largest shopping mall in the country sits near its entrance. And several leading companies—including the Bashundhara Group, a diversified holding, the largest media house of Bangladesh, and the country's biggest electronics exporter—have established their headquarters there.

It does not follow that all East Dhaka will experience a similar dynamism. Much will depend on investments and policies that are beyond the reach of individual developers. A critically important project to support the development of the area would be the construction of the eastern embankment, accompanied by the rehabilitation of canals and the protection of flood retention areas. The area would also benefit from a denser network of mass transit and wider roads as well as targeted policies to attract more high-value activities and boost local agglomeration effects.

A simulation exercise building on a detailed spatial general equilibrium model of the Greater Dhaka area suggests that, in the absence of such critical investments and policies, East Dhaka would attain a population of 1.6 million in 2035 and generate US$10 billion in GDP.

On the other hand, if the embankment were built, the availability of urban land would greatly increase, and the city would rebalance eastward. In this scenario, East Dhaka would host over 5 million people by 2035, and its GDP would reach US$42 billion. A more comprehensive set of road investments and business policies would boost these figures even further. However, such a scenario seems unlikely given the weak capacity of the local authorities (Bird et al. 2018).

Amenities

Beyond high-end housing and open spaces, the Bashundhara Residential Area offers basic urban services, including reliable electricity, gas and water supply, and efficient waste management. A four-lane, well-maintained road runs north–south through the development with links to all sectors. Not all private real estate projects in the area meet such high standards, however.

All private development projects in East Dhaka rely on the public sector for basic infrastructure and social services, including drainage, sewerage, and transportation. The government has certainly invested significant resources in building roads and bridges in East Dhaka. Despite these efforts, transportation infrastructure is falling behind population growth.

In the absence of detailed urban development planning for East Dhaka, potential road corridors may be occupied before any construction takes place. For the few roads that are planned, anecdotal evidence indicates that realignments are needed to meet the land requirements of private developers. And the interface between the private and the public spheres is often inadequate. Even in the otherwise well-functioning Bashundhara Residential Area, the internal road network connects with outside transport infrastructure at only three points (Lamb 2014).

Social and environmental issues

With urban standards substantially above those of the surrounding areas, the Bashundhara Residential Area has attracted a wealthier population, reinforcing the spatial dimension of income inequality. The area is also subject to a different set of norms, focused on security and traffic control. Residents and frequent visitors receive car stickers upon approval by the "welfare society office." They are also required to strictly abide by local security rules.

Organic urbanization eastward has had environmental consequences. Over time, canals and water storage areas that help absorb excess water in times of heavy rainfall have been encroached on by housing construction, clogged by solid waste, or filled with sand (Kamol 2019). Recent assessments indicate only about 2 square kilometers of permanent wetlands remain in East Dhaka, threatening its biodiversity (DWASA 2015; Halcrow Group Limited 2006; World Bank 2018).

Disaster risk has increased as well. Major earthquakes cannot be ruled out in areas outside the Madhupur tract. Their impact could be amplified by large-scale sand-filling, which leads to a loose and segregated soil structure. Ground vibration can make the properties of such soil change rapidly (a process known as liquefaction), destroying urban infrastructure and making buildings sink or fall over (figure 9.1).

FIGURE 9.1 **Massive sand-filling in areas with high seismic risk in East Dhaka, Bangladesh**

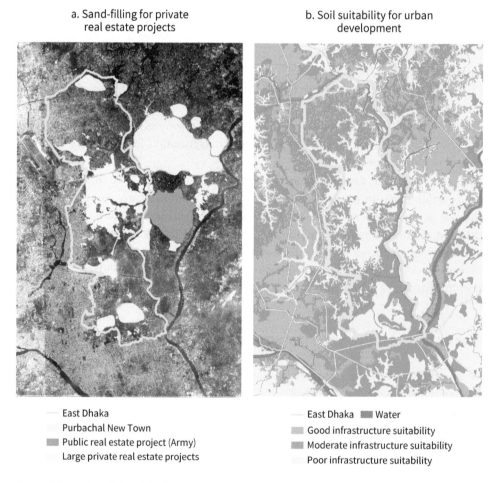

a. Sand-filling for private
real estate projects

b. Soil suitability for urban
development

--- East Dhaka
Purbachal New Town
▧ Public real estate project (Army)
Large private real estate projects

--- East Dhaka ▧ Water
▧ Good infrastructure suitability
▧ Moderate infrastructure suitability
Poor infrastructure suitability

Source: Adapted from Bird et al. 2018.

Land value capture

Land prices have surged in East Dhaka. The price of a square meter in the Bashundhara Residential Area was US$24–83 in 2000 but had increased to US$94–120 by 2016. Ready-to-occupy apartments of a similar quality went from US$19,000–63,000 in 2000 to US$123,000–164,000 in 2016 (Masum et al. 2016). Land prices have likely continued to climb.

Much of the profit the Bashundhara Group and other large developers make comes from the difference between these selling prices and the cost at which they acquired the land. But concerns have been raised about such costs being below the market price. There are reports indicating that landowners have been threatened into selling their land (*Daily Star* 2009). Others suggest that sand-filling results in blurred demarcation lines during the monsoon season, and the resulting uncertainty may have been used by real estate developers to expand the area they control (Halcrow Group Limited 2006; Lamb 2014).

Meanwhile, incomplete and out-of-date land records provide limited protection against eviction or inadequate compensation. A recent study of a *mouza* (a revenue collection unit encompassing several villages) in an area of East Dhaka not yet touched by major real estate projects illustrates the risks. The number of land property records registered with this mouza was indeed much lower than the number of households living there (Bird et al. 2018).

Furthermore, many plots in East Dhaka are *khas* (water bodies and low-lying flood-plains that do not support permanent human settlements). Some of the land titles in the mouza mentioned above fall in this category and are held by the government. Pressure to develop khas for urban uses, potentially at no cost to large developers, cannot be ruled out (Bird et al. 2018).

References

ADB. 1998. *Reforming Dhaka City Management.* Vol. 3 of *Asian Cities in the 21st Century: Contemporary Approaches to Municipal Management.* Manila: Asian Development Bank.

ADB, JICA, UKAID, and World Bank. 2018. *The WEB of Transport Corridors in South Asia.* Washington, DC: World Bank.

Alam, Jahangir. 2014. "The Organized Encroachment of Land Developers—Effects on Urban Flood Management in Greater Dhaka, Bangladesh." *Sustainable Cities and Society* 10: 49–58.

Bashundhara Group. 2022. "Corporate Profile." Accessed March 10, 2022, https://www.bashundharagroup.com/page/corporate-profile.

BBS. 2011. *Bangladesh Population and Housing Census 2011.* Dhaka: Bangladesh Bureau of Statistics.

Bird, Julia, Yue Li, Hossain Zillur Rahman, Martin Rama, and Anthony J. Venables. 2018. *Toward Great Dhaka: A New Urban Development Paradigm Eastward.* Washington, DC: World Bank.

Daily Star. 2009. "Victims Protest 'Land Grabbing' by Bashundhara." *Daily Star* (Dhaka), October 16, 2009.

DWASA. 2015. *Storm Water Drainage Master Plan for Dhaka City.* Dhaka: Dhaka Water and Sewerage Authority.

Halcrow Group Limited. 2006. "Updating/Upgrading the Feasibility Study of Dhaka Integrated Flood Control Embankment cum Eastern Bypass Road Multipurpose Project." Unpublished manuscript. London: Halcrow Group Limited.

Hasan, Faruque. 2008. "From Jahangirnagar to Dhaka." *Forum: A Monthly Publication of the Daily Star* 3, no. 8.

Kamol, Ershad. 2019. "Real Estate Cos Continue to Grab Wetlands." *New Age* (Dhaka), August 22, 2019.

Lamb, Zachary. 2014. "Embanked: Climate Vulnerability and the Paradoxes of Flood Protection in Dhaka." Unpublished manuscript. Cambridge, MA: Massachusetts Institute of Technology, Department of Urban Studies and Planning.

Masum, F., U. E. Chugbu, J. Espiniza, and C. Graffen. 2016. "The Limitations of Formal Land Delivery System: Need for a Pro-Poor Urban Land Development Policy in Dhaka, Bangladesh." Paper presented at World Bank Land and Poverty Conference, Washington, DC.

Rahman, Hossain Zillur. 2017. "Transforming Dhaka East: A Political Economy Perspective on Opportunities and Challenges." Unpublished manuscript. Dhaka: Power and Participation Research Centre.

RAJUK. 2015. *Dhaka Structure Plan 2016–2035.* Dhaka: Rajdhani Unnayan Kartripakkha.

RAJUK. 2022. *Purbachal New Town. Dhaka*: Dhaka: Rajdhani Unnayan Kartripakkha. Last updated December 8, 2022. http://www.rajuk.gov.bd/site/project/fdd1a995-7887-408a-a4da-ac82f7f25bb9/Purbachal-New-Town.

Talukder, S. H. 2006. "Managing Megacities: A Case Study of Metropolitan Regional Governance for Dhaka." PhD diss., Murdoch University, Perth, Australia.

World Bank. 2018. "Enhancing Opportunities for Clean and Resilient Growth in Urban Bangladesh: Country Environmental Analysis." World Bank, Washington, DC.

CHAPTER 10

Bolivia | EL ALTO

Arturo Villegas Limas and Martin Rama*

The city of El Alto sits on a plateau overlooking Bolivia's capital of La Paz. Three times larger than Lhasa in Tibet (China), it is the only million-plus urban agglomeration in the world standing more than 4,000 meters above sea level.

Private actor

El Alto is unique among private cities in that its key private actor was not a large developer or a business association, but rather civil society. The emergence and growth of the city were indeed shaped by a myriad of *juntas vecinales* (neighborhood associations), which brought thousands of people together to fight—sometimes literally—for better urban services and economic opportunities, in a context of neglect by the authorities.

The region of El Alto has a long history of ethnic conflict. In the eighteenth century, a major rebellion against the colonial power took place, led by indigenous leader Julián Apasa, who took the name Túpac Katari to honor illustrious predecessors in the fight against the Spaniards. The city of La Paz was sieged for over six months, and although the rebels were eventually defeated, the episode left a lasting imprint (Albó 2008).

Back then, El Alto was a mostly rural area, but it started densifying in the 1950s. Its population—mostly indigenous Aymara—grew at an annual rate of almost 9 percent in the final decades of the twentieth century, tapping the employment opportunities provided by nearby La Paz. This is how El Alto quickly became one of the biggest cities in Bolivia (Arbona and Kohl 2004). However, basic urban services, such as water supply and street paving, were only partially provided by the municipality of La Paz, leading residents to search for alternative delivery mechanisms.

---

*This private city snapshot is based on Villegas Limas (2021).

An unusually strong civil society movement developed in El Alto—schoolteachers, with former miners, youth, and informal traders building complex relationships among themselves and with the authorities. Their organizations were influenced by a range of ideologies, from Trotskyism in the case of schoolteachers to socialism among former miners, indigenism in the case of youth organizations, and even libertarianism for informal traders (Albó 2008).

Formally, neighborhood associations have their origin in the *sindicatos de inquilinos* (tenant unions) created in the 1950s under the left-leaning government of President Víctor Paz Estenssoro. Residents of El Alto generally saw these associations as representative and tended to follow their lead (Albó 2008). Their number grew steadily, from 6 in 1952 to 44 by 1979, 86 in 1984, 422 by 2004, and more than 600 nowadays.

This proliferation made it necessary to establish increasingly stronger mechanisms to coordinate their action. Thus, the Consejo Central de Vecinos (neighbors' central council) emerged in 1957, followed by the Federación de Juntas Vecinales in 1963 and the Frente de Unidad y Renovación Independiente de El Alto (FURIA, meaning "fury") in 1979 (Fernández 2009; Fernández Rojas 2021).

Interaction with government

Neighborhood associations tried to exert pressure on the municipality of La Paz to boost local investments, focusing on the construction of markets and schools (Poupeau 2010). However, local authorities did not recognize the associations of El Alto, thus reducing their influence on urban policy (Oporto Ordóñez 2018).

Confronted with this limited receptivity at the local level, these associations increasingly took on a prominent role in national politics. In the 1970s and 1980s, they actively participated in movements against military dictatorships (Poupeau 2010). In 2002, they mobilized thousands of citizens to protest privatizations in the gas industry in a so-called Gas War that led to the fall of the government (Albó 2008, Lazar 2008). More recently, they contributed to the ascent of Evo Morales, an Aymara trade unionist who became the country's first indigenous president in 2006 (Makaran 2016).

Over time, the relationship between neighborhood associations and the government became increasingly clientelist. Several politicians have risen to leadership positions in these associations without even living in the areas they serve (Albó 2008).

Location and connectivity

Unlike neighboring La Paz, which sits in a deep canyon, the city of El Alto stands entirely in the Bolivian *altiplano*, a vast uninterrupted highland almost as high above sea level as the Tibetan plateau. The noticeable cliff of La Ceja, where the altiplano ends and the valleys begin, is also an administrative and cultural border, separating

FIGURE 10.1 **El Alto, Bolivia: A vibrant, if somewhat unconventional urban agglomeration**

a. The aerial cable car system

b. The 16 de Julio Street market

c. Freddy Mamani's buildings

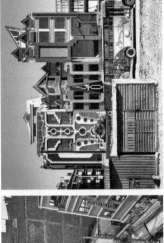

Sources: Panel a: © Leonid Andronov/Alamy Stock Photo. Used with permission of Leonid Andronov/Alamy Stock Photo. Further permission required for reuse; panel b: © Cultura Creative RF/Alamy Stock Photo. Reproduced with permission of Alamy Stock Photo. Further permission required for reuse; panel c: © Tatewaki Nio/Tatewaki Nio Fotos. Reproduced with permission of Tatewaki Nio Fotos. Further permission required for reuse.

a predominately indigenous agglomeration from the more ethnically mixed capital city (Albó 2008).

The area of El Alto was long crossed by roads that connected La Paz to other cities in the highlands. In 1904, a railway station was built where lines from several cities in the highlands come together into a single rail link descending the canyon (Díaz 2016). An airfield was established in the 1940s, and since then it gradually evolved into a full airport, for many years the most important in the country by traffic (Indaburu Quintana 2004).

A significant improvement in El Alto's access to markets came with the construction in 2014 of Mi Teleférico, an aerial cable car system connecting it to La Paz (figure 10.1, panel a). Resources were provided by the national government during the presidency of Evo Morales. With 26 stations along 10 lines, this innovative mass transit system is the longest cable car system in the world, transporting close to 85,000 passengers per day (Martínez, Sánchez, and Yañez-Pagans 2018).

Development time line

Historically, El Alto was home to Aymara communities organized in *ayllus* (villages) that had been subsumed into *latifundios* (large estates) in the late nineteenth century. In feudal fashion, villagers could live on their farmland in exchange for working in the latifundios. However, in the 1950s, the reform-minded government of President Paz Estenssoro transferred land rights to villagers, unsettling the traditional agricultural system.

The acceleration of population growth brought increasing pressure on the land. Traditional inheritance practices led to repeated divisions of plots, hence to the emergence of *minifundios* (tiny farms). Faced with diminishing land returns, many in the younger rural cohorts moved out of agriculture to secure a livelihood. The edge of the plateau overlooking La Paz was a natural migration destination for them (Díaz 2016; Kranenburg 2002).

The population inflow to the area accelerated in the 1980s. In the first part of the decade, two consecutive droughts made agricultural livelihoods even more vulnerable (Poupeau 2010). In the second part, Paz Estenssoro returned to power, this time with a liberalization agenda aimed at tackling Bolivia's hyperinflation. As part of his new package of reforms, he closed many of the state-owned tin mines his first government had nationalized three decades earlier, driving thousands of mostly unionized, laid-off miners into El Alto (Arbona 2007; Poupeau 2010).

Institutional status

For much of its history, El Alto was administratively part of the municipality of La Paz. In 1968, it became a district, designated as an industrial and low-income area. In 1970, a *sub-alcaldía* (ward) was created, with a deputy mayor in charge. And in 1985, more than three decades after it had begun urbanizing, El Alto was named a city.

However, it took another decade for neighborhood associations to be finally recognized. The Law of Popular Participation of 1994 allowed them to contribute to local budget planning processes, especially for resources allocated by the national government (Lazar 2005). The law also transferred some competences to local governments (Thévoz 1999).

Land assembly

The center of El Alto, hosting local government buildings and artisan and commercial enterprises, emerged near the railway station and the airport. The outer rings were gradually populated as low-income families arrived and settled around roads and railway lines (Botton, Hardy, and Poupeau 2017; Fernández 2009; Poupeau 2010). As these settlements densified and developed into full-fledged neighborhoods, El Alto became an unplanned tapestry of areas with uneven urban layouts (Albó 2008).

In some cases, migrants relied on land invasions, which resulted in no clear connection between plot shapes and transport networks (Indaburu Quintana 2004). In others, original landowners divided their mostly uncultivated latifundios into urban-sized land plots and sold them. The practice was illegal at the time, but it helped keep local land prices affordable (Díaz 2016).

Economic activity

The city of El Alto was most successful on economic grounds. From 11,000 inhabitants in 1950, it has grown to more than 1.1 million nowadays. In the early 2000s, it overtook the capital city of La Paz to become Bolivia's second largest city. Its growth was particularly strong between 1992 and 2003, when its population increased by almost 60 percent, and its labor force by a staggering 80 percent (Arbona 2008).

As its population boomed, El Alto gradually became a provider of goods and services to La Paz. Many small manufacturing companies were created, almost all of them informal, with clothing as their main activity. Free-trade zones were established by the national government in the late 1990s, attracting thousands of firms to the area (Arbona 2001; Fernández 2009).

Nowadays, El Alto contributes about 6 percent of Bolivia's GDP, 12 percent of its exports, 16 percent of its industrial employment, and 22 percent of its manufacturing output. About 80 percent of businesses in the La Paz metropolitan area operate from El Alto, and around 200,000 people commute every day between the two cities (Díaz 2016). In addition to garments, the economy of El Alto specializes in furniture production, mechanics, foodstuffs, and textiles.

From an employment viewpoint, however, informal wholesale and retail commerce dominate. Roughly one-third of El Alto's labor force works in this sector, mostly in small family-owned businesses (Poupeau 2010; Rojas and Guaygua 2001). The somewhat chaotic open-air market that operates on 16 de Julio Street on Tuesdays and Sundays, extending for over 5 kilometers, is the biggest of its kind in Bolivia (figure 10.1, panel b).

Amenities

El Alto's record is much weaker when it comes to service delivery. The first urban development plan for El Alto was prepared by the municipality of La Paz in 1976. Two years later, a framework establishing permitted land uses and building heights by area was published. In the 1980s and 1990s, the newly created local government of El Alto developed an urban development model for the city. And in 1999 and 2005 it drafted new plans to improve the urbanization process. But all these initiatives remained on paper (Fernández 2009).

Neighborhood associations effectively improved municipal services for the city. A first needs assessment was prepared in 1964 by the neighborhoods' central council (Fernández Rojas 2021). Over the years, neighborhood associations mobilized private donations and free labor for the development of basic infrastructure and social services, even contributing to teachers' salaries (Díaz 2016; Lazar 2005). Other civil society organizations were successful in changing local policies; for example, in 2007 the student organizations managed to get bars, cantinas, and brothels removed from the vicinity of schools (Risør 2016).

One significant urban upgrading effort was a community-driven development project funded by the World Bank in 1970, with neighborhood associations involved in the prioritization of spending (Kranenburg 2002; Linares 1987; Salmen and Eaves 1989; van Lindert 1986).

However, by the turn of the twenty-first century, 15 percent of El Alto's residents still had no access to electricity, and 94 percent of its roads were not paved. Only 65 percent of the population was connected to the potable water network and 25 percent to the sanitary network, compared to 95 and 80 percent, respectively, in La Paz. To this day many households in El Alto use large containers and rely on distribution networks managed by small cooperatives to access water (Arbona 2007; Botton, Hardy, and Poupeau 2017).

Social and environmental issues

El Alto's remarkable growth cannot obscure the social segregation the city embodies. In 2001, three-quarters of the population ages 15 and above identified themselves as Aymara, compared to half of the population in La Paz. While the unemployment rate is low, the area is disproportionately poor, and ridden with crime.

On the other hand, El Alto has attracted attention for its vibrant culture. This repu-tation is partly associated with the psychedelic-looking buildings by Aymara architect Freddy Mamani, inspired by indigenous fabrics (figure 10.1, panel c). Among these buildings are also dozens of *cholet*, a word meant to be a humorous combination of *chalet* and *cholo*. The latter, a derogatory term to refer to indigenous people, has of late become a sign of pride in El Alto (Boobbyer 2018; Wainwright 2018).

Land value capture

Despite its economic dynamism, El Alto still struggles financially. Although the city is similar in size to La Paz, its tax revenue is six times lower, and its public investment seven times lower. High levels of poverty and informality, together with weak local government capacity, get in the way of higher municipal revenues (Arbona and Kohl 2004; Espinoza and Gozálvez 2003). The municipality has also had difficulties updating its cadastre, and as a result revenue from property tax is almost nil (Kranenburg 2002).

Also underlying the meager revenue of the local government is strong resistance to taxation by the local community. In 2003, violent protests erupted after an attempt to impose a 12.5 percent income tax (Albó 2008). Neighborhood associations argued that the proposed tax aimed to "get more money from the poor" (Arbona 2007).

Neighborhood associations have been somewhat more successful at capturing land value. Even associations that are not yet officially recognized manage to collect money from residents to invest in their neighborhoods.

However, funding urban infrastructure and providing social services remain major challenges that neither the local government nor civil society seems able to effectively address. And corrupt practices involving local leaders—such as the embezzlement of national funds—have been brought into the spotlight. Among them is *obras por votos* (works for votes), whereby political loyalty is demanded in exchange for infrastructure projects, a practice that may have become more common in recent years (Makaran 2016).

References

Albó, Xavier. 2008. "El Alto, la vorágine de una ciudad única." *Journal of Latin American Anthropology* 11 (2): 329–50.

Arbona, Juan M. 2001. *The Political Economy of Micro-enterprise Promotion Policies: Restructuring and Income-Generating Activities in El Alto, Bolivia*. Ithaca, NY: Cornell University.

Arbona, Juan M. 2007. "Neo-liberal Ruptures: Local Political Entities and Neighbourhood Networks in El Alto, Bolivia." *Geoforum* 38 (1): 127–37.

Arbona, Juan M. 2008. "Eso es ser pobre e indio en este país. Repercusiones urbanas e implicaciones sociales de la discriminación y la exclusión: lecciones de El Alto, Bolivia."

In *Pobreza, exclusión social y discriminación étnico-racial en América Latina y el Caribe*, edited by Zabala Arguelles and María del Carmen, 349–72. Bogotá, Colombia: Siglo del Hombre Editores-CLACSO.

Arbona, Juan M., and Benjamin Kohl. 2004. "La Paz–El Alto." *Cities* 21 (3): 255–65.

Boobbyer, Claire. 2018. "High Society: El Alto, Bolivia, Steps into the Spotlight." the *Guardian*, October 17, 2018.

Botton, Sarah, Sebastien Hardy, and Frank Poupeau. 2017. "Water from the Heights, Water from the Grassroots: The Governance of Common Dynamics and Public Services in La Paz–El Alto." Unpublished manuscript. World Bank, Washington, DC.

Díaz, Mariela Paula. 2016. "La dinámica urbana y laboral de la ciudad de El Alto (Bolivia): Entre el mercado y la producción social del hábitat." *Población & Sociedad* 23 (1): 45–77.

Espinoza, Claudia, and Gonzalo Gozálvez. 2003. "Bolivia arrinconada en la azotea de su historia." *Observatorio social de América Latina (Argentina)* 10: 29–36.

Fernández, Gabith Miriam Quispe. 2009. "La formación de la ciudad de El Alto y sus consecuencias." PhD diss., Universidad Autónoma de Madrid.

Fernández Rojas, Johnny. 2021. "Así nació El Alto." Unpublished manuscript. Centro de Formación y Capacitación para la Participación Ciudadana, La Paz.

Indaburu Quintana, Rafael. 2004. *Evaluación de la ciudad de El Alto*. Contract 511-O-00-04-00047-00. Washington, DC: US Agency for International Development.

Kranenburg, Ronald H. 2002. "Buurtconsolidatie en urbane transformatie in El Alto: Een longitudinaal onderzoek naar veranderingsprocessen in de voormalige periferie van La Paz, Bolivia." PhD diss., Utrecht University, the Netherlands.

Lazar, Sian. 2005. "Citizens Despite the State: Everyday Corruption and Local Politics in El Alto, Bolivia." In *Corruption: Anthropological Perspectives*, edited by Dieter Haller and Cris Shore, 212–28. London and Ann Arbor, MI: Pluto Press.

Lazar, Sian. 2008. *El Alto, Rebel City: Self and Citizenship in Andean Bolivia*. Durham, NC: Duke University Press.

Linares, C. 1987. *Bases para la Formulación de una Política Nacional de Vivienda*. PADCO.

Makaran, Gaya. 2016. "La figura del *llunk'u* y el clientelismo en la Bolivia de Evo Morales." *Revista Antropologías del Sur* 3 (5): 33–47.

Martínez, Sebastián, Raul Sánchez, and Patricia Yañez-Pagans. 2018. "Getting a Lift: The Impact of Aerial Cable Cars in La Paz, Bolivia." IDB Working Paper Series 00956. Inter-American Development Bank, Washington, DC.

Oporto Ordóñez, Luis. 2018. "El Alto de pie, nunca de rodillas: de las villas marginales a la urbe industrial." *Fuentes, Revista de la Biblioteca y Archivo Histórico de la Asamblea Legislativa Plurinacional* 12 (55): 71–77.

Poupeau, Frank. 2010. "El Alto: una ficción política." *Bulletin de l'Institut français d'études andines* 39 (2): 427–49.

Risør, Helene. 2016. "Closing Down Bars in the Inner City Centre: Informal Urban Planning, Civil Insecurity, and Subjectivity in Bolivia. *Singapore Journal of Tropical Geography* 37 (3): 330–42.

Rojas, Bruno, and Germán Guaygua. 2001. *El empleo en tiempos de crisis*. Amsterdam: Centre for Latin American Research and Documentation.

Salmen, Lawrence F., and A. Paige Eaves. 1989. "World Bank Work with Nongovernmental Organizations." Policy, Planning and Research Working Papers 305. World Bank, Washington DC.

Thévoz, Laurent. 1999. "Decentralization in Bolivia: A Model under Construction." Communauté d'Études pour l'Aménagement du Territoire, Paris.

van Lindert, Paul. 1986. "Collective Consumption and the State in La Paz, Bolivia." *Boletín de Estudios Latinoamericanos y del Caribe* 41: 71–93.

Villegas Limas, Arturo. 2021. "Case Study: El Alto, Bolivia." Background paper, *Private Cities: Outstanding Examples from Developing Countries and Their Implications for Urban Policy*, World Bank, Washington, DC.

Wainwright, Oliver. 2018. "Party Palaces and Funky Funhouses: Freddy Mamani's Maverick Buildings." the *Guardian*, October 23, 2018.

CHAPTER 11

China | GU'AN

Kun Cheng, Yue Li, Martin Rama, and Siqi Zheng

Next to one of China's most dynamic urban agglomerations, but with its development hampered by administrative boundaries and weak government capacity, Gu'an County entered an unusual public-private partnership (PPP) with a major urban development company focused on investment solicitation and business services.

Private actor

In 1992, Wenxue Wang left a government job to open a hotpot restaurant in Langfang, a city in Hebei Province, a business that allowed him to nurture a close relationship with local authorities. In 1998 he shifted to the construction industry and founded China Fortune Land Development (CFLD). But he soon realized he would not be able to compete with large developers on volume, especially after stricter regulations on purchasing houses were introduced (Cheng 2020; E-House 2018; Jo and Zheng 2020).

To differentiate his company, he adopted a strategy that bears similarities with Michael Porter's "business cluster" notion (Delgado, Porter, and Stern 2010). CFLD's motto became "industry first," meaning that for urbanization projects to be successful they had to attract private businesses. In this view, a new city without a clear economic rationale would run the risk of becoming a bedroom town (E-House 2018; Jo and Zheng 2020).

The Gu'an New Industry City project was CFLD's first—and most successful—application of this strategy. Indeed, making this project work would have been difficult with more sophisticated counterparts, such as the Shanghai municipal authorities, given their high capacity and wealth of business connections. By contrast, county-level governments, such as that of Gu'an, lacked the vision and resources to tap the potential of their localities, and they were often narrowly focused on their city centers. But they were empowered to allocate the surrounding land.

After generating long lists of both locations and industries, CFLD approached local governments to seek support for its urban development projects. To maximize the chances of winning approval, it aligned the proposed industries with the objectives of each local government—especially with those resulting from national directives such as China's 2025 Intelligent Manufacturing Strategy.

Although CFLD outsourced its early work on attracting businesses to international consulting firms, the company grew to employ more than 5,000 people in its Industrial Research Institute in Beijing. A third of them hold master's degrees or higher, and many are former executives and experts from the targeted sectors. Over 3,700 work in the company's corporate solicitation branch, focused on attracting investors to urban development projects. Another 300 help investors with local tax registration, patent applications, and legal services (E-House 2018; Jo and Zheng 2020).

CFLD is publicly traded on the Shanghai Stock Exchange, with Wenxue Wang as its majority shareholder. As of 2016, the company had already invested US$15 billion in urban development projects and delivered 510 million square meters of real estate. To develop international businesses, it set up an international office in Singapore in 2016. There are currently over 30 industry towns built and supported by CFLD in China and overseas.

At the turn of the decade, the company was at the very top of China's industrial park operators, it ranked 45th among the country's real estate developers, and it occupied the 544th position on Forbes Global 2000 list. By then, CFLD's new city approach had become a model that the Chinese government hoped to see develop across the country (Caillavet 2021; E-House 2018; Jo and Zheng 2020).

Interaction with government

At the end of the twentieth century, the Chinese government was trying to address the insufficiency of urban land through the development of satellite cities. The cost of this urbanization strategy—estimated at US$6–7 trillion over two decades—was to be shared with local governments (Cheng 2020).

However, most small municipal authorities lacked the planning expertise and the budget resources to implement the strategy. According to one study, the authorities of Gu'an would have had to spend close to US$2.5 billion to transform their locality into a satellite city. The debt service associated with such oversized investment would have absorbed the entire fiscal revenue of the county for many years (Wei 2017, cited by Cheng 2020).

To overcome their budget constraints, local governments turned to borrowing, using their land as collateral, but this approach resulted in rapidly growing municipal debt. Besides, the effort was not always sufficient to attract successful private companies, which were looking for skilled labor and support services, and not only for tax breaks.

The satellite city strategy stalled in 2002, when the Ministry of Finance, in an attempt to deleverage local governments, barred them from selling land to repay their debts. The focus then shifted to PPPs for urban development. In 2004, the Ministry of Housing and Urban-Rural Development standardized their legal requirements, payment processes, and conflict resolution mechanisms for such PPPs. Importantly, it barred local governments from intervening in the large developers' operations, except when there was a significant risk for the public interest (E-House 2018).

Location and connectivity

As a small county in Hebei Province, Gu'an was ideally placed to seize the opportunities created by the new PPP model. The province wraps like a kidney around Beijing and Tianjin, two large urban agglomerations that together form one of the richest regions in China. However, the population of the two cities was growing at full tilt—it reached 45 million in 2016—thus placing significant strain on infrastructure and affordable housing.

Gu'an had weak capacity and limited budget resources, but it was just two hours by car from Beijing's city center and barely 50 kilometers from its international airport. If appropriately developed, it could attract businesses and talent from its very large neighboring cities and along the way help them decongest (Cheng 2020; E-House 2018; Jo and Zheng 2020).

Development time line

Success was far from guaranteed. In 2002, Gu'an was one of the poorest counties in Hebei, with a population of 380,000 and a per capita GDP of just US$1,000. Land was cheap, as it was in other counties in the vicinity. The area was mostly agricultural, with almost no industrial presence. Yet, based on its research, CFLD concluded that the county should focus on advanced display manufacturing, aviation and aerospace, and biomedical research and development.

This ambitious proposal contrasted with the modest interest expressed by China's largest developers: Vanke, Evergrande, and Sunac. Their focus was on building residential communities with public spaces and shopping malls. Gu'an County was simply too poor to support an urban concept tailored to an aspiring middle class (Jo and Zheng 2020).

In 2002, a PPP agreement was signed between the municipal government of Gu'an and CFLD. Under its terms, CFLD would be responsible for the master plan for the

New Industry City, the construction of its infrastructure, and the provision of amenities. It would also be accountable for operating and maintaining urban services and would commit to a full handover of all facilities after 50 years. The local government, in turn, would have responsibility for approvals and the supervision of the project (Cheng 2020; E-House 2018; Jo and Zheng 2020).

CFLD relocated its headquarters to Gu'an and engaged in active solicitation to attract companies from the three selected sectors to the locality. To this effect, it established industry-specific venture funds, partnerships with dozens of prestigious universities and research institutes, and an incubator to aid high-growth firms.

This full-service package had an impact on firms' decisions to relocate to Gu'an. For example, for Eternal Material Technology—a large manufacturer of organic light-emitting diodes—meeting clean room manufacturing standards was a priority. Whereas competing localities offered it land and tax subsidies, CFLD brought in clean room manufacturing experts from its aerospace clients to secure the investment (Jo and Zheng 2020).

Only five years after the signing of the PPP agreement did companies begin arriving in Gu'an in large numbers. But once that happened a momentum was built. Thus, when the BOE Technology Group—a leader in panel manufacturing—decided to build a new production base for mobile display in Gu'an, 30 of its suppliers and partners followed (E-House 2018).

For first-tier firms such as BOE Technology Group, CFLD offered discounts on land, tax breaks, subsidized housing for employees, or office space in a start-up incubator. The offers had to be approved by the local government, but the negotiations were confidential and much more flexible than the process through which state-owned industrial parks evaluated corporate applications for entry (Jo and Zheng 2020).

Institutional status

Under the terms of the 2002 PPP agreement, Gu'an New Industry City was run by a special purpose vehicle wholly owned by CFLD. In parallel, the municipal government established a management committee, the most typical institutional arrangement in the case of new towns (Cheng 2020). Ultimately, the decision-making process for the area relies on a collaboration between these two entities (figure 11.1).

As Gu'an developed, the Chinese government began to recognize the important contribution the New Industry City could make to the broader region. In 2013, it approved the construction of Beijing's second international airport at the border of Beijing and Hebei Province, only about 12 kilometers from Gu'an. This decision allowed CFLD to further prioritize aviation and aerospace as key sectors and to attract top businesses to the area, both public and private (Jiao and Yu 2020; Jo and Zheng 2020).

Then, in 2014, the government announced that an integrated urban and economic megaregion would be formed between Beijing, Tianjin, and Hebei Province.

FIGURE 11.1 **The partnership structure underlying urban development in Gu'an, China**

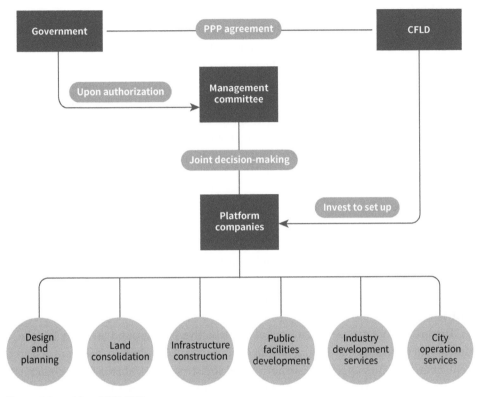

Source: Adapted from CFLD 2018.

Note: CFLD = China Fortune Land Development; PPP = public-private partnership.

Familiarly known as "Jing-Jin-Ji," this vast urban region is comparable in scale and ambition to the Greater Tokyo area or the northeast corridor from Boston to Washington, DC (Taylor 2019).

Land assembly

The municipal authorities of Gu'an initially allocated 60 square kilometers of rural land for CFLD to develop its project. Much of this land was vacant because it was too sandy to farm. Over time, through land acquisitions, the project area was expanded to more than 170 square kilometers. Competing large developers claim that CFLD enjoyed preferential treatment whenever the Gu'an government held land auctions. Allegedly, local authorities were also lenient toward the project in other ways, such as endorsing its conversion of industrial land into residential uses (Jo and Zheng 2020; Wen et al. 2017).

Economic activity

Gu'an was dramatically transformed in barely two decades. Land prices reveal the magnitude of the change. When the PPP agreement was signed, land in Gu'an cost about US$160 per square meter; by 2019, the price was in the vicinity of US$3,000.

With over 520 companies attracted to the locality and 30,000 new jobs created, Gu'an ranks as one of China's top-100 counties to invest in. By 2019 the county's population had climbed to 500,000 and its per capita GDP exceeded US$7,300. Government revenue increased from US$20 million in 2002 to US$1.2 billion in 2016 (Cheng 2020; E-House 2018; Jo and Zheng 2020).

Amenities

So far, CFLD has invested about US$4.8 billion in Gu'an County, constructing 300 kilometers of roads, six water supply plants, four thermal power plants, a sewage disposal plant, two lakes, three parks, and 2.3 million square meters of linked greenways around the city, as well as several public squares, hospitals, high schools, and commercial districts.

The urban core primarily consists of an attractive park around an artificial lake, a downtown main street and plaza, and an exhibition hall. In addition, there are research centers and business parks for airport-based logistics, an incubator for commercializing scientific research from Tsinghua University, and thermal hot springs (Jo and Zheng 2020).

Social and environmental issues

New cities such as those developed by CFLD have been criticized as privatized, commodified, and homogenized products of corporate profit-seeking. However, it may be too early to assess their social and environmental impacts. Gu'an is not yet halfway into the 50-year time horizon envisioned in its PPP. And early indications seem less negative than the new-city criticism suggests. For example, in 2018 Gu'an was listed among the 60 "people-first PPPs for sustainable development" by the United Nations Economic Commission for Europe (*China Daily* 2018; Jo and Zheng 2020).

Land value capture

The PPP agreement between the government of Gu'an and CFLD was an unusual but effective mechanism to split between the two parties the economic surplus from urbanizing the county. Under the terms of the agreement, CFLD would receive a series of clearly specified monetary transfers in exchange for its investments and services. Every year, the Gu'an municipality would compensate CFLD for 115 percent of the investments it had made in the locality in the previous year, and for 110 percent of the planning and design costs it had incurred. Most important, the local government would pay CFLD a commission fee of 45 percent of the value of the fixed investments made by the companies it had attracted to the locality.

These terms created a very strong incentive for CFLD to engage in solicitation. Indeed, infrastructure investments and advisory services were compensated on a cost-plus basis, with a relatively modest margin, but the margin for industrial development activities was significant.

However, these terms also posed a challenge for the Gu'an municipal government, as it had to compensate CFLD for substantial expenditures at a time when it still had limited fiscal revenue. The challenge was amplified by the several years it would take for companies to relocate to Gu'an and start paying taxes locally. The solution was to allocate land to large developers—including CFLD itself—interested in real estate projects, or to charge them one-time user fees for the right to undertake housing construction on municipal land. This gamble succeeded, and the local government was able to honor its commitments under the PPP agreement (Jiao and Yu 2020; Jo and Zheng 2020).

Its success in Gu'an encouraged CFLD to replicate the model elsewhere, in China and overseas. Its focus was on locations that were 50–80 kilometers away from major urban agglomerations, but where urban development had been hampered by ill-defined administrative boundaries. However, how much of the success in Gu'an owes to this innovative business strategy and how much to its extraordinary location is still an open question (E-House 2018; Jo and Zheng 2020).

Perhaps as a result of having stretched itself too far, in 2021 CFLD failed to repay US\$530 million to its bondholders, triggering its downgrade to a restricted default rating. An additional US\$1.2 billion in fresh defaults followed a few months later (Caillavet 2021; Yu and Yoon 2021).

With US\$9.8 billion of bonds outstanding—including US\$4.6 billion offshore—CFLD's difficulties have cast a shadow on the future urban development of Gu'an. They also raise the prospect that bondholders in China and abroad may end up footing part of the bill for its extraordinary development over the past two decades.

References

Caillavet, Christopher. 2021. "China's CFLD Defaults on Fresh \$1.2B to Bring Overdue Debts to \$14.7B." *Mingtiandi*, November 2, 2021.

CFLD (China Fortune Land Development). 2018. "CFLD: Operator of New Cities." PowerPoint presentation, United Nations Commission for East Asia and the Pacific, Bangkok.

Cheng, Kun. 2020. "Private Involvement in City Making: A Preliminary Historical Review." Background paper, *Private Cities: Outstanding Examples from Developing Countries and Their Implications for Urban Policy*, World Bank, Washington, DC.

China Daily. 2018. "UN Selects Gu'an New Industry City as One of Sustainable Development PPP Cases." *China Daily*, May 15, 2018.

Delgado, Mercedes, Michael E. Porter, and Scott Stern. 2010. "Clusters and Entrepreneurship." *Journal of Economic Geography* 10 (4): 495–518.

E-House. 2018. "CFLD's Gu'an New Industry City: A New Kind of Public-Private Partnership." Wharton Case Study. University of Pennsylvania, Wharton School, Philadelphia.

Jiao, Yongli, and Yang Yu. 2020. "Rising Private City Operators in Contemporary China: A Study of the CFLD Model." *Cities* 101: 102696.

Jo, Angie, and Siqi Zheng. 2020. "New Planned Cities as Economic Engines: Global Trend and Our Conceptual Framework." In *Toward Urban Economic Vibrancy: Patterns and Practices in Asia's New Cities*, edited by Siqi Zheng and Zhengzhen Tan. Cambridge, MA: MIT Press.

Taylor, Jon. 2019. "Five Years On: The Beijing-Tianjin-Hebei Urban Agglomeration." *Asia Dialogue*, University of Nottingham Asia Research Institute, March 15, 2019.

Wei, Huang. 2017. "A Case Study of the Apply of Public-Private Partnership (PPP) into the Industrial Town Development." Unpublished manuscript. Southwest Jiaotong University, Chengdu.

Wen, Hou, Huang Rong, Yu Ning, and Han Wei. 2017. "Once-Poor County Builds New Model for Property Development." *Caixing Global*, March 23, 2017.

Yu, Xie, and Frances Yoon. 2021. "Chinese Developer's $4.6 Billion in Offshore Debt Is in Doubt after Default." *Wall Street Journal*, March 3, 2021.

CHAPTER 12

Egypt, Arab Republic of | CAIRO FESTIVAL CITY

Kareem Ibrahim, Tamer Elshayal, Sohaib Athar, and Martin Rama*

Cairo Festival City is a mixed-use community that offers high-end residential accommodations, retail, services, and office space in the proximity of the Egyptian capital. Closer in size to the private cities of advanced economies, it is more upscale than most of its developing country counterparts.

Private actor

The large developer behind Cairo Festival City is Majid Al Futtaim. His company, the Al Futtaim Group Real Estate (AFGRE), is a branch of a family-owned conglomerate that was founded in the 1930s and has over 200 subsidiaries in a range of sectors, from automotive to retail and from banking to insurance. With US$16 billion in assets and over 40,000 employees worldwide, the group is well established in the Middle East, East Africa, and South and South-East Asia regions. However, the death of Majid Al Futtaim in 2021 triggered a family dispute among his 10 heirs that is yet to be resolved (Kerr 2022).

Cairo Festival City belongs to a model of mixed-use, high-end urban communities that the group has also developed in Doha (Qatar) and Dubai (United Arab Emirates). In all these cases, AFGRE has been responsible for urban planning, architectural design, building construction, and marketing and sales. It has also taken charge of parts of the operation and maintenance of urban infrastructure and amenities (Kanna 2011).

---

*This private city snapshot is based on Ibrahim, Elshayal, and Athar (2021a).

The approach followed by AFGRE for Cairo Festival City contrasts somewhat with that of other private investors involved in urban development projects in the Arab Republic of Egypt. Other developers generally start with off-plan sales of residential units, with the proceeds generated from those sales then used to finance infrastructure and services. By contrast, AFGRE incurs the full cost of the project up front, arranging the finance needed for this purpose. In the case of Cairo Festival City, total investment is expected to reach about US$2.2 billion by 2023. With all land parcels enjoying plug-and-play infrastructure status from the outset, the functionality of the city is not disrupted by subsequent development work.

Interaction with government

Traditionally, all new urban areas in Egypt were planned and built exclusively by the government. Unsatisfactory urban conditions were pushing many current and potential city dwellers to seek residence outside major agglomerations (Bayat and Denis 2000). Therefore, the focus was on the development of state-owned vacant land in the vast desert areas surrounding major metropolitan centers. However, limited government capacity and institutional coordination failures prevented significant progress in that direction (Nada 2014; Sims 2008).

This is how the importance of leveraging private sector resources and expertise started being acknowledged (Nada and Sims 2020). An important change in the urban policy framework took place in 1979, when the development of new urban centers and communities in Egypt—whether using resources that are public or private—was put under the purview of the New Urban Communities Authority (NUCA), an agency of the Ministry of Housing, Utilities and Urban Communities. In this new framework, NUCA is involved in the identification of locations, oversees the land allocation and acquisition process, interfaces with prospective developers, issues technical guidelines for the projects, and monitors their financial performance (Omar 2018; UN-Habitat 2015).

The new approach to urban development policy took off in practice in the 1990s, following the introduction of market-oriented economic reforms. To attract foreign investment, developers were encouraged to buy significant tracts of vacant, state-owned desert land for new urban development projects. These tracts were generally within large areas administratively notified by NUCA as "new urban communities" and earmarked for urban development. One of them was purchased by AFGRE in 1997 for its Cairo Festival City project (Ibrahim, Elshayal, and Athar 2021b).

Over time, however, the interaction between the government and AFGRE has evolved into ongoing negotiations. The issues at stake include requests for further land acquisition or access to infrastructure, as well as financial and technical contributions to be made by each of the two parties.

Location and connectivity

Cairo Festival City is strategically located at the entrance of New Cairo City, one of Egypt's most-affluent new urban communities developed by NUCA since 2000. In terms of transport networks, the area lies at the intersection of a ring road connecting the different parts of the Greater Cairo region with the main axis road of New Cairo City (figure 12.1). The area is also connected by a major highway to downtown Cairo, a city that dominates the Egyptian economy (Sims 2012).

Locations with a similar potential for urban development are hard to come by, especially for a private city that functions as a commercial and recreational center serving

FIGURE 12.1 **Cairo Festival City, Arab Republic of Egypt: Nested in a new urban community within a metropolis**

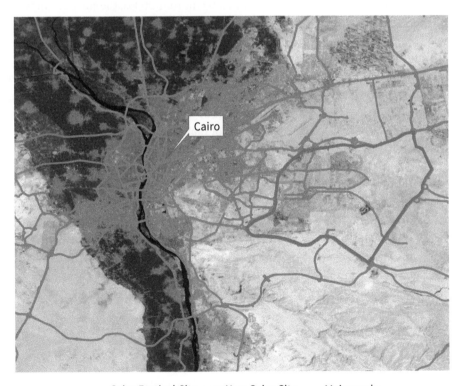

—— Cairo Festival City —— New Cairo City —— Main roads

Source: Original figure for this book.

a major urban agglomeration. This makes Cairo Festival City a notable case in Egypt's real estate landscape.

Development time line

The development of Cairo Festival City began in 1997, even before the official inception of New Cairo City in 2000, but initial progress was slow. Construction activity only picked up in 2007, and faced unexpected delays shortly after. Large-scale land and real estate transactions with private developers started to attract increasing public and media scrutiny. Some of them were even challenged in court.

In 2010, in a landmark ruling, the Egyptian Administrative Court annulled contracts the government had signed with several large private developers. In this context, government authorities put on hold the issuance of new construction permits in Cairo Festival City, which in turn led to a legal dispute between AFGRE and NUCA.

These delays failed to deter small-scale private developers, who remained upbeat about the prospects of the project. Their frantic construction in the areas around it strongly stimulated the local property market. By the mid-2000s, the surroundings were much more developed than the AFGRE site itself, which up to that point had remained almost vacant.

On-site work continued only on the projects that had been previously approved by NUCA. Among them was the CFC Mall, Egypt's first megamall and the anchor development of this private city project. Its inauguration in 2013, the completion of several office buildings in the area, and the settlement of the dispute between AFGRE and the government in 2014 finally triggered a phase of rapid real estate construction.

Cairo Festival City also became more integrated within itself, and more interdependent with the urban context around it. Gradually, its self-reliant infrastructure, together with its high-quality services and amenities, gave it a clear advantage over neighboring areas.

As of 2020, about 70 percent of the original project had been completed. By that time, the total built-up area approved for construction, for all types of buildings, was 1.3 million square meters. Of that total, 43 percent was reserved for residential uses and 50 percent for commercial uses (295,000 square meters of retail space and 361,000 square meters of office space). Construction was expected to be finalized in 2023.

Institutional status

Administratively, Cairo Festival City is part of New Cairo City, a broader new urban community. One of NUCA's subsidiaries oversees and coordinates municipal governance for the entire area. Its board of trustees includes representatives from citizens and major investors, although they are appointed through an informal process supervised by NUCA rather than directly elected. The trustees' influence on city budgets, finances, and decision-making processes is limited anyway, as those processes are directly managed by the public sector officials of the new city administration (Ibrahim, Elshayal, and Athar 2021a).

This nested relationship between Cairo Festival City and New Cairo City should, in principle, help coordinate urban development decisions in the private and public parts of the agglomeration. In practice, however, Egypt's urban planning framework for new cities still faces challenges. There is not always a clear overall vision regarding synergies in land use at the broader metropolitan level. The process for preparing land use and infrastructure plans and issuing permits is cumbersome. And government is often slow in fulfilling its commitments (UN-Habitat 2015).

As the primary developer of Cairo Festival City, AFGRE is responsible for the operation and maintenance of its infrastructure and services, either directly or through special arrangements with various service providers. It also interfaces with NUCA on decisions related to the immediate perimeter of the private city, including access points, vehicle traffic, and impact on utilities.

Land assembly

AFGRE acquired much of the vast tract of vacant desert land it needed to develop Cairo Festival City in 1997, using a direct purchase mechanism that was common at the time. The land assembly process for new cities was both discretionary and transactional. The specifics (offerings, pricing, allocation, and titling) were influenced by the attractiveness of the projects, the investors' relative bargaining power, and the priorities of the government (Ibrahim, Elshayal, and Athar 2021b, Sims 2014).

The purchase agreement with NUCA stipulated that AFGRE would pay for the land in installments over a period of 10 years, would have to complete the project within that time horizon, and would only then receive the corresponding land title. The completion deadline was extended in 2007. As part of the 2014 settlement of their legal dispute, AFGRE agreed to make supplementary retroactive payments to the government, while at the same time acquiring the right of use for surrounding land and receiving a new extension of the project completion deadline.

Since then, the government has been aiming to move away from such direct purchase mechanisms as those used for Cairo Festival City, in the direction of revenue-sharing schemes. These tend to be more transparent and also more attractive to private investors. Indeed, they substantially lower the cost of land acquisition, as the public agency generally contributes its own land. And they strengthen the commitment of public agencies to expedite implementation and the provision of connecting infrastructure, given that the government has a stake in the success of the partnership (Ibrahim, Elshayal, and Athar 2021b, Nada and Sims 2020).

Economic activity

Amid Egypt's rapidly changing consumer culture, the CFC Mall became a key driver of economic activity in Cairo Festival City (Abaza 2006). AFGRE's main line of business is retail, with the conglomerate being the agent and distributer of many global brands throughout the Middle East. The CFC Mall leverages this comparative advantage by serving as a hub of high-end stores, including the first branch of IKEA in Egypt, a Marks & Spencer department store, and outlets for Honda, Lexus, and Toyota cars.

The city also hosts well-known entertainment facilities such as KidZania. And with its high-end office facilities, its central business district has become the chosen location for the Egyptian headquarters of several notable multinational companies, including Air France, British Petroleum, PepsiCo, and Procter & Gamble.

While Cairo Festival City is expected to be home to a relatively modest 13,000 residents once completed, it is expected to have a daily working population of 50,000. These numbers may not look impressive, but they are associated with household incomes and labor earnings that are substantially above the Egyptian average.

Amenities

The city also stands out for the quality of its infrastructure and services. It has a dense network of roads and pedestrian walkways, an independent electricity station, a potable and irrigation water network, its own sewerage system, a natural gas network, and a state-of-the-art telecommunication system.

Amenities meet high standards as well. Cairo Festival City hosts an international school with a reputation for being among the best in Egypt. It also accommodates an automotive park, a world-class sports club, multiple movie theaters, and a landscaped environment.

Social and environmental issues

On the other hand, infrastructure and utilities in the surrounding area escape the control—even the influence—of AFGRE. Until recently, Cairo Festival City suffered from congestion at its main entry point from New Cairo City. Due to the lack of adequate public transportation, it also struggles to accommodate the overflow of private cars accessing its premises. And flooding in the surrounding area has directly affected the city, regardless of the measures taken by its management.

Similar to other areas built by large developers in and near the Egyptian capital, Cairo Festival City caters to high- and upper-middle-income population segments

(Wahdan 2009). Its residential offerings are gated, with private accesses separating those who live there from general visitors. Once completed, each of these areas will be managed by a private company offering security services, coordinating utilities, managing landscaped areas, and ensuring the maintenance of residential units.

When asked whether the existing business model could incorporate middle-income residents to increase the inclusiveness of the city, the management of Cairo Festival City noted that socio-economic diversity is not an urban feature desired by its current population. Mixedness could in fact deter potential clients who are willing to pay a premium for an exclusive residential environment.

Land value capture

Government resources devoted to the development of new urban communities such as Cairo Festival City have been deemed too large, and NUCA's budgetary surplus too small (Tadamun 2015). However, this assessment does not factor in the impact on general tax revenue. It focuses only on direct land value capture, which has mainly been through the land purchase agreements NUCA signed with large developers.

Beyond explicit monetary transfers, other mechanisms have also been used to enhance the economic surplus generated by Cairo Festival City, and to share this surplus between the public and private partners in mutually beneficial ways.

For example, AFGRE agreed to relinquish a prime piece of land to allow the construction of a flyover crossing the New Cairo ring road in front of Cairo Festival City, also contributing to the design of the flyover and its associated infrastructure. The government, in turn, funded the construction. Similar arrangements have allowed the construction of a pedestrian bridge over the ring road, and of a publicly funded monorail line passing through Cairo Festival City.

When feasible, AFGRE also entered into partnerships with public or parastatal utility providers to improve the provision of public services into the city. For example, it invested in an on-site electrical substation that was built by the electricity distribution company, with a revenue-sharing scheme allowing it to recoup some of the cost. In other cases, the government directly asked AFGRE to extend infrastructure networks into Cairo Festival City, in exchange for retaining a fraction of utility bills. However, at times such arrangements have resulted in residents paying duplicate service charges.

Some of the land value gains have taken place in areas outside the development. By virtue of its success in becoming a shopping and recreational center, and through its offerings of high-quality retail and office spaces, Cairo Festival City has supported higher property values in its vicinity. The average price of office spaces and retail shops has surged, despite few noticeable changes in the urban environment.

References

Abaza, Mona. 2006. *Changing Consumer Cultures of Modern Egypt: Cairo's Urban Reshaping.* Leiden: Brill.

Bayat, Asef, and Eric Denis. 2000. "Who Is Afraid of *Ashwaiyyat*? Urban Change and Politics in Egypt." *Environment and Urbanization* 12 (2): 185–99.

Ibrahim, Kareem, Tamer Elshayal, and Sohaib Athar. 2021a. "Cairo Festival City: A Case Study of Private Cities in Egypt." Background paper, *Private Cities: Outstanding Examples from Developing Countries and Their Implications for Urban Policy,* World Bank, Washington, DC.

Ibrahim, Kareem, Tamer Elshayal, and Sohaib Athar. 2021b. "Private Cities in Egypt." Background paper, *Private Cities: Outstanding Examples from Developing Countries and Their Implications for Urban Policy,* World Bank, Washington, DC.

Kanna, Ahmed. 2011. *Dubai: The City as Corporation.* Minneapolis: University of Minnesota Press.

Kerr, Simeon. 2022. "Dubai Ruler Steps In over Retail Empire's Inheritance Dispute." *Financial Times,* February 13, 2022.

Nada, Mohammed. 2014. "The Politics and Governance of Implementing Urban Expansion Policies in Egyptian Cities." *Égypte/Monde arabe* 11: 145–76.

Nada, Mohammed, and David Sims. 2020. *Assessment of Land Governance in Egypt.* Washington, DC: World Bank.

Omar, Dina. 2018. "Urban Growth Management Policies—The Rise of New Town Policy to Deal with Urban Growth: The Case of Egypt." Master's thesis, Politecnico di Milano.

Sims, David. 2008. *Towards an Urban Sector Strategy. Vol. 2 of Arab Republic of Egypt Urban Sector Note.* Report 44506-EG. Washington, DC: World Bank.

Sims, David. 2012. *Understanding Cairo: The Logic of a City out of Control.* Cairo: American University in Cairo Press.

Sims, David. 2014. *Egypt's Desert Dreams: Development or Disaster?* Cairo: American University in Cairo Press.

Tadamun. 2015. "Egypt's New Cities: Neither Just nor Efficient." Cairo Urban Solidarity Initiative, December 31, 2015. http://www.tadamun.co/egypts-new-cities-neither-just-efficient/?lang=en#or.Y3J6x-zMLuQ.

UN-Habitat. 2015. *Legislative Analysis to Support Sustainable Approaches to City Planning and Extension in Egypt.* New York: United Nations Human Settlements Programme.

Wahdan, Dalia. 2009. "Planning Egypt's New Settlements: The Politics of Spatial Inequities." Cairo Papers in Social Sciences. Cairo: American University in Cairo Press.

CHAPTER 13

Honduras | SAN PEDRO SULA

Arturo Villegas Limas and Martin Rama*

San Pedro Sula rose with the banana trade, as foreign companies twisted government policies in support of their investments there. Over time, local industrialists became the key players, leveraging national economic reforms to transform the plantation town into Central America's biggest manufacturing hub.

Private actor

Bananas became a valued delicacy at the turn of the twentieth century. By devising efficient logistics to bring them to markets before they ripened, Samuel Zemurray became one of the most successful entrepreneurs in the global banana trade, eventually buying United Fruit.

As Samuel Zemurray ventured into banana production, acquiring large tracts of suitable agricultural land in the San Pedro Sula area, he aimed to ensure a favorable policy environment. He recruited mercenaries who overthrew the president of Honduras and, in 1912, installed an exiled politician in his place. In exchange, he was rewarded with generous tax, land, and infrastructure concessions. This is how the term "banana republic" came to be (Cohen 2013).

Samuel Zemurray's political engagements continued for decades. In the US, he helped draft agricultural policies for President Franklin D. Roosevelt's New Deal. In Honduras, he lent money to the government on multiple occasions, he represented it four times in foreign debt negotiations, he bribed officials to ensure low taxes on banana

---

*This private city snapshot is based on Villegas Limas (2021).

exports, and he supported two rebellions over the terms of use of rivers and railroads (Cohen 2013; Euraque 1990; García-Buchard 1997a, 1997b; Morris and Ropp 1977).

His and other fruit companies also shaped the development of San Pedro Sula. They did so in part by advising its weak municipal government on local development policies. More important, they directly invested in local infrastructure and provided basic services.

As the banana business started losing momentum after World War II, other private actors surfaced. The Chamber of Commerce and Industry of Cortés (CCIC) had been established in 1916, mainly by European and US immigrants to the San Pedro Sula region. But immigrants of Lebanese descent, mainly garment producers, gradually gained more prominence (Crowley 1984; Euraque 1990, 2001).

This local business community became directly involved in city matters by building drainage and levees, paying for teachers and municipal public servants, and even funding studies to reform municipal fiscal management (Castle-Miller 2014; Euraque 2001).

With its growing economic stature, CCIC also became influential at the national level, helping propel the liberal reforms of the 1950s and 1960s. The gradual reorientation of the economy toward industrialization and global integration favored a region with above-average infrastructure and redundant land and labor from the banana plantations. The *maquila* (export-oriented manufacturing) boomed in the area, and so did San Pedro Sula (Euraque 1993, 2001).

Interaction with government

Municipal autonomy was traditionally limited in Honduras, with the central government designating local authorities and approving all significant expenditures (Vélez and Herrera 2016). Yet the economic might and entrepreneurial spirit of San Pedro Sula gave it a different status. From 1884 to 1920, 28 of its 35 mayors were banana plantation owners. More recently, the mayoral seat of San Pedro Sula has been coveted by politicians with national ambitions (Aguirre 1992; Euraque 1993; Lippman 1998).

The key private actors of San Pedro Sula have thus interacted more with the central government than with the municipality, which they most often controlled anyway. And they did so mainly through political channels. This interaction contributed to the development of the city by mobilizing support for local infrastructure projects, securing tax exemptions, and influencing broader economic policies.

Location and connectivity

San Pedro Sula is located in the coastal lowlands north of Tegucigalpa, the capital of Honduras, to which it is connected by the country's main arterial road. The city is also linked by a highway and a railway line to the Caribbean port of Puerto Cortés. And it is at the center of a dense system of smaller agglomerations with deep economic ties.

Development time line

Although San Pedro Sula was founded by Spanish conquistadors in 1520, by 1860 it was still an impoverished town of barely 600 inhabitants (Euraque 1993). Local dynamics started to change in the mid-nineteenth century, with a project to build a railway connecting the Pacific and Caribbean coasts. While only 56 kilometers of tracks were completed, San Pedro Sula's access to Puerto Cortés was greatly improved (Croner 1973; Euraque 1993, 2001).

Several local infrastructure projects followed, funded mostly by the private sector. In 1893, German and Italian immigrants involved in agricultural production and trade built an aqueduct to bring water to the city. And in 1904, together with others, they gave a loan to the municipality to expand local water supply (Euraque 1990; Pastor Fasquelle 1990).

The role of the private sector was reinforced during the boom years of the banana trade. On Samuel Zemurray's initiative, plantation owners agreed on a tax on their exports to finance local infrastructure, including roads, a market, and a hospital (Castle-Miller 2014). Banana companies made substantial infrastructure investments in their plantations too. Of the 65,000 hectares United Fruit held in the locality in the 1950s, 20,000 were cleared, drained, and had roads (May and Plaza 1958).

However, foreign banana companies became increasingly concerned about labor unrest and the prospect of nationalist policies. The introduction of new banana varieties and technologies allowed them to drastically reduce their workforce and remain profitable. But their local activity mostly ceased in the 1970s, when the government abolished their concessions and tightened industry regulations (Croner 1973; Del-Cid 1988; May and Plaza 1958).

Local manufacturing was gaining momentum by then. Rather than having their cargo ships return empty, banana companies became importers of basic goods. They established *comisariatos* (local shops) and paid their workers in tokens that could only be exchanged there. But they also partnered with immigrants from Europe and the Middle East to produce goods, allowing them to diversify their product mix (Del-Cid 1988; Euraque 2001).

As the banana companies collectively employed 12,000 workers, their downsizing and subsequent departure created a vast pool of cheap labor. The small workshops that used to supply the comisariatos evolved into full-scale factories catering to the Honduran domestic market, and San Pedro Sula gradually became a manufacturing city (Davidson 1994; Euraque 1990; Shirey 1970).

This was also the time when the national government started to encourage industrialization and export orientation. The 1957 Law of Industrial Development and the 1960

Central American Common Market granted tax exemptions and reduced import tariffs. The supply response was swift: by 1968, half of the manufacturing industry of Honduras was in San Pedro Sula (Euraque 1990).

Other reforms followed. In 1977, the creation of the Puerto Cortés free trade zone granted tax exemptions to companies in the municipality, with the benefits soon extended to its vicinity. In 1987, the Export Processing Zone Law provided incentives to companies investing in industrial parks (Engman 2011; Torres Ramírez 1997). And in 2005, the Dominican Republic–Central America–US Free Trade Agreement greatly facilitated access to markets. These reforms transformed San Pedro Sula into a maquila powerhouse, and the second urban agglomeration in Honduras (figure 13.1).

FIGURE 13.1 **Expansion of San Pedro Sula, Honduras, in recent decades**

a. Built-up area

| 1984 | 1989 | 1994 | 1999 | 2004 | 2016 |

(Figure continues on next page)

FIGURE 13.1 **Expansion of San Pedro Sula, Honduras, in recent decades** *(continued)*

b. Manufacturing sites *(maquilas)*

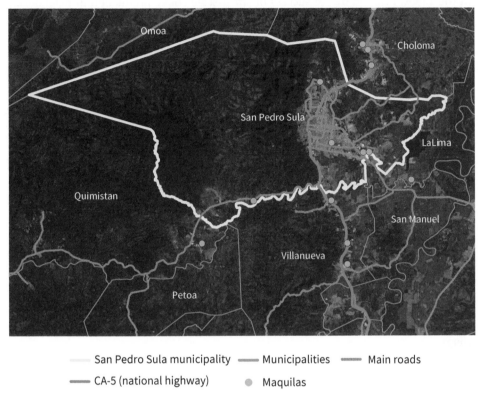

| San Pedro Sula municipality | Municipalities | Main roads |
| CA-5 (national highway) | Maquilas | |

Sources: Original figures for this book based on data from San Pedro Sula Municipality and Villegas Limas 2021 (panels a and b) and Asociación Hondureña de Maquiladores directory, http://www.ahm-honduras.com/ (panel b).

Institutional status

While San Pedro Sula has been administratively a city throughout its recent history—and an influential one—the formal empowerment of local authorities is relatively recent in Honduras. Only since 1990 have local governments been directly elected and allowed to set their priorities and budgets. Under the new rules, they can establish and levy local fees, allocate their portion of national funding, and manage land under their jurisdiction (Cienfuegos Salgado and Guzmán Hernández 2008; Lippman 1998).

Land assembly

In the 1880s, inspired by the success of small-scale coffee production in neighboring countries, the government of Honduras authorized the conversion of *ejidos* (commons used for cattle grazing) into land concessions (COCOCH 2008; Euraque 1990).

The new mechanism had limited uptake among small farmers but laid the ground-work for large-scale banana production (Del-Cid 1988; Stokes 1947). By 1915, 60 percent of San Pedro Sula's plantations were established in former ejidos (Euraque 1993). More than half of them had over 20 hectares of land, and the top 16 combined held over 1,000 hectares (García-Buchard 1997a, 1997b; Soluri 2000, 2005).

Land was often allocated in connection with infrastructure concessions. For example, the Tela Railroad Company—owned by United Fruit—received 6,000 hectares of land for every 12 kilometers of tracks laid; and a company subsequently purchased by Samuel Zemurray was granted 5,000 hectares on each side of its 5-mile-long railroad (Euraque 1993, 2001; Soluri 2005).

Control of the railways was then turned into a tool for further land assembly. Foreign banana companies would not allow others to use their trains. Local producers were often ruined and had to sell their land at a discount (Del-Cid 1988; Euraque 2001).

As banana corporations retreated in the 1950s, vast amounts of plantation land were left up for grabs. In 1955, the United Fruit company donated most of its local landholdings to the Honduran government. Other plots simply remained vacant (Guillén Romo 1992).

With its weak capacity, the municipality of San Pedro Sula was not able to tap this windfall. Instead, jobless agricultural workers and internal migrants squatted on the former plantation land around the city (Aguirre 1992; Frye 2011; May and Plaza 1958). Industrialists also chose to relocate their facilities to the newly vacant land, especially around the highways to Tegucigalpa and Puerto Cortés (Aguirre 1992; Shirey 1970).

Economic activity

While structural transformation has remained elusive for many developing countries, San Pedro Sula went from impoverished town to center of the global banana trade to manufacturing powerhouse. What is more, this remarkable economic journey happened in a country that is the second poorest in Latin America and the Caribbean.

As a result, San Pedro Sula has become the second biggest city in Honduras, hosting the largest number of internal migrants nationwide (Engman 2011; Flores Fonseca 2008). Its region accounts for one-quarter of the country's population but contributes half of its exports and almost two-thirds of its GDP (Lagos Pineda 2020; Maria et al. 2017).

Amenities

The record is more mixed when it comes to amenities. The departure of the banana companies pushed thousands of jobless plantation workers to the city, while the manufacturing attracted large numbers of internal migrants. These large-scale population movements overwhelmed the local infrastructure and the capacity of the city to provide services (Aguirre 1992; Clichevsky 2003).

By the end of the 1980s, 37 percent of the dwellings in San Pedro Sula were over-crowded and 53 percent of the population lived in informal settlements (Cantarero et al. 1995, Sandoval, Romero, and Suazo 1990). Despite urban development plans, efforts to upgrade the capacity of the municipality, and large-scale regularization of land plots, improvements on the ground have been modest so far (Aguirre 1992, Baquedano 2020, Clichevsky 2003).

Social and environmental issues

San Pedro Sula has also struggled with high levels of crime and has even been named "the murder capital of the world" (Kahn 2013; Ralph 2014). Limited policing capacity has allowed illegal organizations to flourish in the city. While crime rates have declined in recent years, moving across low-income neighborhoods remains dangerous, and the city virtually shuts down at night (González Díaz 2018; Grayson and Cotroneo 2018; Hernandez Ore, Sousa, and Lopez 2015; Lafuente 2017).

Meanwhile, sprawling urbanization is gradually encroaching on the mountainous area of El Merendón, whose watershed provides 80 percent of the water San Pedro Sula consumes. Formally an ejido, El Merendón was acquired by an affluent local family and converted into a national park in 1918 by one of its members, as he became mayor of the city. But high-end housing construction is leading to deforestation, while informal settlements proliferate on riverbanks (Figueroa 2022; *La Prensa* 2021; Radio Progreso 2019).

Land value capture

Concessions were the key land value capture mechanism used in San Pedro Sula during the plantation phase. Whereas the government contributed land, private investors had to build infrastructure and then, supposedly, pay taxes on their revenue. In most cases, one centavo was owed to the central government for each bunch of bananas exported, and half a centavo to the originating municipality (Euraque 2001).

However, tax collection was met with staunch resistance in practice. An analysis of eight years of San Pedro Sula's budgets between 1901 and 1935 shows that in only two opportunities was there any tax revenue collected from local banana businesses.

Most of the city's income came from the local commercial activity indirectly supported by the banana industry (Euraque 2001).

The workers on the banana plantations also tried to raise their share of the local surplus by mobilizing for higher wages. Labor unrest was swiftly contained in the 1920s and 1930s, but the landmark 1954 strike lasted for more than two months and spread into other regions (Coleman 2016). While defeated, it led to the adoption of the first labor code of Honduras. It also prompted the banana companies to drastically reduce their workforce and, eventually, to move out of the country (Euraque 2001).

Several measures aimed to boost local government revenue. In 1940, property owners were authorized to contribute up to a third of the cost of paving projects benefiting them. In 1958, the control of property taxes was transferred to municipalities. And in 1984, San Pedro Sula became the second locality in the country—after Tegucigalpa—allowed to collect betterment contributions (Aguirre 1992; Smolka 2013).

Municipalities also benefited from large-scale infrastructure projects. The major highways linking San Pedro Sula to Tegucigalpa and Puerto Cortés were financed by multilateral development organizations, and therefore reimbursed through general tax revenue. Manufacturing companies settled around these highways, which are key to their profitability. However, free trade zones and export processing zones are exempted from multiple taxes, limiting land value capture.

References

Aguirre, Carlos. 1992. "Ciudad y municipio de San Pedro Sula, Honduras: síntesis del informe final del estudio de caso." Unpublished manuscript, Comisión Económica para América Latina y el Caribe, Santiago.

Baquedano, Kleymer. 2020. "Más de 11,800 títulos entregó el Instituto de la Propiedad en 2019." *La Prensa*, January 1, 2020.

Cantarero, Ada, Nelson Lagos, José Ramón Mejia, and Fernando Heredia. 1995. "San Pedro Sula: cálculo y análisis de indicadores socioeconómicos y demográficos, con aplicación de ZONPLAN y REDATAM PLUS." Unpublished manuscript, Centro Latinoamericano de Demografía, Santiago.

Castle-Miller, Michael. 2014. "Banana Colony: San Pedro Sula, Honduras under the U.S. Banana Empires, 1875–1960." Unpublished manuscript. https://ssrn.com/abstract=2459167.

Cienfuegos Salgado, David, and Esperanza Guzmán Hernández. 2008. "Honduras: Régimen municipal." In *Régimen jurídico municipal en Iberoamérica*, edited by David Cienfuegos Salgado, 399–427. Mexico City: Universidad Nacional Autónoma de México.

Clichevsky, Nora. 2003. *Pobreza y acceso al suelo urbano. Algunas interrogantes sobre las políticas de regularización en América Latina*. Santiago: Comisión Económica para América Latina y el Cairbe.

COCOCH. 2008. "Reforma Agraria, Agricultura y Medio Rural en Honduras: La Agenda Pendiente del Sector Campesino." Working paper. Consejo Coordinador de Organizaciones Campesinas de Honduras, Tegucigalpa.

Cohen, Rich. 2013. *The Fish That Ate the Whale: The Life and Times of America's Banana King*. Paperback edition. London: Picador.

Coleman, Kevin 2016. *A Camera in the Garden of Eden: The Self-Forging of a Banana Republic*. Austin: University of Texas Press.

Croner, Charles Marc. 1973. "Spatial Characteristics of Internal Migration to San Pedro Sula, Honduras." Unpublished manuscript, Michigan State University, East Lansing.

Crowley, William K. 1984. "The Palestinian Community in Honduras." *Yearbook. Conference of Latin Americanist Geographers* 10: 35–47.

Davidson, William V. 1994. "Honduras: Historical Profiles of Major Cities." In *Latin American Urbanization: Historical Profiles of Major Cities*, edited by Gerald Michael Greenfield, 313–30. Westport, CT, and London: Greenwood Press.

Del-Cid, Jose Rafael. 1988. "Populating a Green Desert: Population Policy and Development. Their Effect on Population Redistribution. Honduras, 1876–1980." PhD diss., University of Texas at Austin.

Engman, Michael. 2011. "Success and Stasis in Honduras' Free Zones." In *Special Economic Zones: Progress, Emerging Challenges, and Future Directions*, edited by Thomas Farole and Gokhan Akinci. Washington, DC: World Bank.

Euraque, Darío A. 1990. "Merchants and Industrialists in Northern Honduras: The Making of a National Bourgeoisie in Peripheral Capitalism, 1870s–1972." PhD diss., University of Wisconsin, Madison.

Euraque, Darío A. 1993. "San Pedro Sula, actual capitán industrial de Honduras: su trayectoria entre villorrio colonial y emporio bananero, 1536–1936." *Mesoamérica* 14 (26): 217–52.

Euraque, Darío A. 2001. *El capitalismo de San Pedro Sula y la historia política hondureña (1870–1972)*. Tegucigalpa: Editorial Guaymuras.

Figueroa, Jessica. 2022. "La cordillera del Merendón sufre depredación similar a Río Plátano." *El Heraldo*, September 19, 2022.

Flores Fonseca, Manuel Antonio. 2008. "Migración interna intermunicipal de Honduras." *Población y desarrollo-Argonautas y caminantes* 3: 16–26.

Frye, Alex. 2011. "Hondurans in Tacamiche Resist Eviction by Chiquita Banana Company, 1994–1997." Global Nonviolent Action Database, June 5, 2011. https://nvdatabase.swarthmore .edu/content/hondurans-tacamiche-resist-eviction-chiquita-banana-company-1994-1997.

García-Buchard, Ethel. 1997a. "Empresa bananera e intervención política en Costa Rica (1899–1939) y Honduras (1912–1933)." *Revista de historia* 35: 9–41.

García-Buchard, Ethel. 1997b. *Poder político, interés bananero e identidad nacional en Centro América: un estudio comparativo. Costa Rica (1884–1938) y Honduras (1902–1958)*. Tegucigalpa: Editorial Universitaria.

González Díaz, Marcos. 2018. "Honduras: ¿Cómo se vive realmente en san Pedro Sula desde que no es la ciudad más violenta del mundo?" *BBC News Mundo*, May 30, 2018.

Grayson, Catherine-Lune, and Angela Cotroneo. 2018. *Displaced in Cities: Experiencing and Responding to Urban Internal Displacement Outside Camps*. Washington, DC: International Committee of the Red Cross.

Guillén Romo, Héctor. 1992. "Gestión urbana en San Pedro Sula, Honduras: la perspectiva del municipio." Unpublished manuscript, Comisión Económica para América Latina y el Caribe, Santiago.

Hernandez Ore, Marco Antonio, Liliana D. Sousa, and Humberto J. Lopez. 2015. *Honduras: Unlocking Economic Potential for Greater Opportunities. Systematic Country Diagnostic.* Washington, DC: World Bank

Kahn, Carrie. 2013. "Honduras Claims Unwanted Title of World's Murder Capital." *Morning Edition,* NPR, June 12, 2013.

La Prensa. 2021. "Exigen a alcaldía plan para Frenar Nuevas Invasiones en Bordos." *La Prensa,* July 15, 2021.

Lafuente, Javier. 2017. "La Violencia, El Estigma Eterno de San Pedro Sula." *El País,* November 22, 2017.

Lagos Pineda, Nelson Javier. 2020. "La dinámica demográfica y el impacto del bono demográfico de la región del Valle de Sula." PhD diss., Universidad Nacional Autónoma de Honduras, Tegucigalpa.

Lippman, Hal. 1998. *Democratic Local Governance in Honduras.* Washington, DC: US Agency for International Development.

Maria, Augustin, Jose Luis Acero, Ana I. Aguilera, and Marisa Garcia Lozano. 2017. *Central America Urbanization Review: Making Cities Work for Central America.* Washington, DC: World Bank.

May, Stacey, and Galo Plaza. 1958. *United Fruit Company in Latin America.* Washington, DC: National Planning Association.

Morris, James A., and Steve C. Ropp. 1977. "Corporatism and Dependent Development: A Honduran Case Study." *Latin American Research Review* 12 (2): 27–68.

Pastor Fasquelle, Rodolfo. 1990. *Biografía de San Pedro Sula, 1536–1954.* San Pedro Sula: Centro Editorial.

Radio Progreso. 2019. "Imparable deforestación del Merendón." Radio Progreso, September 25, 2019.

Ralph, Jeremy. 2014. "Dispatch from Honduras: What It's Like to Live in the Murder Capital of the World." *Business Insider,* October 30, 2014.

Sandoval, Jerónimo, Rigoberto Romero, and Humberto F. Suazo. 1990. "Cómo enfocar una política de desarrollo de la tierra urbana: Caso de San Pedro Sula." Unpublished manuscript, US Agency for International Development, Washington, DC.

Shirey, Ruth Irene. 1970. "An Analysis of the Location of Manufacturing: Tegucigalpa and San Pedro Sula, Honduras." PhD diss., University of Tennessee, Knoxville.

Smolka, Martin O. 2013. *Implementing Value Capture in Latin America: Policies and Tools for Urban Development.* Cambridge, MA: Lincoln Institute of Land Policy.

Soluri, John. 2000. "People, Plants, and Pathogens: The Eco-Social Dynamics of Export Banana Production in Honduras, 1875–1950. *Hispanic American Historical Review* 80 (3): 463–501.

Soluri, John. 2005. *Banana Cultures: Agriculture, Consumption, and Environmental Change in Honduras and the United States*. Austin: University of Texas Press.

Stokes, William S. 1947. "The Land Laws of Honduras." *Agricultural History* 21 (3): 148–54.

Torres Ramírez, Esther Olga. 1997. "Honduras: La industria maquiladora." Unpublished manuscript. Comisión Económica para América Latina y el Caribe, Santiago.

Vélez, Anarella, and Iván Herrera. 2016. "Historia de la municipalidad de Tegucigalpa: años 1870–1903." Unpublished manuscript, Universidad Nacional Autónoma de Honduras, Tegucigalpa.

Villegas Limas, Arturo. 2021. "Case Study: San Pedro Sula, Honduras." Background paper, *Private Cities: Outstanding Examples from Developing Countries and Their Implications for Urban Policy*, World Bank, Washington, DC.

CHAPTER 14

India | GURGAON

Balakrishnan Balachandran, Arjun Joshi, and Yue Li*

Gurgaon is an urban agglomeration of well over 2 million people located 30 kilometers southwest of Delhi, in the neighboring state of Haryana. With its gleaming skyscrapers, upscale apartments, shopping malls, and golf courses, it has become an aspirational destination for India's fast-growing middle class.

Private actor

In the late 1990s, large real estate developers led by Delhi Lease and Finance (DLF) seized the opportunities created by the emerging outsourcing of business processes to build a private city. Since then, it has grown into a thriving metropolitan area. By 2015, Gurgaon hosted more than half of the Fortune 500 companies and had gained a reputation as the start-up capital of India (Bhardwaj 2015; Rajagopalan and Tabarrok 2014).

DLF was initially joined by Ansal and then by Unitech and several other developers. However, DLF was arguably the most important private actor. Its chairman at the time, K. P. Singh, generated no shortage of controversy as an ex-army officer with close ties to its top brass, a leader of national-level business associations, and an acquaintance of former prime minister Rajiv Gandhi (Singh, Menon, and Swamy 2015). When DLF went public, in 2007, it raised nearly US$2 billion, making K. P. Singh one of the richest persons in India (PTI 2017).

The national government is said to have prevailed upon the government of the state of Haryana so that it would adopt key changes to urban development policies. Such changes greatly benefited DLF. In most states in India, assembling agricultural land and

*This private city snapshot is based on Balachandran, Joshi, and Li (2021).

converting it to urban uses are fraught with legal, political, and bureaucratic hurdles. Laws restrict a shift away from agriculture, and where the shift is possible, the procedures to follow are cumbersome. But Gurgaon emerged thanks to clever ways to circumvent those barriers.

Interaction with government

The most critical actors on the government side were at the state level. In 1975, the Haryana Development and Regulation of Urban Areas Act made it possible to give licenses to private developers to directly purchase land from landowners and build townships on land parcels greater than 40 hectares in specific areas. And in 1977, the Haryana Urban Development Authority (HUDA) was established, with the state's chief minister as its chair.

Public actors did not totally relinquish the traditional roles of local governments in urban development, as they did prepare master plans for the area and conduct some land assembly and housing construction. There were even periods when tensions arose, with licenses previously granted to large developers being canceled and land that had been acquired by them being reclaimed by HUDA for low-income housing. There were also changes to master plans that disrupted investment projects by large developers. Overall, however, the government's role in building and managing the city was of secondary importance.

Location and connectivity

One of Gurgaon's main attractions is its proximity to Delhi, a metropolis of 17 million inhabitants, with one of the highest income levels across all India. The district also sits next to the Delhi–Mumbai corridor, the busiest branch of the Golden Quadrilateral network of expressways connecting the biggest agglomerations in the country (Ghani, Goswami, and Kerr 2016).

Gurgaon's access to markets was further boosted in recent years by major investments made by both large developers and various levels of government. Thus, the modern Terminal 3 of Indira Gandhi International Airport, which lies just outside the city limits toward Gurgaon, was inaugurated in 2010. And the Dwarka Expressway connecting Gurgaon to Delhi—built through a partnership between DLF and HUDA—was completed in 2016.

Some of the most significant developments in terms of connectivity have concerned mass transport. In 2010 Delhi's metro system reached the area and in 2013, the Rapid Metro Rail system became operational within Gurgaon. The latter was the first fully private light-rail train line in India, jointly planned, financed, and executed by DLF and Infrastructure Leasing & Financial Services (figure 14.1).

FIGURE 14.1 **Public and private investments in connectivity in Gurgaon, India**

a. Connecting Gurgaon to Delhi

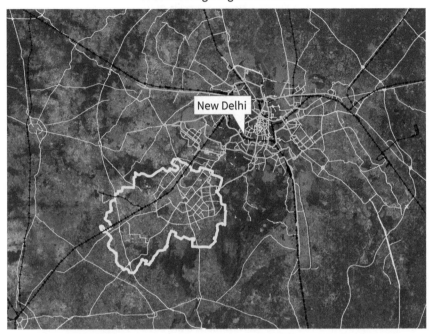

Gurugram Metropolitan ——— Delhi Metro Rail ——— Main roads +‒+ Railway network
Development Authority

b. Privately financed Rapid Metro Gurgaon

(Figure continues on next page)

FIGURE 14.1 **Public and private investments in connectivity in Gurgaon, India** *(continued)*

c. New roads built, 2001–11

d. New roads built, 2011–21

Gurugram Metropolitan Development Authority area — Existing roads — New roads

Sources: Panels a, c, and d, original figures for this book. Panel b, © Sudhir Deshwal, licensed under CC BY -SA 2.0, https://www.flickr.com/photos/127241256@N07/15320823772/.

Development time line

Three phases stand out in Gurgaon's development. From the 1970s to the late 1990s, enabling legislation allowed converting agricultural land in the area for urban development purposes. In 1979, the city of Faridabad was separated from the Gurgaon district, which remained mostly rural. Given that its land was not particularly fertile, the district became very attractive to large developers—especially at a time when the size of parcels they could own had been capped in the urban areas of Delhi.

By 1990, DLF had licenses for 713 hectares of land, and Ansal and Unitech for 374 and 82 hectares, respectively. The establishment of the Maruti Suzuki car factory in the area, in 1982, also helped boost its dynamism. Yet by the end of this phase, the population of Gurgaon was still a relatively modest 120,000 inhabitants.

The second phase, from the late 1990s to the late 2000s, saw the arrival of major international companies interested in outsourcing their business operations to India. Jack Welch, CEO of General Electric, visited in 1989, meeting the then–telecommunications minister and the prime minister (Rajagopalan and Tabarrok 2014). This visit led to a partnership with DLF to set up General Electric's operations in Gurgaon, a business model that was followed by American Express, IBM, Microsoft, Oracle, Bank of America, and many other prominent multinational companies (Mehtani 2012).

Private developments in Gurgaon offered distinct advantages to these multinational companies. Business parks were set up with plug-and-play infrastructure. Importantly, leases involved no hassles, contrary to what is often the case in India. According to K. P. Singh, had these advantages not been provided, these multinational companies would not have come (Yardley 2011a).

New large developers arrived on the scene in the second phase and continued their expansion in the third (most recent) phase. They included major players like Emaar MGF, Chintels, Raheja, Vatikaus, and others, who between them acquired over 1,300 hectares in 2001–10 and nearly 1,000 hectares in 2011–20. This period also saw progress in large real estate developments such as DLF Cyber City. With 186,000 square meters of office space, it became the glittering, iconic image of Gurgaon.

Institutional status

In the third period, new urban governance entities were set up, indicating the authorities' intention to play a bigger role in the development of Gurgaon, and to transform the city into a mainstream metropolis with its own government.

Despite having met the conditions to be deemed urban by the time of the 1991 population census, the Gurgaon district remained administratively rural until 2008. Until then, HUDA had been the sole government agency in charge of local development. It was only four decades after its establishment that the Municipal Corporation of Gurgaon was created, with the industrial township of Manesar next to it.

Another decade elapsed until the Gurugram Metropolitan Development Authority (GMDA) was established, in 2017. GMDA covers over 54 percent of the Gurgaon district and encompasses Gurgaon, Manesar, and several smaller nearby municipalities. The municipal corporation and the district were renamed Gurugram, but the name Gurgaon remains widely used to designate the broad urban agglomeration.

Land assembly

The Gurgaon district was uncharacteristically exempted from the clearances that are usually required in India before agricultural land can be converted into urban uses. Instead, HUDA and the Town and Country Planning Department of Haryana state were given the full authority to grant licenses to developers, approve land use plans, and issue construction permits. HUDA was also put in charge of building the necessary urban infrastructure in the area.

Licenses were granted predominantly for residential land use, although from the late 1990s there was a surge in land-use licenses for commercial purposes and information technology. By law, a fifth of the housing had to be reserved for disadvantaged population groups, and another quarter had to be sold at cost, but the remaining dwellings could be placed at market price. Developers were required to provide schools, hospitals, and other community buildings at their expense, or pay the government for their provision.

Economic activity

Undoubtedly, Gurgaon's most important outcome was economic growth. It has been argued that the city's private developments—with their own backup power generators, water supply, sewage treatment plants, transport services, and even post offices—were individually successful, whereas the overall agglomeration remained essentially dysfunctional (Yardley 2011b). However, these private islands were able to operate at a level that satisfied the requirements of multinational companies, in contrast to conventional cities elsewhere in India.

There are seven special economic zones for information technology in Haryana, and all of them are in Gurgaon (Government of India 2020). In addition, Gurgaon's agglomeration produced 99 percent of the automobiles manufactured in Haryana state, 96 percent of its sewing machines, 92 percent of its sporting goods, and 86 percent of its hosiery products. Along the way it contributed 70 percent of the state's GDP. This level of economic activity is nationally significant, as it corresponds to about 2 percent of India's GDP (IBEF 2020; Kumar 2015). Not surprisingly, the population of Gurgaon grew by over 400 percent in the first decade of the twenty-first century.

Amenities

Gurgaon has not done so well when it comes to amenities. There is a consistent time lag between a private investor submitting plans for a new development and the necessary trunk infrastructure being delivered by HUDA (*Civil Society* 2018). No real public transport system was in place until 2010. By then, Gurgaon had 200 kilometers of roads, but only 23 percent of them had sidewalks.

There are challenges in relation to service provision as well. As of 2013, only 50 percent of the city was covered by the sewerage network. As of 2017, only two-thirds of Gurgaon residents had access to piped water, and its availability was intermittent. And power supply has never stopped being an issue, as demand has increased consistently faster than supply (CSE 2013; Rajagopalan and Tabarrok 2014; Roychowdhury and Puri 2017).

Social and environmental issues

While Gurgaon has undeniably become one of the most prosperous and dynamic urban agglomerations in India, the not-so-bright spots are undeniable as well. Socially, Gurgaon is perceived as a city of the elite, where middle- and upper-class residents enjoy gated housing enclaves, with access to high-quality privatized services, while large numbers of migrant workers live in crammed housing, with minimal access to basic amenities like water and electricity (Gururani 2013; Naik 2015).

Depletion of groundwater has been another matter of concern in Gurgaon for many years. The water level was about 19 meters below the surface in 2005 and went down to about 35 meters by 2014, and to 38 meters more recently (Alam 2021; Roychowdhury and Puri 2017). Groundwater is extracted through private borewells to meet both residential and commercial requirements, including construction. But the rate of extraction is much higher than the rate of aquifer recharge from rainwater.

Surface water is also increasingly polluted due to industrial effluents, disposal of untreated sewage, and unscientific disposal of solid waste (Roychowdhury and Puri 2017). Because insufficient drainage has been built, and traditional water bodies have disappeared over the course of development, many locations in Gurgaon get consistently flooded during the monsoon season (Rawat et al. 2021).

It is not by chance that Gurgaon ranks 31st among 62 cities of similar size in India's latest Ease of Living Index (MOHUA 2021). It also had the dubious distinction of being considered the world's most polluted city in 2018 (IQAir 2021).

Land value capture

As a result of its extraordinary dynamism, Gurgaon saw its land prices soar from negligible when it was still rural to about US$2,000 per square meter nowadays. Much of the land value gain was captured by the large developers involved, through their sales of residential properties and leases of commercial and information technology space. However, the local government has also appropriated some of the bonanza through property taxes and stamp duties and, especially, through the license fees and external development charges for infrastructure paid by private investors (Government of Haryana 2015). Over a longer-term horizon, Gurgaon has become a major source of general tax revenue for India's government (Kumar 2015).

To some extent, the original residents of Gurgaon benefited as well, as large developers relied on creative arrangements to reduce the risk of litigation. Thus, some farmers lent money to developers in the form of deposits at attractive interest rates (Singh, Menon, and Swamy 2015). And the original settlements of the area continue to exist in the form of urban villages, providing affordable housing supply for low-income groups. As of 2011, there were 94 of them in the area (Census of India 2011). Given their privileged location, the value of land in these urban villages has increased considerably.

Not all land value capture took place legally, however. Media reports of corruption involving large developers and politicians have been frequent (Yardley 2011a). Weak links include changes in land use, sales of development licenses, and the issuance of building permits (Gupta 2016; Rajagopalan and Tabarrok 2014). In parallel, housing that was supposedly reserved for disadvantaged population groups has been resold and reregistered illegally, then developed in violation of the regulations (*Economic Times* 2019). Thus, as many as 110 illegal colonies might have emerged in and around Gurgaon (Singh 2019).

References

Alam, Shahnawaz. 2021. "Gurugram's Water Table Dipped 5m in 2 Years." *Times of India*, March 22, 2021.

Balachandran, Balakrishnan, Arjun Joshi, and Yue Li. 2021. "Gurgaon: A Case Study of Private Cities in India." Background paper, *Private Cities: Outstanding Examples from Developing Countries and Their Implications for Urban Policy*, World Bank, Washington, DC.

Bhardwaj, Deepika. 2015. "What Makes Gurgaon the Country's Start-Up Capital?" *Times of India*, August 26, 2015.

Census of India. 2011. *District Census Handbook, Gurgaon, Village and Town Directory*. Delhi: Office of the Registrar General and Census Commissioner, India.

Civil Society. 2018. "Gurugram Must Be Dealt with as a Single City." *Civil Society*, October 25, 2018.

CSE. 2013. "Gurgaon: The Water-Waste Portrait." *The Water-Waste Portrait*. Delhi: Centre for Science and Environment.

Economic Times. 2019. "Why Illegal Construction Is Rampant in Gurugram: Unauthorised Residential Areas." *Economic Times*, January 25, 2019.

Ghani, Ejaz, Arti Grover Goswami, and William R. Kerr. 2016. "Highway to Success: The Impact of the Golden Quadrilateral Project for the Location and Performance of Indian Manufacturing." *Economic Journal* 126 (591): 317–57.

Government of Haryana. 2015. *Whitepaper on State Finances*. Chandigarh: Finance Department, Government of Haryana.

Government of India. 2020. *List of Operational SEZs in India, September 2020*. Delhi: Department of Commerce, Government of India.

Gupta, Vishal. 2016. "Indian Administrative Service and Crony Capitalism." In *Crony Capitalism in India: Establishing Robust Counteractive Institutional Frameworks*, edited by Naresh Khatri and Abhoy K. Ojha, 177–205. London: Palgrave Macmillan.

Gururani, Shubhra. 2013. "Flexible Planning: The Making of India's 'Millennium City', Gurgaon." In *Ecologies of Urbanism in India: Metropolitan Civility and Sustainability*, edited by Anne M. Rademacher and K. Sivaramakrishnan, 118–43. Hong Kong SAR, China: Hong Kong University Press.

IBEF. 2020. *About Haryana: Information on Industries, Geography, Economy & Growth*. Delhi: India Brand Equity Foundation.

IQAir. 2021. *World Air Quality Report 2020: Region & City PM2.5 Ranking*. Goldach, Switzerland: IQAir.

Kumar, Ashok. 2015. "Gurgaon Becomes Haryana's Golden Goose." the *Hindu*, October 9, 2015.

Mehtani, Pooja Chowdhary. 2012. "Growth, Development, and Sustainability of Cities: A Case Study of Gurgaon." PhD diss., University of Delhi.

MOHUA. 2021. *Ease of Living Index 2020: Assessment Report*. Delhi: Ministry of Housing and Urban Affairs.

Naik, Mukta. 2015. "Informal Rental Housing Typologies and Experiences of Low-Income Migrant Renters in Gurgaon, India." *Environment and Urbanization ASIA* 6 (2): 154–75.

PTI. 2017. "Kushal Pal Singh: DLF's K P Singh Tops Realty Rich List, M P Lodha Second." *Economic Times*, October 5, 2017.

Rajagopalan, Shruti, and Alexander T. Tabarrok. 2014. "Lessons from Gurgaon, India's Private City." Working Paper in Economics no. 14-32, George Mason University, Fairfax, VA. https://ssrn.com/abstract=2514652.

Rawat, Abhilash, M. P. Govind, Jawale Madhuri Vasudev, and Preetam Karmakar. 2021. "Developing Strategies for Mitigating Pluvial Flooding in Gurugram." In *Hydrological Extremes: River Hydraulics and Irrigation Water Management*, edited by Ashish Pandey, S. K. Mishra, M. L. Kansal, R. D. Singh, and V. P. Singh, 19–41. Cham, Switzerland: Springer International Publishing.

Roychowdhury, Anumita, and Shubhra Puri. 2017. *Gurugram: A Framework for Sustainable Development*. Delhi: Centre for Science and Environment.

Singh, K. P., Ramesh Menon, and Raman Swamy. 2015. *Whatever the Odds: The Incredible Story behind DLF*. Delhi: HarperCollins Publishers India.

Singh, Rao Jaswant. 2019. "110 Illegal Colonies Built in Gurugram Last Year, DTCP Says 32 Violators Booked." *Times of India*, August 22, 2019.

Yardley, Jim. 2011a. "In India, Dynamism Wrestles with Dysfunction." *New York Times*, June 8, 2011.

Yardley, Jim. 2011b. "The Gurgaon Story: A Mirror to India's Growth." New Delhi Television (NDTV), June 9, 2011. https://www.ndtv.com/gurgaon-news/the-gurgaon-story-a-mirror-to-indias-growth-458043.

CHAPTER 15

India | JAMSHEDPUR

Balakrishnan Balachandran, Arjun Joshi, and Yue Li*

Founded in 1907 as a steel company town in the backwaters of eastern India, Jamshedpur evolved from an experiment in green and social urbanism into a large-scale, award-winning city. To this day, it is run by a private industrial conglomerate, not by a local government.

Private actor

The city of Jamshedpur is indissolubly associated with the name of Jamshedji Tata, an entrepreneur often referred to as "the father of Indian industry." Born to a family of priests in the Parsi minority (Zoroastrians who arrived in India fleeing persecution in today's Iran), he had a Western education and traveled regularly to China for business. The group of companies he created thrived for more than a century under his descendants (Lala 2004).

Dealing initially in cotton and steel, Jamshedji Tata became an early convert to *swadeshi* (self-sufficiency). He was so influential in the world of Indian industry that Jawaharlal Nehru referred to him as "a one-man Planning Commission" (Raianu 2018b). By one account, he was the greatest philanthropist of all time, with US$102 billion in donations, adjusted for inflation (Hurun Report 2021).

Jamshedpur was the first successful experiment with heavy industrial production in the interior of the subcontinent, in what is still today one of India's poorest areas (World Bank 2018). It was also the first company town to be established and run by an Indian firm—the Tata Iron and Steel Company (TISCO), later renamed Tata Steel.

*This private city snapshot is based on Balachandran, Joshi, and Li (2021).

The design of the city is inspired by a paternalistic vision, departing from the colonial urbanism of military cantonments and hill stations (Raianu 2018a). "Be sure to lay wide streets planted with shady trees. Be sure that there is plenty of space for lawns and gardens. Reserve large areas for football, hockey and parks. Earmark areas for temples, mosques and churches," wrote Jamshedji Tata in 1902. Jamshedpur was planned and built following this guidance (Tata Steel, n.d., 1).

Interaction with government

More than 110 years after its founding, Jamshedpur is not yet run by a local government. The site of the largest integrated steel mill in the British Empire and then of the largest private company in India, it has preserved its autonomy through a political revolution, near-bankruptcy, communal riots, and one nationalization attempt. The persistence of this unusual status might be due to British rulers believing that Jamshedpur was essential to their defense industry, and to the Indian government seeing it as a national treasure run by men of integrity for the benefit of the nation (Kling 1998).

When Jamshedpur was established, colonial rulers allowed it to function with autonomy from the British administrative system. The conditions under which Jamshedpur operated were also at odds with the laws of independent India, according to which land-use changes—especially from agriculture to urban activities—and land development were matters to be handled by states, whereas service delivery was under the purview of local authorities.

Jamshedpur's autonomy was thus legally challenged, resulting in a 30-year-long court battle. In 1984, the land of the city was finally vested in the state government, in accordance with the law. But it was at the same time leased back to TISCO, with the condition that municipal services would be provided in the city. This was when the Jamshedpur Utilities and Services Co. Ltd. (JUSCO) was created by the company to look after Jamshedpur's trunk infrastructure and service provision. The land lease was most recently renewed in 2005 (Raianu 2018a).

Location and connectivity

Jamshedpur was built away from existing economic hubs to tap the local availability of the raw materials needed for steelmaking: coal, iron ore, and limestone. The villages around also hosted a large number of blacksmiths with indigenous knowledge of local mineral resources (Kumar 2015).

Despite being remote, Jamshedpur is well connected. The city is only 5 kilometers from a railway line linking Mumbai to Kolkata, and it is also close to the Kharkai and Subarnarekha rivers. Nowadays, it takes four hours to reach Kolkata from Jamshedpur, by either road or train (Sinha and Singh 2011).

Development time line

For more than seven decades, TISCO's urban development unit was entrusted with planning, building, and managing the city of Jamshedpur. It did so by mobilizing reputable international expertise, including urban planners and social scientists.

The first blueprint for the city was prepared in 1911 by a US firm from Pittsburgh, hence familiar with steel towns. The proposed layout devoted special attention to the topography of the site, placing housing on an elevation to avoid dust from the plant. A spacious recreation ground and a bazaar with European and Indian shops were foreseen for the center of the town.

As the local population grew, the urban development plan was expanded in 1917 by a British sanitary engineer. Influenced by the Garden City principles, he aimed to respect the ecology of the area. Accordingly, the streets and drainage networks he designed created a system of parks and parkways distributed throughout the town.

The next urban development phase was led by a British military engineer who was familiar with North American planning principles and understood the urban dynamics of industrial expansion. In 1937 he adopted a concentric design for the growth of the city, placing residential neighborhoods for workers near the central business district.

Finally, the city hired the German chief architect of Mysore, a state whose ruling kings were great patrons of the arts. His contribution, in 1945, was to design two additional areas for the city—one residential and the other commercial—while also laying the ground for linear development along transport corridors (Sinha and Singh 2011).

In parallel with this incremental planning process, the Tata group of companies expanded its manufacturing activities in the city. By 1912, the steel plant anchoring the town was in full production. In 1945, Tata Motors was established as a manufacturer of locomotives, and in 1954, it entered automobile production, becoming over time a reputable manufacturer of trucks and buses. While nowadays Tata Motors has multiple production plants in India and abroad, the one in Jamshedpur is still among the largest. More recently, production of aviation steel also began in the city as part of the broader venturing of the Tata group into the aerospace industry (Shukla 2022).

Institutional status

For most of its history, Jamshedpur has been a "notified area," meaning a jurisdiction where the roles and responsibilities of local authorities are much more limited than in a standard city. The Jamshedpur Notified Area Committee was established in 1924 and is currently led by the collector of the mostly forest-covered district the private city sits in.

Even after the land-lease agreement with TISCO was signed, several attempts were made to convert Jamshedpur into a full-fledged municipality. In 1989 the Supreme Court directed the state government to declare its intention to do so. But the subsequent notification was challenged by TISCO.

Then, in 1993, the 74th constitutional amendment allowed industrial townships to be considered urban areas, which the state government tried to do. Multiple other legal iterations followed, but as of today the matter is still pending with the Supreme Court (Balachandran, Joshi, and Li 2021).

Land assembly

The process through which TISCO managed to assemble the land needed for Jamshedpur has been described as "a mass of anomalies" (Raianu 2018a). The original plot—more than 14 square kilometers—was obtained from the colonial government. The transaction took place in 1908, under the auspices of the Right to Acquisition Act of 1894. According to this act, which has remained in force in independent India, the transaction can only be for public purposes.

With TISCO being a for-profit company, the "public purpose" interpretation may seem far-fetched. What was typically meant by that was infrastructure development, or the planning of a new urban settlement. Yet, steel production was considered strategically important at the time. And in this case, it also involved the creation of a new township in an impoverished area.

Additional land for Jamshedpur was acquired by taking advantage of the multiple legal regimes in force under the colonial administration. For example, there were laws specifically applying to princely states and to the *zamindar* (landlords). TISCO used the latter to lease land from 21 villages under the purview of a local zamindar. Relying on a third-party syndicate, it eventually bought most of that land (Raianu 2018a).

Economic activity

In 1949, a visitor to Jamshedpur wrote: "It would appear the town rose as in an Arabian Night's Dream out of airy nothing, the wild bushes wherein lurked the tiger and the jackal giving place to fiery furnaces, boilers and power-houses foundries and tall chimneys, all the creation of one single firm, illustrating Marx's famous statement that Capitalism has accomplished wonders far surpassing Egyptian pyramids, Roman aqueducs [*sic*] and Gothic Cathedrals" (M. D. Darookhanavala, quoted by Raianu 2018a, 367).

Some of the hyperbole in this quotation can easily be discounted, as the writer was a former employee of the Tata group. Still, Jamshedpur undoubtedly became a dynamic city, attracting over time major international investors, including Lafarge Cement, Indian Steel and Wire Products, TRF Limited, Timken, Agrico, Praxair, and Brin Oxygen Company.

This remarkable performance shows in aggregate figures. While the Jamshedpur's notified area has about 700,000 inhabitants, the overall urban agglomeration is twice as large, which makes it the biggest urban center in the state of Jharkhand. The significance of the city transcends the state, as it is also one the largest manufacturing hubs in eastern India (Balachandran, Joshi, and Li 2021).

Amenities

Jamshedpur urban infrastructure is clearly above the India average. JUSCO supplies potable and raw water to all residents within the notified area, as well as clarified and raw water to local industrial units. The city's water management system is certified by the International Standards Organization, metered connections were introduced in 2007, and water consumption per capita is twice the national mean. Power is available 99 percent of the time, and 90 percent of the electricity cable network of the city lies below ground (JUSCO, n.d.).

Local service delivery is strong as well. Jamshedpur has become one of the foremost educational centers of the eastern India region. The city counts 183 schools, 13 colleges, several well-reputed learning institutions, and a few popular auditoriums. The Meherbai Tata Memorial Hospital offers specialized cancer care, and the JRD Tata sports complex is one of the best in the country (Balachandran, Joshi, and Li 2021).

Social and environmental issues

The notified area of Jamshedpur has done well on the social front. In addition to housing, TISCO provides its employees with water, sanitation, electricity, schools, and medical and recreational facilities free of cost. The city had the second highest quality-of-life index of all of India in 2013 (*Pioneer* 2013). It was also ranked India's second cleanest city in 2019 (*Hindu* 2019).

The same can be said about the city's environmental performance. The Jamshedpur's notified area has 37 percent green cover, with its over 45 community parks having a total surface of more than 160 hectares. The Jubilee Park and the Tata Steel Zoological Park are popular recreation spaces. Despite this prevalence of green space, the population density of the notified area exceeds 10,000 inhabitants per square kilometer (Census of India 2011). In 2005, the city was selected to be part of the United Nations Global Compact Cities Pilot Project (Tata Steel 2005).

At the same time, there is an obvious social divide between the notified area and its surroundings. Jamshedpur's prosperity attracted substantial internal migration and, over time, the surroundings urbanized in an organic manner, with encroached land and substandard housing being common (figure 15.1). Jamshedpur's outgrowths thus represent its antithesis: formally urban areas without adequate planning, infrastructure, or services (Kumar 2015).

FIGURE 15.1 **Jamshedpur, India: A well-planned company town amid poorly planned conventional cities**

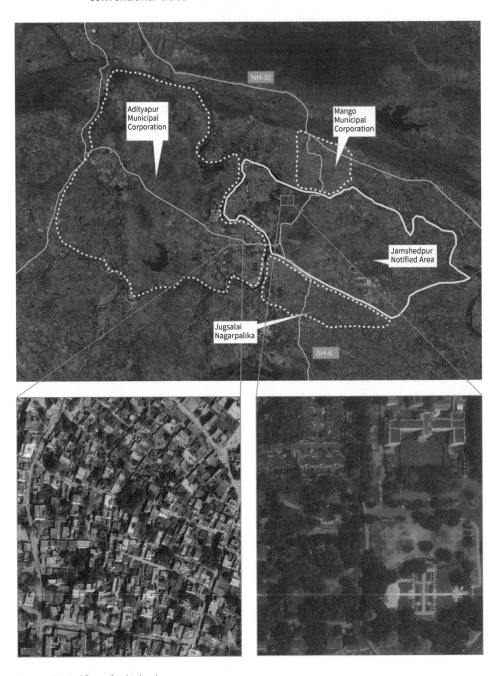

Source: Original figure for this book.

Land value capture

The Tata group has benefited in various ways from the development of Jamshedpur. Its companies can access high-quality urban land for their operations, and they can more easily attract the complementary firms, skills, and labor they need. On the other hand, more direct benefits from urban development—such as selling land plots—have been less central to Jamshedpur's value proposition.

Preserving this successful business model requires both keeping control of the land and preserving its high quality. The 30-year-long court battle with the state government in the aftermath of India's independence can be interpreted in this light. Having to pay leasing fees for the land reduced the surplus the Tata group derives from Jamshedpur, and having to take responsibility for local infrastructure and services may have reduced it even further. However, the loss for the Tata group would have been even bigger if Jamshedpur had become a conventional city, closer in nature to its current outgrowths.

An even more radical socialization of the surplus generated by the locality could have been accomplished by nationalizing TISCO, its owner. This is what the minister of mines and the minister of industries tried to do in 1978, at a time when India's government had a resolutely socialist orientation. Remarkably for the Tata group, the high quality of life Jamshedpur provided to its workers acted in its favor. The strongest opposition to TISCO's nationalization came from its own trade union, and on the face of it the government decided not to proceed (Khanna 2021).

References

Balachandran, Balakrishnan, Arjun Joshi, and Yue Li. 2021. "Private Cities in India." Background paper, *Private Cities: Outstanding Examples from Developing Countries and Their Implications for Urban Policy*, World Bank, Washington, DC.

Census of India. 2011. *District Census Handbook, Purbi Singhbhum, Village and Town Directory*. Jharkhand: Directorate of Census Operations. https://censusindia.gov.in/nada/index.php/catalog/556.

Hindu. 2019. "Indore, Jamshedpur Lead Swachh 2020 Table." *Hindu*, December 31, 2019.

Hurun Report. 2021. "EdelGive Hurun Philanthropists of the Century." Unpublished manuscript, EdelGive Foundation, Mumbai. https://www.hurunindia.net/philanthropy-2021.

JUSCO. 2011. "24x7 Urban Water Supply at Jamshedpur." Presentation to Working Group on Urban and Industrial Water Supply for 12th Five-Year Plan (2011–2017), New Delhi, March 18, 2011. http://mohua.gov.in/upload/uploadfiles/files/JUSCO_PPP_Jamshedpur_PPT_0.pdf.

JUSCO. n.d. "Jamshedpur Utilities & Services Company Ltd.—JUSCO, A Tata Enterprise." Company website. Accessed March 18, 2020. https://www.tatasteeluisl.com/.

Khanna, Sundeep. 2021. "Backstory: The Near-Nationalisation of Tata Steel." CNBC-TV18, July 26, 2021.

Kling, Blair B. 1998. "Paternalism in Indian Labor: The Tata Iron and Steel Company of Jamshedpur." *International Labor and Working-Class History* 53: 69–87.

Kumar, Rajnish. 2015. "Spatial Evolution of Jamshedpur City and Its Agglomeration Effects." In *Third Conference: GIS-Based Global History from Asian Perspectives*. Tokyo, June 5, 2015.

Lala, Russi M. 2004. *The Creation of Wealth: The Tatas from the 19th to the 21st Century*. Gurgaon: Penguin Books India.

Pioneer. 2013. "Jamshedpur Ranks 2nd in 'Quality of Life' Survey." *Pioneer*, June 8, 2013.

Raianu, Mircea. 2018a. "A Mass of Anomalies: Land, Law, and Sovereignty in an Indian Company Town." *Comparative Studies in Society and History* 60 (2): 367–89.

Raianu, Mircea. 2018b. "The Incorporation of India: The Tata Business Firm between Empire and Nation, ca. 1860–1970." *Enterprise and Society* 19 (4): 816–25.

Shukla, Ajai. 2022. "Tata Aerospace Is Boeing 'Supplier of the Year,' Picked out of 11,000 Firms." *Business Standard*, June 24, 2022.

Sinha, Amita, and Jatinder Singh. 2011. "Jamshedpur: Planning an Ideal Steel City in India." *Journal of Planning History* 10 (4): 263–81.

Tata Steel. 2005. "Jamshedpur Becomes the First South Asian City to Join the United National Global Compact Cities Pilot Programme." Press release, March 7, 2005. https://www.tatasteel.com/media/newsroom/press-releases/india/2005/jamshedpur-becomes-the-first-south-asian-city-to-join-the-united-national-global-compact-cities-pilot-programme/.

Tata Steel. n.d. "Jamshedpur: A City Guide." https://www.tatasteel.com/media/7155/jamshedpur-brochure_revised_final.pdf.

World Bank. 2018. "India States Briefs." World Bank news, February 1, 2018. https://www.worldbank.org/en/news/feature/2016/05/26/india-states-briefs.

CHAPTER 16

Indonesia | BATAM

Mulya Amri, Tony Hartanto Widjarnarso, Mark Roberts, and Yue Li*

Batam embodies the successful transformation of a set of large industrial parks into a full-fledged city. From a small fishing village half a century ago, it has become an economic powerhouse and one of Indonesia's top-15 urban agglomerations by population.

Private actor

The establishment of Batam was motivated by a deliberate strategy by the government of Indonesia to boost local economic development in a remote area. Initially, the focus was on oil exploitation, with responsibilities handed over to Pertamina, a large state-owned enterprise. But it did not take too long before Pertamina's own financial difficulties opened the way for a change in approach.

The leading actor behind the new approach—and a key force behind the subsequent rise of Batam—was the government of Singapore, together with its affiliated businesses, also known as government-linked companies (GLCs). In a paradoxical way, Batam is an example of a private city whose key nongovernment actor is not a domestic large developer or business association, but rather a foreign government—albeit an unusually entrepreneurial one.

The idea of strengthening regional economic ties through a Singapore-Johor-Riau (SIJORI) Growth Triangle was proposed in 1989 by the Singaporean deputy prime minister of the time, Goh Chok Tong. Just across the straits from the land-constrained city state, the island of Batam was ideally suited to accommodate sprawling industrial plants.

---

*This private city snapshot is based on Amri et al. (2021).

The main goal was to relocate GLC production facilities from Singapore. But Batam was also expected to attract large local investors (Heng 2006; Wong and Ng 2009).

Shortly after, the governments of Indonesia and Singapore signed a cooperation agreement to develop the island. Under the terms of the agreement, Singaporean GLCs would be responsible for master plans and overall urban design, tapping their reputation for quality flagship projects to boost the confidence of potential investors. The Indonesian government, in turn, would contribute infrastructure investments and ensure regulatory certainty. The area covered by the agreement was massive, implying that even self-contained development projects could have significant local spillovers (Peachey, Perry, and Grundy-Warr 1998).

Not only did the government of Singapore negotiate protection by the government of Indonesia for the planned industrial parks, but also it participated in the selection of the consortia that would develop the parks and actively marketed them to its own business community (Pereira 2007; Yeoh, How, and Lin Leong 2005). It has even been argued that the government of Singapore influenced the policy agenda of what was then Riau province—where Batam was located—through both diplomatic channels and Indonesian conglomerates that had good access to policy makers (Smith 1996).

Interaction with government

The government of Indonesia also made important contributions to the development of the area. It did so mainly through the Batam Industrial Development Authority (BIDA), which had been established in 1971 to coordinate local infrastructure projects and approve foreign and domestic investment applications (Hutchinson 2017).

Based in the capital city of Jakarta, BIDA was initially linked to Pertamina, the state-owned oil company that had been given a leading role in local development (Hutchinson 2017). Struggling with financial difficulties, Pertamina gradually withdrew, and in 1978, Bacharuddin Jusuf Habibie, a protégé of then-president Soeharto, was appointed as BIDA's chairman. Rather than continuing Batam's competitive stance related to Singapore, he shifted to a collaborative stance, focusing BIDA's role on local infrastructure development (BP Batam 2017a).

Location and connectivity

Location plays an important role in the success of Batam. The island's proximity to Singapore, next to some of the world's most important shipping lines, gives it a clear advantage over alternative locations. In addition, key connectivity investments by the government of Indonesia dramatically improved its access to markets.

BIDA developed the Hang Nadim International Airport, inaugurated in 1996 and significantly expanded since then. The airport was servicing 6.3 million passengers annually before the COVID-19 crisis. BIDA also built six world-class bridges that connect the islands of Batam, Galang, and Rempang. These bridges are part of a local road network that is almost 1,700 kilometers long (BIFZA 2019; BP Batam 2017a).

Development time line

Batam was essentially rural until the 1970s. Malay settlers had occupied the island since around 231 AD (JDIH Pemerintah Kota Batam, n.d.). However, by the time BIDA was established, the local population was estimated at a mere 6,000 people. A majority of them were from an indigenous tribe called the *orang laut* (sea men) that was engaged in fishing and agriculture. The landscape was mostly forested; basic infrastructure was almost nonexistent (BP Batam 2017a).

Except for some land acquisition and oil exploration by Pertamina, not much happened in Batam until 1978, when a presidential decree converted the entire island into a bonded area (Hutchinson 2017; Lee 2018; Wong and Ng 2009). Under this regime, goods can be imported and reexported without paying tariffs, and are exempt from value added tax and excises as long as they are not sold somewhere else in Indonesia.

The bonded-area declaration aligned with Habibie's intent for Batam to become a duty-free zone that could serve as the outsourcing and logistics hub for Singapore's growing manufacturing base. However, restrictive regulations on investments, equity, and landownership remained a major roadblock to implementing this vision. By one account, the island hosted only 13 foreign companies by 1988, one decade after the introduction of the bonded-area regime (Wulandari 2013).

The main transformation took place in 1989, when foreign corporations were allowed to independently operate industrial parks in Batam and to retain majority ownership of their facilities. The government of Singapore followed up by mobilizing two GLCs—SembCorp Industries and Jurong Town Corporation—to develop the 500-hectare Batamindo industrial park. An Indonesian company, Salim Group, was associated with the project to guarantee regulatory control (Yeoh, How, and Lin Leong 2005).

While Batamindo was not the first industrial park to be established on the island, it was much better serviced than its predecessors, featuring its own power supply and water treatment plants, a sewerage system, telecommunication facilities, commercial centers and markets, shops and banks, as well as restaurants and a mosque. Batamindo also had a residential area for contracted laborers and an executive village providing accommodations and recreation facilities for managers and professional staff (Yeoh, Cai, and Wee 2003; Yeoh, How, and Sim 2010).

In addition to Batamindo, three other flagship projects were undertaken as part of the Indonesia-Singapore collaboration. These were the Bintan Industrial Estate, the Bintan Beach International Resort, and the Karimun Marine and Industrial Complex. All three were developed by consortia that included Singaporean GLCs and Indonesian firms, in some cases alongside other foreign investors (Gallant Ventures 2014; Grundy-Warr, Peachey, and Perry 1999). Other private investors followed suit, and by 2019, the island had a total of 26 industrial estates, all with their own infrastructure services, in addition to dormitories, housing, and commercial facilities (BIFZA 2019).

The Asian financial crisis of the late 1990s and the associated political events in Indonesia opened a phase of uncertainty for Batam. Top-down arrangements that had allowed direct intervention by the central government in the development of the island were confronted with radical decentralization. Under the new form of governance, significant authority was transferred to municipal governments that often had a reputation for low capacity (Amri 2016).

However, even under the new arrangements, Batam remained a part of the Indonesian territory operating under different rules. Already a bonded area since 1987, in 2007 it joined two nearby islands as part of the broader Batam-Bintan-Karimun region, an enclave that was declared a free trade zone for a period of 70 years (Putri 2019; Zaenuddin 2012).

Institutional status

Administratively, Batam remained a small subdistrict of Riau province until 1983. At that point it was upgraded to a city, with a mayor elected by the local constituency for a five-year period, just as in other Indonesian cities and localities. It only became a self-governing city in 1999, as part of the decentralization process that also led to the establishment of the Riau Islands province in 2004 (Wong and Ng 2009).

Consistent with this institutional transformation, some of BIDA's authority was transferred to the new municipal government. In addition, its headquarters were moved from Jakarta to the island, with the intention of responding more quickly to local decision-makers (Hutchinson 2017). But even this most recent phase culminated a series of somewhat unconventional governance arrangements for Batam (figure 16.1).

Until very recently, the highly influential BIDA did not report to local authorities. It was first under the direct authority of Indonesia's president and then under the Board of Special Economic Zones (SEZs), chaired by the minister of economic affairs (Amri 2016; BP Batam 2017b). Only in 2019, in an attempt to alleviate the tension between the administrative and economic arrangements in place, was it decided that the mayor of Batam would also serve as BIDA's chairperson.

FIGURE 16.1 **An enabling institutional environment for Batam, Indonesia**

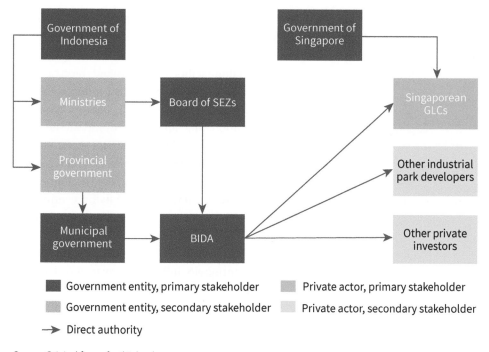

Source: Original figure for this book.

Note: BIDA = Batam Industrial Development Authority; GLC = government-linked company; SEZ = Special Economic Zone.

Land assembly

The earliest record of land acquisition for industrial development in Batam dates back to 1969, when 300 hectares were transferred to Pertamina by the Riau provincial government. In 1973, the decision-making power to manage land on the island was also assigned to BIDA, thus bypassing the need to abide by standard land acquisition procedures (BP Batam 2017b; Smith 1996).

This move was met with little or no resistance. At that time, the island was virtually uninhabited, with the existing population base being too small—and too poor—to effectively voice opposition. Had the standard procedures to acquire land for public purposes been followed, there would have been months of public consultations, followed by value appraisal for compensation, appeal and grievance proceedings, and administrative decisions by various government entities (Smith 1996).

However, the fact that the amount of land reserved for industrial use has remained stable since 2003, despite the growing demand for industrial plots, suggests the declining power of BIDA, especially in the aftermath of Soeharto's resignation from power in 1998 (Paranoan 2011).

Economic activity

Batam represents an unquestionable economic success. Following the 1989 decision to allow foreign ownership and management of industrial parks in Batam, large numbers of Singapore-based firms—many of them subsidiaries of American, European, and Japanese multinationals—established production facilities on the island. Electrical and electronic firms were heavily represented at the beginning, with their number growing from 4 in 1990 to 62 in 1997 to around 80 in 2009. Subsequently, Batam's economic activities expanded into shipbuilding, accommodating almost half of Indonesia's shipyards by the early 2010s. More recently, the focus shifted to the tourism sector and the digital economy (Hutchinson 2017; Negara and Hutchinson 2018; Wong and Ng 2009).

These investments drew in large numbers of migrants from across the Indonesian archipelago. The population of Batam grew from a few thousand half a century ago to 80,000 in 1990, to more than 250,000 in 1997, and close to 1.2 million in 2020 (BPS Batam 2021; Hutchinson 2017).

With the exception of the 2008–10 period, Batam's GDP growth outpaced that of the Indonesian economy as a whole. The continuous inflow of foreign direct investment even allowed the island to withstand the Asian financial crisis better than the rest of the country. As Indonesia's GDP contracted by 13 percent in 1998, that of Batam increased by 3 percent. As of 2018, the GDP per capita of Riau Islands province was almost twice the Indonesian average (BPS 2019). And its minimum wage was also substantially higher than the median across Indonesian provinces (BPS 2021).

Amenities

Batam also stands out in terms of its service delivery. The island possesses 33 power plants, 10 water reservoirs, extensive gas networks, 16 public and private hospitals, 64 public health centers, eight universities and one polytechnic institute (BIFZA 2019; BP Batam 2017a). A public maritime university also exists on the nearby island of Bintan, presumably to support the shipbuilding industries that thrived in Batam during the mid-2000s (Smiling Hill Team 2015).

Social and environmental issues

But the island has also been a prominent site for industrial unrest, particularly after it was declared a free trade zone. A couple of notable industrial protests involving violence occurred in the 2010s, one in reaction to a racially discriminatory remark to workers by an expatriate, the other in response to a minimum wage increase perceived as insufficient (Ford 2013). At the same time, employers have complained that minimum wages are too high for Batam to remain competitive (*Jakarta Post* 2017).

Rapid population growth has also led to environmental concerns. In addition to the emission of pollutants typically associated with a strong manufacturing base, high housing prices have pushed many migrants to live in *rumah liar* (informal settlements). These often encroach upon forests, water catchment zones, and conserved land areas. And they became so pervasive that 50,000 were identified in 2000 (Gallant Ventures 2014; Haryati 2017; Lee 2018).

Land value capture

Remarkably for a private city that has been so dynamic from an economic standpoint, no land value capture mechanisms are recorded in Batam. The development of infrastructure and services was primarily done by the public sector, through BIDA, using national government budgets. Beyond paying taxes, the only transfers of resources by the direct beneficiaries of Batam's extraordinary development have been the lease payments they had to make to BIDA for the plots of land they used.

References

Amri, Mulya. 2016. "A Periphery Serving Three Cores: Balancing Local, National, and Cross-Border Interests in the Riau Islands." In *The SIJORI Cross-Border Regions: Transnational Politics, Economics and Culture*, edited by F. E. Hutchinson. Singapore: ISEAS–Yusof Ishak Institute.

Amri, Mulya, Tony Hartanto Widjarnarso, Mark Roberts, and Yue Li. 2021. "Batam: A Case Study of Private City Development in Indonesia." Background paper, *Private Cities: Outstanding Examples from Developing Countries and Their Implications for Urban Policy*, World Bank, Washington, DC.

BIFZA. 2019. *Development Progress of Batam 2019*. Batam Indonesia Free Trade Authority. https://bpbatam.go.id/wp-content/uploads/2020/12/dpob-sem-1-2019-v3.pdf.

BP Batam. 2017a. *Latar Belakang*. Badan Pengusaha Batam. Accessed August 3, 2020. https://batamport.bpbatam.go.id/latar-belakang/

BP Batam. 2017b. *Sejarah Batam*. Badan Pengusaha Batam. Accessed July 1, 2020. https://bpbatam.go.id/tentang-batam/sejarah-batam/.

BPS Batam. 2021. *Jumlah Penduduk Menurut Kelompok Umur dan Jenis Kelamin Berdasarkan Sensus Penduduk 2020*. Batam: Badan Pusak Statistik.

BPS. 2019. *[Seri 2010] Produk Domestik Regional Bruto Per Kapita Atas Dasar Harga Konstan 2010 Menurut Provinsi, 2010–2018 (Ribu Rupiah)*. Jakarta: Badan Pusak Statistik.

BPS. 2021. *Upah Minimum Regiona/Propinsi 1997-2020*. Jakarta: Badan Pusak Statistik.

Ford, Michele. 2013. "Violent Industrial Protest in Indonesia: Cultural Phenomenon or Legacy of an Authoritarian Past?" In *New Forms and Expressions of Conflict at Work*, edited by G. Gall, 171–90. Basingstoke, UK: Palgrave Macmillan.

Gallant Ventures. 2014. *Realising Indonesia Focused Strategies: Annual Report 2014*. Singapore: Gallant Ventures.

Grundy-Warr, Carl, Karen Peachey, and Martin Perry. 1999. "Fragmented Integration in the Singapore-Indonesian Border Zone: Southeast Asia's 'Growth Triangle' against the Global Economy." *International Journal of Urban and Regional Research* 23 (2): 304–28.

Haryati, Dewl. 2017. "Rumah Liar di Kota Batam Akan Ditata Tahun 2017. Ini Target ke Depan." *Tribun Batam*, January 19, 2017.

Heng, Toh Mun. 2006. *Development in the Indonesia-Malaysia-Singapore Growth Triangle*. Singapore: National University of Singapore, Singapore Centre for Applied and Policy Economics.

Hutchinson, Francis E. 2017. *Rowing against the Tide? Batam's Economic Fortunes in Today's Indonesia*. Singapore: ISEAS–Yusof Ishak Institute.

Jakarta Post. 2017. "Batam Economy in a State of Emergency, Mayor Says." *Jakarta Post*, June 16, 2017.

JDIH Pemerintah Kota Batam. n.d. "Sejarah Batam [History of Batam]." Jaringan Dokumentasi dan Informasi Hukum Kota Batam. Accessed February 6, 2023. https://jdih.batam.go.id/?page _id=500#:~:text=Pulau%20Batam%20dihuni%20pertama%20kali,minyak%20bumi%20di%20 Pulau%20Sambu.

Lee, Poh Onn. 2018. *Reconciling Economic and Environmental Imperatives in Batam*. Singapore: ISEAS–Yusof Ishak Institute.

Negara, Siwage Dharma, and Francis E. Hutchinson. 2018. *Batam: Life after the FTZ?* Singapore: ISEAS–Yusof Ishak Institute.

Paranoan, Fesly. 2011. "An Alternative Approach of Industrial Land Valuation in Batam." Thesis, University of Twente, Faculty of Geo-Information Science and Earth Observation, Enschede, the Netherlands. http://essay.utwente.nl/84983/1/paranoan.pdf.

Peachey, Karen, Martin Perry, and Carl Grundy-Warr. 1998. "The Riau Islands and Economic Cooperation in the Singapore-Indonesian Border Zone." Unpublished manuscript, University of Durham, UK, Department of Geography.

Pereira, Alexius A. 2007. "State Entrepreneurship and Regional Development: Singapore's Industrial Parks in Batam and Suzhou." *Entrepreneurship and Regional Development* 16 (2): 129–44.

Putri, Rizqi Apriani. 2019. "Estimate Batam's Paradiplomacy in Free Trade Area through Content Analysis Regulatory." *Journal of Islamic World and Politics* 3 (2): 651–69.

Smiling Hill Team. 2015. *Batam, Now and Tomorrow*. Batam Okusi Associates. https:// okusiassociates.com/public/BatamInBrief-OkusiAssociates.pdf.

Smith, Shannon L. D. 1996. *Developing Batam: Indonesia's Political Economy under the New Order*. PhD diss., Australian National University, Canberra. https://openresearch-repository .anu.edu.au/handle/1885/12854?mode=full.

Wong, Poh Kam, and Kwan Kee Ng. 2009. "Batam, Bintan and Karimun: Past History and Current Development towards Being a SEZ." Lee Kuan Yew School of Public Policy, National University of Singapore, August 24, 2009. https://www.academia.edu/3796844/Batam_Bintan_and _Karimun_Past_History_and_Current_Development_Towards_Being_A_SEZ.

Wulandari, Sri. 2013. *Batam Free Trade Zone*. Asia Monitor Resource Centre (AMRC), Hong Kong SAR, China. https://www.yumpu.com/en/document/view/17433173/batam-free-trade -zonepdf-asia-monitor-resource-center.

Yeoh, Caroline, Charmaine Jialing Cai, and Julian Ching Wei Wee. 2003. "Transborder Industrialization and Singapore's Regionalization Strategy: Singapore's Industrial Parks in Indonesia and China—Boom, Bane, or an Ongoing Game." Hawaii International Conference on Business, 3rd, Honolulu, June 18–21, 2003. Accessed September 2, 2020. https://core.ac .uk/download/pdf/13250800.pdf.

Yeoh, Caroline, Wilfred Pow Ngee How, and Ai Lin Leong. 2005. "'Created' Enclaves for Enterprise: An Empirical Study of Singapore's Industrial Parks in Indonesia, Vietnam and China." *Entrepreneurship & Regional Development* 17 (6): 479–99.

Yeoh, Caroline, Wilfred Pow Ngee How, and Victor Sim. 2010. "Re-Engineering Economic Space: The Case of Singapore's Transborder Industrialization 'Gambits' in Asia." *Journal of Asia Business Studies* 1 (1): 34–45.

Zaenuddin, Muhammad. 2012. "Kajian Free Trade Zone (FTZ) Batam-Bintan-Karimun (Permasalahan, Implementasi, dan Solusinya)." *Eko-Regional Jurnal Pembangunan Ekonomi Wilayah* 7 (2): 79–90.

CHAPTER 17

Indonesia | KOTA BARU MAJA

Tony Hartanto Widjarnarso, Mulya Amri, Mark Roberts, and Yue Li*

Because of its location and history, Kota Baru Maja may seem a standard edge city. However, it owes its rapid growth to flexible urban policies that created opportunities for large developers while mandating that they provide local services and helping keep land and housing affordable.

Private actor

The main private actor behind the rapid emergence of Kota Baru Maja is PT. Ciputra Development Tbk (the Ciputra group hereafter), a major holding company specializing in urban real estate. Another large developer—PT. Permata Mutiara Maja—has been involved, as well as three others that have been slower to begin construction, despite owning substantial tracts of land in the area.

The Ciputra group was created by Tjie Tjin Hoan, a descendant of Chinese merchants whose ancestry goes back to Fujian Province and who was known as Pak Ciputra in the local language. Trained as an architect, he worked for many years for a construction company partially owned by Jakarta's local government, before establishing his own family holding in 1981 (Maulia 2019).

Since then, the Ciputra group has become the most significant developer in Indonesia. Involved in more than 44 major urban projects at home and abroad, it has gained a solid reputation for the quality of its products (Leaf 2015). One of the company's main tenets, ever since the Asian financial crisis, has been not to own land, but instead to develop real estate on land acquired by other private entities (Widjarnarso et al. 2021).

---

*This private city snapshot is based on Widjarnarso et al. (2021).

The Asian financial crisis dealt a severe blow to the highly leveraged Ciputra group, forcing it to restructure its debts. But it also affected many other smaller developers. Several of them were absorbed by PT. Hanson International, a local company operating in the industrial and trade sector that ended up amassing substantial amounts of land in the vicinity of Jakarta, the capital city.

The Ciputra group's involvement in Kota Baru Maja began in 2013, when PT. Hanson International approached it to tap its real estate expertise. Their joint development in the area—the Citra Maja Raya township—takes up almost one-fifth of the surface originally planned for the city.

The city has also managed to attract the interest of other private sector actors, which have undertaken considerable investments in infrastructure, including roads and electricity.

Interaction with government

Urban development policy in Indonesia changed considerably with the "big bang" decentralization of the late 1990s and early 2000s, when the private sector was explicitly recognized as a key player. Since then, a significant number of townships and gated communities have been built by large developers with almost no interference from the government (Amri, Roberts, and Li 2021). These new urban entities cater to an emerging middle class in search of comfort, safety, and prestige (Leisch 2002).

There have also been more ambitious initiatives, truly on a city scale. The flagship development plan of President Susilo Bambang Yudhoyono identified six major economic corridors in Indonesia (Bappenas 2011). Kota Baru Maja was mentioned in that plan as part of the Java Corridor. Initially conceived as a dormitory town for Jakarta, it was subsequently described by the Ministry of Agrarian Affairs and Spatial Planning (MAASP) as a regional hub that would connect to growing economic centers nearby (Amin 2010).

Kota Baru Maja had been officially established in 1998 by a decree of what is now the Ministry of Public Works and Housing (MPWH) even before being mentioned in the development plan (Hermawan 2010). The process itself was exceptional, as the creation of new cities is supposed to require formal approval by both the highest legislative body and the president, not just a ministerial decision.

More strikingly, Kota Baru Maja's boundaries were only loosely defined at the beginning. There was a reference to a bulletin published by MAASP, featuring a map where the city's delineation is based on the boundaries of the land that large developers had acquired in the area (Bappenas 2011). A subsequent revision expanded the city from 109 square kilometers to 155, to incorporate new areas reserved for real estate projects by the private sector (Widjarnarso et al. 2021).

This spatial fluidity was aligned with the view of MPWH that the city would be built by private investors, rather than by the government. And indeed, most master plans for Kota Baru Maja have been prepared by large developers for the areas under their purview.

However, MPWH conducted a series of meetings with private developers and local governments to coordinate on the necessary infrastructure development. The process led in 2016 to a memorandum of understanding between all the relevant stakeholders (Ministry of Public Works 2016).

Relying on the private sector helped overcome what would have otherwise been a major coordination challenge. The area selected for the new city is located across three *kabupatens* (districts) in two provinces. Therefore, no single government entity would have had the full authority to lead Maja's overall planning and infrastructure development.

Several central government agencies served as the key public sector counterparts for the large developers (figure 17.1). MPWH played the most active role overall, with its Regional Infrastructure Development Body leading the planning and development of the necessary regional infrastructure, such as roads and dams. The Ministry of Transport established the railway service to Kota Baru Maja, effectively enabling transit-oriented urban development. And MAASP organized detailed spatial planning workshops for large developers to coordinate their plans.

FIGURE 17.1 Interaction between private and public sectors in Kota Baru Maja, Indonesia

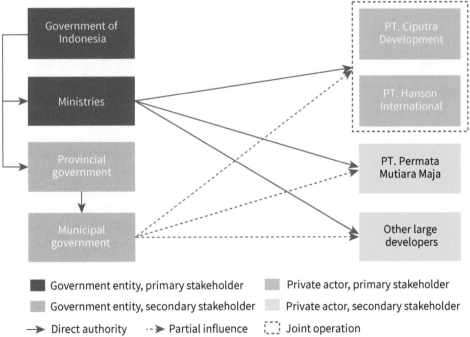

Source: Original figure for this book, based on Widjarnarso et al. 2021.
Note: PT. = Perseroan Terbatas.

Location and connectivity

Kota Baru Maja lies at the border between Banten and West Java provinces, about 70 kilometers west of Jakarta, to which it is well connected through recently completed toll roads. The city can also be accessed by a 90-minute commuter train ride thanks to the newly built line.

The city may not be exclusively dependent on Jakarta's dynamism, however. Kota Baru Maja is close to the Banten Industrial Zone, the port of Bojonegara, and the industrial hubs of Balaraja and Rangkasbitung—none of which lies within the capital city's metropolitan area.

Development time line

When Kota Baru Maja was first conceptualized as an affordable satellite town to accommodate Jakarta's growing population, the area was mostly rural. Some developers had already launched real estate projects by the time Kota Baru Maja was formally established in 1998. However, most construction was halted in the aftermath of the Asian financial crisis, and much of the land that had been acquired for urban development remained vacant (Hermawan 2010). Some of the former residents who had been relocated elsewhere even moved back, squatting on land to resume agricultural activities. As a result, Kota Baru Maja remained largely rural until the early 2010s.

In contrast to the relative inactivity of private sector actors, the public sector was busy building major infrastructure links to Kota Baru Maja, including toll roads and the commuter rail line connecting the city to central Jakarta. The launch of the commuter train service, in 2013, triggered a resumption of interest in the area by large developers.

In Ciputra group's case, the focus was on the Citra Maja Raya project, which relied on a joint operation agreement with PT. Hanson International and other landowners. Featuring a 2,600-hectare mixed-use development and catering to the middle class, this was the first major private real estate project in the area. In 2016, another partnership agreement was signed for the development of Citra Maja Raya 2 (PT. Ciputra Residence 2019). Master plans for these two projects were prepared by the Ciputra group, and communications with local governments dealt mainly with permit processing (Widjarnarso et al. 2021).

Other large developers had started their projects earlier, but in a modest, slow, and fragmented manner. In 2009, only 100 new residential units were built altogether (Amin 2010). However, during that same period, private investors were actively involved in public-private partnerships to build provincial toll roads that greatly benefited Maja's development (Agustine 2018; Kencana 2019).

Institutional status

Kota Baru Maja was established by ministerial decrees and decisions, but has yet to be formally recognized by the government as a city. It does not possess its own local government, nor is it formally listed as a municipality by the Ministry of Home Affairs, the Indonesian Statistics Office, or the National Geospatial Agency.

Land assembly

Other locations had been considered for a new city supporting Jakarta's growth, including Depok toward its south and Bekasi on its eastern side. However, Kota Baru Maja was preferred due to the greater availability of land. Even two decades after the establishment of the city, density in one of its central kabupaten was still below 800 people per square kilometer, and most of the local workforce was still in agriculture (BPS 2018).

With the Asian financial crisis, most of the real estate projects in the Kota Baru Maja area had to be canceled, with several developers being unable to service their debts and some of them going bankrupt. In 1998, as the crisis unfolded, the government used the Indonesian Bank Restructuring Agency (IBRA) to stabilize the financial system. IBRA confiscated assets that belonged to the closed banks and their debtors—many of whom were small-scale real estate developers—and auctioned them off to repay creditors. Land was prominent among those assets (Widjarnarso et al. 2021).

However, the land assembly process itself was entirely managed by private actors. This was not unusual: the experience of gated communities in Jakarta shows that the consolidation of land parcels was mostly done by private facilitators working for the developers (Zhu 2010). In Kota Baru Maja's case, private corporations such as PT. Hanson International acquired land not only through IBRA auctions but also by purchasing it directly from local owners and from developers in distress.

Economic activity

Kota Baru Maja remains less developed than Jakarta's immediate periphery, and agriculture is still the main economic activity for the majority of the population in the area. Despite significant public and private investments, its overall economic growth during the period 2011–18 has not been notably higher than that of its surrounding areas.

Remarkably, though, this rural area—whose development only started in earnest in 2013—became a major urban center in less than one decade. As of 2016, MPWH estimated that Kota Baru Maja hosted a population of 500,000 inhabitants (Djamal and Naufal 2016). This number is projected to grow to 1.5 million by 2035, close to the size of Indonesia's 12th biggest city at present (BPS 2021).

Amenities

On the one hand, Indonesia's law on settlements and housing mandates that private investors provide public services and facilities in the areas they develop. These assets, together with their operation and maintenance, are to be handed over to the local government upon the completion of the projects. On the other hand, the law on regional governance makes the government responsible for the necessary infrastructure. For example, MPWH built the Sindangheula and Karian dams, which provide raw water to Kota Baru Maja and its surroundings (BPIW 2016; Djamal and Naufal 2016).

These legal mandates, and the often-weak capacity of local governments, have encouraged the Ciputra group and other large developers to incorporate multiple amenities into their real estate business model. Depending on the case, the list includes roads and sewerage, education and health care facilities, security personnel, waste management, and cleaning and landscaping—even if some of these should in principle be provided by local authorities (Dieleman 2011).

However, there is also some degree of interaction between public and private actors in relation to local services. In Kota Baru Maja's case, the Ciputra group benefited from partial subsidization by the central government (Atim 2016). At the same time, it supported local government agencies that are formally responsible for specific services. For example, to expedite the completion of its real estate project, the Ciputra group helped the local water company with the provision of the necessary equipment and associated works (Widjarnarso et al. 2021).

To cover the operation costs of some of these services—in particular, facilities' maintenance, security personnel, and shuttle buses to the commuter train station—the Ciputra group collects fees from Citra Maja Raya residents. The level of the fee is determined by the size of the parcel. Other amenities included in the area master plan—from shopping malls to private schools to amusement parks—finance themselves on a commercial basis.

Social and environmental issues

Kota Baru Maja does not suffer from the market segregation typically plaguing urbanization projects by large developers. Almost 90 percent of the dwellings in Citra Maja Raya fall in the category of affordable housing. Relatively cheap land prices during the Asian financial crisis and good connectivity to Jakarta may partly explain this outcome (Winarso and Firman 2002). But the flexibility characterizing urban development policies in Indonesia may play a role as well (Monkkonen 2013; Roberts, Sander, and Tiwari 2009).

There is limited physical segregation as well. Residential clusters may be gated, but not the city itself. This allows the general public, including inhabitants from neighboring communities, to access public areas and amenities such as shopping malls and theme parks (Amri, Roberts, and Li 2021). The constant presence of construction workers and service personnel from the surrounding region adds to Kota Baru Maja's social diversity (Sabrina 2019).

No studies are publicly available on the environmental impacts of Kota Baru Maja's development. This might be due to its residential and commercial nature, as the city was designed to support surrounding industrial areas rather than to accommodate industrial activities within its boundaries (Amin 2010). So far at least, environmental concerns do not seem to be high in the public debate.

Land value capture

Explicit land value capture mechanisms have not yet been leveraged in Kota Baru Maja's case. Instead, the Ciputra group has engaged in informal cooperation with authorities to coordinate the city's development in a way that is mutually beneficial.

Thus, the central government has financed most of the regional transport networks that make it possible for the city to thrive. In exchange, the Ciputra group has provided amenities that benefit the entire area and are often managed by the local government. And it has cooperated with public utilities to help deliver services—from water to electricity—that residents value, hence increasing the market value of housing units in the area (Widjarnarso et al. 2021).

References

Agustine, Irene. 2018. "Ini Progres Rencana Proyek Jalan Tol Serpong—Maja." Bisnis.com, May 9, 2018. https://ekonomi.bisnis.com/read/20180509/45/793259/ini-progres-rencana -proyek-jalan-tol-serpongmaja.

Amin, Mirna. 2010. "Kota Kekerabatan Maja dan Masa Depan." *Buletin Tata Ruang* 53: 41–48.

Amri, Mulya, Mark Roberts, and Yue Li. 2021. "Private Cities in Indonesia." Background paper, *Private Cities: Outstanding Examples from Developing Countries and Their Implications for Urban Policy,* World Bank, Jakarta.

Atim, Ahmad Hakiki. 2016. "Analisis Kebijakan Pembangunan Kota Kekerabatan Maja di Kabupaten Lebak." Thesis, Sultan Ageng Tirtayasa University, Faculty of Social and Political Science, Serang. https://eprints.untirta.ac.id/760/1/ANALISIS%20KEBIJAKAN%20PEMB ANGUNAN%20KOTA%20KEKERABATAN%20MAJA%20DI%20KABUPATEN%20 LEBAK%20-%20Copy.pdf

Bappenas. 2011. *Masterplan Percepatan dan Perluasan Pembangunan Ekonomi Indonesia* (MP3EI) 2011–2025. Jakarta: Indonesian Coordinating Ministry of Economic Affairs. https:// peraturan.bpk.go.id/Home/Details/41157/perpres-no-32-tahun-2011.

BPIW. 2016. "Mewujudkan Pemerataan Hunian Untuk Semua Kalangan Masyarakat." *Buletin Sinergi BPIW,* June: 38–43. [Badan Pengembangan Infrastruktur Wilayah (Regional Infrastructure Development Body), Jakarta.]

BPS. 2018. *Kecamatan Maja Dalam Angka 2018*. Rangkasbitung: Badan Pusat Statistik, Kabupaten Lebak. https://lebakkab.bps.go.id/publication/download.html?nrbvfeve=OGNkM zcwYTk5MmY5OTRhYTcwMmExNGQz&xzmn=aHR0cHM6Ly9sZWJha2tYi5icHMuZ28u aWQvcHVibGljYXRpb24vMjAxOC8wOS8yNi84Y2QzNzBhOTQ0ZjNjNGFzNzE0Z0ZDM va2VjYW1hdGFuLW1hamamEtZGFsYW0tYW5na2EtMjAxOC5odG1s&twoadf.

BPS. 2021. *Hasil Sensus Penduduk 2020*. Jakarta: Badan Pusat Statistik.

Dieleman, Marleen. 2011. "New Town Development in Indonesia: Renegotiating, Shaping, and Replacing Institutions." *Bijdragen tot de Taal-, Land- en Volkenkunde* 167 (1): 60–85.

Djamal, Hendra, and Ichlasul Naufal. 2016. "Interview with Hermanto Dardak, Head of Badan Pengembangan Infrastruktur Wilayah (BPIW)." *Buletin Sinergi BPIW*: 16–19. [Kementerian PUPR: Harmonisasi Pengembangan Infrastruktur dan Kawasan Kota Baru Publik Maja.]

Hermawan, Asep. 2010. "Stagnasi Perkembangan Permukiman (Studi Kasus Kawasan Siap Bangun di Kecamatan Maja, Kabupaten Lebak Banten)." Thesis, Universitas Diponegoro, Urban and Regional Development Post-Graduate Program, Semarang. http://eprints.undip .ac.id/23612/1/ASEP_HERMAWAN.pdf.

Kencana, Maulandy Rizky Bayu. 2019. "Tol Serpong-Balaraja Dukung Pengembangan Kota Baru Maja." Liputan6.com, September 21, 2019. https://www.liputan6.com/bisnis/read/4068068/to l-serpong-balaraja-dukung-pengembangan-kota-baru-maja.

Leaf, Michael. 2015. "Exporting Indonesian Urbanism: Ciputra and the Developmental Vision of Market Modernism." *South East Asia Research* 23 (2): 169–86.

Leisch, Harald. 2002. "Gated Communities in Indonesia." *Cities* 19 (5): 341–50.

Maulia, Erwida. 2019. "Billionaire Indonesian Property Tycoon Ciputra, Dies at 88." *Nikkei ASIA*, November 27, 2019.

Ministry of Public Works. 2016. *Kesepakatan Bersama tentang Percepatan Pembangunan Infrastruktur Bidang Pekerjaan Umum dan Perumahan Rakyat Dalam Rangka Pengembangan Kota Baru Publik Maja*. Agreement. Jakarta: Ministry of Public Works. https://eppid.pu.go.id /assets/common/pdf/infopublik20160909132748.pdf.

Monkkonen, Paavo. 2013. "Urban Land-Use Regulations and Housing Markets in Developing Countries: Evidence from Indonesia on the Importance of Enforcement." *Land Use Policy* 34: 255–64.

PT. Ciputra Residence. 2019. *Building a Resilient Future—2018 Annual Report*. Jakarta: PT. Ciputra Residence. https://ciputraresidence.com/wp-content/uploads/2015/05/AR-CTRR _2018-Final.pdf.

Sabrina, Alfi Qolbi. 2019. "Dampak Pembangunan Kota Baru Publik Maja Pada Kehidupan Sosial Ekonomi Masyarakat di Kecamatan Maja Kabupaten Lebak." Thesis, University of Sultan Ageng Tirtayasa, Faculty of Social and Political Science, Serang. http://eprints.untirta.ac.id/1296/1 /DAMPAK%20PEMBANGUNAN%20KOTA%20BARU%20PUBLIK%20MAJA%20FIX%20 1%20-%20Copy.pdf.

Widjarnarso, Tony Hartanto, Mulya Amri, Mark Roberts, and Yue Li. 2021. "Maja New Town: A Case Study of Private City Development in Indonesia." Background paper, *Private Cities: Outstanding Examples from Developing Countries and Their Implications for Urban Policy*, World Bank, Jakarta.

Winarso, Haryo, and Tommy Firman. 2002. "Residential Land Development in Jabotabek, Indonesia: Triggering Economic Crisis?" *Habitat International* 26 (4): 487–506.

Zhu, Jieming. 2010. "Symmetric Development of Informal Settlements and Gated Communities: Capacity of the State, the Case of Jakarta, Indonesia." Working Paper Series 135, Asia Research Institute, Singapore.

CHAPTER 18

Nigeria | EKO ATLANTIC

Yue Li and Martin Rama

Currently being built on a reclaimed peninsula the size of Manhattan, Eko Atlantic aspires to be a tidy Dubai-style city off the coast of sprawling Lagos, one of the biggest urban agglomerations worldwide. Its name—the precolonial designation of the area— evokes ecology, in reference to the project's massive oceanic wall to stop coastal erosion.

Private actor

Eko Atlantic was designed, is being built, and will be managed by South Energyx Development F.Z.E (SEDFZE)—previously South Energyx Nigeria Ltd—a company created to implement this project by the powerful Chagoury group. The funding is entirely private. Domestically, it has involved the Bank of Nigeria, the First City Monument Bank, and the Guaranty Trust Bank, among others. Internationally, resources have been mobilized by the African Development Bank (AfDB), BNP Paribas, Fortis, and KBC Bank (AfDB 2018; Oduntan 2015; Seymour 2010).

The main force behind this large-scale development is Gilbert Chagoury, a Nigerian entrepreneur with Lebanese roots. Together with his brother Ronald, he founded the Chagoury group in 1971. Since then, their conglomerate has ventured into multiple sectors, including real estate, manufacturing, hospitality, telecommunications, and insurance. The Chagourys have been listed among the 30 richest African dynasties of Lebanese descent (Masseguin and Marbot 2020).

Gilbert Chagoury is also known as a philanthropist, having made significant contributions to the Louvre Museum in France, and to St. Jude Children's Research Hospital and the Clinton Foundation in the US. His political forays have been more controversial. In 2000, a Swiss court convicted him of money laundering during the time of Nigerian

211

dictator Sani Abacha. And in 2021, he entered a deferred prosecution agreement with the US government in relation to his illegal campaign contributions there (Lipton and Eder 2016; Urevich 2010; US Department of Justice 2021).

Interaction with government

The Land Use Act of 1978, enshrined in Nigeria's constitution, vests the management and control of land in any state of the federation in the governor of that state. Accordingly, the development of Eko Atlantic is being carried out as a public-private partnership (PPP), with the Lagos state government being the public partner. The Nigerian federal government plays a supporting role (Eko Atlantic, n.d.).

This arrangement is somewhat unbalanced, as the initiative and the action stem mostly from the private partner. The vision for Eko Atlantic had been articulated earlier, but not much had been done to follow up on it. As with other projects for satellite cities and large urban developments in Sub-Saharan Africa, Eko Atlantic only gained momentum in recent years, on the heels of a determined push by the private investor (Watson 2013).

Location and connectivity

Eko Atlantic is located on an infill site south of Victoria Island, with its artificial peninsula as an appendage to the city's renowned Bar Beach shoreline. It also stands next to the Commodore Channel, which is the only significant connection between the Lagos Lagoon and the Atlantic Ocean, and is the main entrance to one of the busiest ports in Africa. Therefore, the development can be considered peripheral to the city only to the extent that it is situated on newly created land that projects into the sea (Oduntan 2015; Watson 2013).

Thanks to its central location, Eko Atlantic stands next to an estimated population of 18 million and an annual GDP of around US$43 billion. Lagos is also considered the start-up capital of Africa, home to the continent's largest e-commerce company and a vibrant "fintech" scene (Adeoye 2021; Oduntan 2015; World Economic Forum 2022).

Development time line

Eko Atlantic's defining feature is the reclamation of 10 square kilometers of land, an engineering feat that requires moving 140 million tons of sand (figure 18.1). To protect this large artificial peninsula from coastal erosion and storm flooding, its southern shore will be bordered by the "Great Wall of Lagos," a sea defense barrier made of 100,000 five-ton concrete blocks. When completed, this structure will be 8.5 kilometers

FIGURE 18.1 **Massive land reclamation in Eko Atlantic, Nigeria**

Source: Original figure for this book.

long, stand 8.5 meters above sea level, and comprise a wave deflector (Eko Atlantic, n.d.; Lukacs 2014).

Coastal erosion has been a recurrent challenge for Victoria Island, with the shoreline receding up to 2 kilometers locally over the past century. As recently as 2006, the sea rise was strong enough to damage the road infrastructure along Bar Beach. Natural erosion has been compounded by the blocking of coastal sediment transport by the moles built by the British colonial government in 1908 and 1912 to consolidate the Commodore Channel (Adeoti, Nweke, and Obienyi 2020; AfDB 2018).

SEDFZE commissioned a diverse set of international organizations and companies to undertake different components of the Eko Atlantic project. The modeling of the coastal defense system was done by the DHI Institute in Copenhagen, Denmark, with testing required for 1-in-100-year ocean surges and up to 1-in-1,000-year storms. The master plan for the city was done by Dar al Handasah Shair and MZ Architects, from Dubai, and traffic analysis was conducted by Royal Haskoning DHV, from Indonesia (Eko Atlantic, n.d.; Watson 2013).

The contractor for the land reclamation component of the Eko Atlantic project is the China Communications Construction Group, a company that works in the field of marine dredging and landfill operation. Activities started in 2009, with two-thirds of the sand-filling completed by 2020, and 6.5 kilometers of the sea wall built by 2022 (Eko Atlantic, n.d.).

The urban development component of the project started in 2013, a milestone commemorated with the participation of Nigerian president Goodluck Jonathan and former US president Bill Clinton. The first building towers—including that of British Petroleum—were inaugurated in 2016. Work on the urban component is expected to continue until 2040 or beyond (Adeoti, Nweke, and Obienyi 2020; AfDB 2018; Akinsanmi 2013; Lukacs 2014).

Institutional status

In a clear departure from the local governance arrangements in force in Nigeria, Eko Atlantic will not be managed by the urban authorities of Lagos, but rather by the Eko Atlantic Management Company. Under the terms of the PPP agreement underlying the project, this arrangement is expected to remain in place for a period of 78 years (AfDB 2018).

There have been calls to push this institutional innovation even further, by granting Eko Atlantic a charter city status. Doing so would require the delegation of federal regulatory authority to Lagos State, which in turn would transfer the new powers to the project's management company. Eko Atlantic would then become a special zone of reform, able to attract larger investment volumes (Oduntan 2015). However, no real progress has been made in this direction so far.

Land assembly

By virtue of its reliance on reclaimed land, Eko Atlantic did not face the resettlement and compensation issues that often plague urban development projects in Sub-Saharan Africa. Elsewhere, the sense of urgency created by rapid urbanization has at times led to fast-tracked city construction and bypassed land laws. The dual property system inherited from colonial times—a combination of formalized land rights in the cities' central areas and customary rights in their peripheries—only complicates matters further (Pieterse and Parnell 2014, van Noorloos and Kloosterboer 2018). However, with all the land needed for the project being created through sand-filling, those institutional constraints to land assembly have been irrelevant in this case.

Economic activity

Upon completion, Eko Atlantic is expected to host around 300,000 residents and attract about 200,000 commuters daily. Its main axis, Eko Boulevard, will be 2 kilometers long and 60 meters wide, encompassing a total area of 700,000 square meters.

Along this sweeping avenue will stand mixed-use towers that could, in principle, turn the district into a powerhouse for corporate, financial, and retail activity (Eko Atlantic, n.d.).

This significant scale, together with its privileged location, planned layout, and careful implementation, raise high expectations for Eko Atlantic's economic potential. In the words of a World Bank country director, the city could become "the future Hong Kong of Africa" (Liu 2018).

Eko Atlantic can also relieve some of the pressure on Lagos, one of the largest and fastest-growing urban agglomerations in the world. Its vast artificial peninsula should allow local businesses to relocate out of Lagos, reducing overall congestion (Adeoti, Nweke, and Obienyi 2020). The large addition of functional urban land is even more valuable when considering the sprawling nature of Lagos, whose low land intensity and irregular layout are characteristic of Sub-Saharan African cities with a British colonial past (Baruah, Henderson, and Peng 2021).

Not surprisingly, assessments about the project's economic returns are sanguine. For one of its funders, "Eko Atlantic will substantially provide employment, income and skills development, it will have considerable positive effects on surrounding businesses, on the value of land, and last but not least on Government revenues" (AfDB 2018, 30). This positive assessment is not backed by a quantitative economic analysis, but it is nonetheless plausible.

Amenities

Eko Atlantic aims to offer its residents a range of world-class infrastructure services. The road network includes elevated street levels to accommodate basement parking above groundwater. There will be an underground storm water drainage system, water and sewage treatment, and a fiber-optic telecom network. Electricity will be generated specifically for the city to ensure a reliable power supply.

The independent utilities to manage these services are already in place. Land plots are expected to be delivered with connection to utility services, and a seamless process to approve deeds of assignment construction permits is being promised (Eko Atlantic, n.d.).

Beyond infrastructure, the project also envisions multiple consumption amenities. The waterfront promenade will be 10.2 kilometers long, and there will be two large marinas connected by an internal waterway network. The city will host the largest shopping mall in West Africa, and progress has been made in attracting schools, colleges, and hospitals to the area (Adeoti, Nweke, and Obienyi 2020; Eko Atlantic, n.d.).

A specialized international group will provide security services for the entire city. No cars will be allowed to park on the street, and closed-circuit cameras mounted across the city will feed monitoring information to a central control room (Adeoti, Nweke, and Obienyi 2020).

Social and environmental issues

Assessments of Eko Atlantic's social and environmental implications have also been sanguine. For example, in 2009, the Lagos State government and SEDFZE jointly received the Clinton Global Initiative Commitment Certificate, awarded to those who "create and implement solutions to the world's most pressing challenges" (Clinton Foundation 2022; Eko Atlantic 2009). And in 2018, one of the project's international funders concluded that "the new city will set an example of how creating a high standard of living can be combined with concern for the environment. Its new infrastructure will reduce the level of carbon emissions and improve sustainability" (AfDB 2018, 30).

These positive assessments are more controversial than those concerning the project's economic impacts. Indeed, the newly emerging satellite cities of Sub-Saharan Africa have been criticized as higher-class consumption enclaves, rather than solutions to the region's urbanization challenges (van Noorloos and Kloosterboer 2018). Some have even referred to the associated social divide as "a type of *nouveau apartheid* or segregationist society" (Falk 2012).

Beyond supporting segregation by wealth, Eko Atlantic could also be characterized by norms that depart from Nigeria's legal architecture. According to David Frame, SEDFZE's managing director, "any vehicle seen on the street will be termed abnormal either that it was stolen or to be used for criminal purposes. In that way such vehicles will be towed away and never to get back to the owner" (quoted by Adeoti, Nweke, and Obienyi 2020). Thus, an idiosyncratic take on the presumption of innocence cannot be ruled out.

Whereas the detrimental impacts of coastal erosion and storm surges are well understood, there is less agreement on whether the Eko Atlantic project will lead to greater urban resilience and sustainability. One analysis suggests that it will support short-term storm mitigation on Victoria Island, but in the longer run it will reshape coastal Lagos in a way that harms marginalized communities (Ajibade 2017; Amadi et al. 2012).

Land value capture

The straightforward nature of the PPP agreement underlying Eko Atlantic makes the division of the local economic surplus quite transparent. The agreement in force is such that SEDFZE bears the entire cost of the project, but it also owns all its associated land. SEDFZE may strategically decide to modulate plot sales over time, but its profit basically stems from the difference between the selling price of land and its reclamation and development cost.

As for the government, it will eventually capture the tax revenue generated by the new locality, but it will not directly appropriate any land value gains. A relevant question is whether the additional tax revenue could overestimate the government's share of the surplus, due to the movement of capital and labor from Lagos to Eko Atlantic. But it is too early to tell whether the two locations will operate as complements or substitutes in terms of their economic activity.

References

Adeoti, Femi, Maduka Nweke, and Chinwendu Obienyi. 2020. "Eko Atlantic City to Put Nigeria among 20 Economic Power—Frame." *Sun News Online*, January 10, 2020.

Adeoye, Aanu. 2021. "Lagos Finally Grows into Its Role as Africa's Silicon Valley." *Rest of World*, July 16, 2021.

AfDB (African Development Bank). 2018. "Project: Eko Atlantic City Development, Lagos, Nigeria: Shore Protection, Land Reclamation and City Masterplanning." Environmental and Social Impact Assessment (ESIA) summary. African Development Bank, Abidjan, Côte d'Ivoire.

Ajibade, Idowu. 2017. "Can a Future City Enhance Urban Resilience and Sustainability? A Political Ecology Analysis of Eko Atlantic City, Nigeria." *International Journal of Disaster Risk Reduction* 26: 85–92.

Akinsanmi, Gboyega. 2013. "Clinton: Eko Atlantic City, Destination for Global Investment." *This Day Live*, February 24, 2013.

Amadi, Ako, David Aradeon, Margaret Okorodudu-Fubara, and Olanrewaju A. Fagbohun. 2012. "Eko Atlantic Project—Opinion Papers." *Africa Portal*, January 1, 2012.

Baruah, Neeraj G., J. Vernon Henderson, and Cong Peng. 2021. "Colonial Legacies: Shaping African Cities." *Journal of Economic Geography* 21 (1): 29–65.

Clinton Foundation. 2022. "Clinton Global Initiative." ClintonFoundation.org. Accessed April 6, 2022. https://www.clintonfoundation.org/programs/leadership-public-service/clinton-global -initiative.

Eko Atlantic. 2009. "Fashola Receives Clinton Award for Eko City." News release, September 29, 2009. https://www.ekoatlantic.com/latestnews/press-clipping/fashola-receives-clinton -award-for-eko-atlantic-city/.

Eko Atlantic. n.d. "Prime Real Estate and Infrastructure in Africa." EkoAtlantic.com. Accessed March 28, 2022. https://www.ekoatlantic.com.

Falk, Tyler. 2012. "How Satellite Cities Are Reshaping East Africa." *CityLab*, Bloomberg, May 9, 2012.

Liu, Dong. 2018. "Mega-Urbanization in the Global South: Fast Cities and New Urban Utopias of the Postcolonial State." *Urban Geography* 39 (9): 1449–51.

Lipton, Eric, and Steve Eder. 2016. "2009 Emails Reveal Intersection of Clinton Family Interests." *New York Times*, August 10, 2016.

Lukacs, Martin. 2014. "New, Privatized African City Heralds Climate Apartheid." the *Guardian*, January 21, 2014.

Masseguin, Léa, and Olivier Marbot. 2020. "Lebanese in Africa: A Look at 30 Family Dynasties." *Africa Report*, December 4, 2020.

Oduntan, Gbenga. 2015. "Why Nigeria's Plans for a Dream Eldorado City Are Not Radical Enough." CNN, August 10, 2015.

Pieterse, Edgar, and Susan Parnell. 2014. "*Africa's Urban Revolution* in Context." In Africa's Urban Revolution, edited by Edgar Pieterse and Susan Parnell, 1–17. London: Zed Books.

Seymour, Richard. 2010. "A Shiny New Lagos Rises from the Sea. *African Business* 365: 52–56.

Urevich, Robin. 2010. "Chasing the Ghosts of a Corrupt Regime: Gilbert Chagoury, Clinton Donor and Diplomat with a Checkered Past." *Frontline/World*, PBS, January 8, 2010.

US Department of Justice. 2021.

"Lebanese-Nigerian Billionaire and Two Associates Resolve Federal Probe into Alleged Violations of Campaign Finance Laws." Press release, US Attorney's Office for the Central District of California, March 31, 2021. https://www.justice.gov/usao-cdca/pr /lebanese-nigerian-billionaire-and-two-associates-resolve-federal-probe-alleged.

van Noorloos, Femke, and Marjan Kloosterboer. 2018. "Africa's New Cities: The Contested Future of Urbanisation." *Urban Studies* 55 (6): 1223–41.

Watson, Vanessa. 2013. "African Urban Fantasies: Dreams or Nightmares?" *Environment & Urbanization* 26 (1): 215–31.

World Economic Forum. 2022. "Lagos: A Look at Africa's New Startup Capital." WEForum.org, January 25, 2022. https://www.weforum.org/agenda/2022/01/lagos-africa-startup-capital.

CHAPTER 19

Pakistan | BAHRIA TOWN KARACHI

Nadia Qureshi and Yue Li*

Bigger in surface than Manhattan, at the edge of one of the most populous cities in the world, Bahria Town Karachi has been designed to host more than 1 million people. Its developer has unusual planning and implementation autonomy, and a strong track record on amenities. Its land assembly methods have been more controversial.

Private actor

Bahria Town is a large company owned by Malik Riaz, one of Pakistan's wealthiest persons. As a teenager, when his family's business collapsed, he took a clerical job with the country's Military Engineering Services. From there he worked his way up, becoming a small contractor in the 1980s, establishing his own company in 1996, and eventually building what became one of Asia's biggest real estate businesses (Anjleena 2020; *Dawn* 2012; *Mélange Magazine* 2018).

The company's first major undertaking was a partnership with the Charitable Trust of the Pakistan Navy to build a gated community for military personnel, under the name of Navy's Bahria Foundation. However, due to a falling out, the contract was canceled, and a protracted legal battle ensued. In the end, the Supreme Court dismissed the claims by the Charitable Trust, and in 2000 the Pakistan Navy transferred its entire shareholding in the joint venture to Malik Riaz (*Pakistan Today* 2012).

Two decades later, Bahria Town has more than 50,000 employees and has delivered about US$5 billion in real estate developments (Bahria Town 2020). No reliable figures are available on the company's total value. However, the difference between the market

---

*This private city snapshot is based on Qureshi and Li (2021a).

price and the acquisition cost of its landholdings, estimated at US$800 million, provides a lower bound (Qureshi and Li 2021a). Malik Riaz's wealth is said to be in the range of US$1.0–1.5 billion (*Citybook* 2020; Khan 2022).

Resources for the development of Bahria Town's urban projects are mobilized through the company's main affiliated financial institution, the Escorts Investment Bank Limited. Established in 1996, regulated and supervised by the Securities and Exchange Commission of Pakistan, and listed on the Pakistan Stock Exchange, it has operated with a majority shareholding and under management control by the Bahria Town company since 2018 (Qureshi and Li 2021a).

There are several Bahria towns—urban development projects by the company—at different stages of completion in Pakistan nowadays. All of them combine residential options with business activities and high-quality amenities. Security, together with uninterrupted electricity, gas, and water supply, distinguishes these urban developments from other cities in Pakistan. The newest and by far the most ambitious of the company's undertakings is Bahria Town Karachi (Qureshi and Li 2021a).

Interaction with government

In Pakistan, the responsibility for urban development sits with local government authorities. Building on the colonial legacy, cities are supposed to be run as municipalities, military cantonments, or improvement trusts (Government of Pakistan 1956).

While local authorities initially focused on providing public housing and land plots, over time they shifted toward building infrastructure and delivering services. The share of the urban development budget allocated to housing fell from almost 60 percent in the 1960s to less than 20 percent in the 1980s. In parallel, the share allocated to utilities increased from less than a quarter to roughly 40 percent. This shift coincided with a surge in remittances from Pakistani labor migrants to Gulf countries, which triggered an unprecedented boom in private housing construction and considerable speculation in land markets (Qadeer 1996).

In parallel, a new urban development policy paradigm gradually emerged, one placing a greater emphasis on the private sector. The Constitution of Pakistan allows large developers to build local infrastructure and provide housing solutions. However, the government is supposed to remain the enabler, articulating the framework under which private actors must operate. This framework emerged in 1976, when development authorities were introduced to support municipalities in their urban planning efforts (Ahmad and Anjum 2012).

Weak implementation capacity has remained the main challenge. There has been no dearth of urban policies, programs, and plans in Pakistan, yet the outcomes have not matched expectations (Ellis and Roberts 2016). The overlapping functions and powers of the government agencies involved in urban development may explain the slow progress on the ground (Ahmad and Anjum 2012).

Outdated planning legislation, zoning regulations, and city bylaws add to the challenge. Not favoring mixed land use, high population density, and public spaces, the current framework for urban development "has seriously affected the quality of architecture and urban design and has suppressed initiatives for design creativity and excellence" (Planning Commission 2011, 11).

The flip side of weak local authorities has been the emergence of an unconventional but effective semipublic urban developer, the Defense Housing Authority (DHA). Established in 1975, DHA was originally entrusted with providing housing to military personnel. The Charitable Trust of the Navy, the key partner in the Bahria Town company's first urban undertaking, is an illustration of the model.

Since then, however, DHA has converted parts of cantonment areas and large tracts of agricultural land into major urban development projects for civilians, on a for-profit basis. Along the way it has become one of Pakistan's largest real estate businesses. There are several major DHA developments at present; the largest one, in Lahore, had 378,000 inhabitants in the most recently available count (Qureshi and Li 2021b).

Location and connectivity

Bahria Town Karachi is located in the province of Sindh, at the north edge of the largest city in Pakistan—and one of the biggest cities in the world. The entire development lies within the administrative boundaries of the Karachi Metropolitan Corporation, the government authority in charge of developing and managing the city (figure 19.1, panel a).

The site is adjacent to the Karachi-Hyderabad Motorway and 25 kilometers from Jinnah International Airport. The area is crossed by a tributary of the seasonal Malir River, part of the broader Indus River delta on which Karachi sits.

Development time line

Bahria Town Karachi was launched in 2014, so its population is still modest. But its scale is not. Spanning over 72 square kilometers, it is the largest urban development project of its kind in Pakistan, with an area larger than that of Manhattan in the US (figure 19.1, panel b).

Given that the city is still at an early stage of construction, the time line of milestone events to report is thin. But its master plan, and the trajectory of other, more advanced Bahria towns, gives a clear sense of what to expect in the coming years.

The master plan foresees that 36 percent of the land will be devoted to residential uses, 16 percent to commercial uses and public buildings, and 12 percent to green areas. Parcel sizes will on average be smaller than in other Bahria towns, with 60 percent

FIGURE 19.1 **The unusually large footprint of Bahria Town Karachi, Pakistan**

a. Relative to Karachi   b. Relative to Manhattan, United States

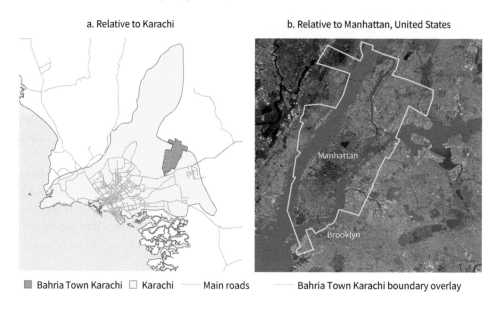

⬛ Bahria Town Karachi ☐ Karachi ⎯ Main roads   ⎯ Bahria Town Karachi boundary overlay

Source: Original figure for this book, based on Qureshi and Li 2021a.

of them having less than 1,000 square meters. All internal roads will be more than 9 meters wide.

Bahria Town Karachi is planned to host trade and business zones, as well as markets, warehouses and storage services, and an off-dock terminal. It is also attracting investments through partnerships with international players. For example, two high-end hotels are being built in partnership with Sheraton, at an estimated cost of US$200 million.

Other partnerships are used by the Bahria Town company to offer high-quality amenities in its developments. Services such as electricity, water, sewerage, gas, and security are provided in collaboration with public utilities and government agencies. Partnerships with domestic private actors are typically behind high-end schools, colleges, and hospitals (Qureshi and Li 2021a).

Institutional status

Much the same as other developments by the company, Bahria Town Karachi is regulated by its own detailed bylaws. Once the city's master plan is approved by the local development authority, decisions on land use, building standards, parking requirements, and design criteria are thus made by the large developer.

Land assembly

Given the vast amount of land needed for Bahria Town Karachi, the location chosen for its development is relatively distant from the city's central business district. This is despite the significant investment the company has made downtown to build Pakistan's tallest skyscraper—the 62-story Bahria Opal Tower (Qureshi and Li 2021a).

The land on which the development sits used to be mostly agricultural, and it was mainly in the hands of small farmers and community landholdings. Plots were acquired by the Bahria Town company supposedly at market prices, or through bilateral negotiation, without government intervention.

The transfer of land rights to the company required the issuance of nonobjection certificates by the relevant local development authority, in line with the regulations in force in Pakistan. After property taxes were levied on the transactions, permissions to use the land for urban development purposes needed to be granted as well, in accordance with the prevailing regime for private housing schemes (Government of Sindh 2014).

The process through which some of the land was assembled has been the subject of much debate in Pakistan. There have been farmers' demonstrations against alleged land evictions, media reports on suspected corruption, and court litigation on the legality of some of the permissions (Bhatti 2018).

In 2018, the Supreme Court issued a verdict restricting Bahria Town Karachi to a maximum of 24 square kilometers of land, noting that the local development authority had overstepped its powers. This decision was reversed in 2019, and the legality of the disputed land acquisition confirmed, after Bahria Town paid US$3.1 billion as a compensation to the government (Hafeez and Musyani 2021).

The United Kingdom's National Crime Agency also froze more than US$240 million of assets belonging to Malik Riaz, for alleged "bribery and corruption overseas." The case was settled without admission of wrongdoing, and the money was returned to the government of Pakistan. Malik Riaz claimed that the transfer counted toward the compensation agreed upon with the Supreme Court (Neate 2019).

Economic activity

With the urbanization rate rapidly increasing in Pakistan, Bahria towns are bound to see their population soar. The company's housing products have already been chosen by over 100,000 households, a relatively small fraction of the country's population. Over time, however, Bahria Town Karachi alone could host more than 1 million people, which is approximately the size of the 10th biggest city in Pakistan at present (Qureshi and Li 2021a, 2021b).

In addition to residential solutions, Bahria towns attract a considerable number of businesses, with a focus on commerce, hospitality, education, health, and leisure. Their sheer scale also generates a sizable demand for the construction industry. And their high-quality urban environment makes them attractive to foreign investors. In all these ways, Bahria towns contribute to economic growth in Pakistan.

However, by sitting relatively distant from central business districts, Bahria towns are more suburban than DHA developments. For example, the Bahria Opal Tower is contiguous to a downtown DHA development but one hour away by road from Bahria Town Karachi. Not surprisingly, land values are consistently lower in Bahria towns than in DHA developments (Qureshi and Li 2021b).

The focus on low-rise, suburban garden cities has been said to incentivize urban sprawl while neglecting downtown development. In the words of an eminent Pakistani policy maker, "cities appear to have no downtowns or city centres—dense areas of mixed use concentrate residential, office, commercial and entertainment within an almost walkable district" (Haque 2015, 5).

Amenities

Bahria towns have been successful at providing high-quality amenities. Uninterrupted electricity and water supply, efficient and timely solid waste collection and disposal, good sanitation, gas supply not suffering from the usual pressure instability, rescue and fire services, and 24-hour security are among the services that differentiate these developments from other urban areas in Pakistan. In addition, Bahria towns offer abundant retail choices, public spaces, and green areas.

With obvious hyperbole, Bahria towns have been described by the media as a "functioning state within a non-functioning one" (Magnier 2011). And they have even been dubbed Pakistan's "gateway to paradise" (*Newsweek* 2013). More down-to-earth, perhaps, they are seen as the places "where Pakistan's new middle class takes refuge from the Taliban attacks and endless power cuts that plague the rest of the country" (*Emirates 24/7* 2022).

Social and environmental issues

Media reports like those just cited make it obvious that significant social segregation exists between the orderly and well-functioning urban environment of Bahria towns and the messier conventional cities around them. And the spatial layout of Bahria towns, with curve-shaped streets and frequent dead ends, is deliberately planned for a population that travels by private cars, which is the case only among the upper echelons of Pakistan's society (Qureshi and Li 2021a).

Land value capture

Bahria Town Karachi covers the cost of the amenities and services it provides by charging fees to its residents. The fees are in addition to the property tax residents pay to the local government and amount to 25 percent of the annual rental value. While the tax obligation is determined by the Sindh Urban Immovable Property Tax Act of 1958, the fees are set by the Bahria Town company, without government intervention (Qureshi and Li 2021a).

The profit the Bahria Town company makes out of developments such as Bahria Town Karachi results in part from the high quality of its urban products—a source of monopoly power in the context of a messy urbanization process. But profits are also boosted when agricultural land can be acquired at a discount and converted to urban land with low transaction costs.

The recent Supreme Court rulings, and the compensation payment agreed upon with the Bahria Town company, should allow society at large to recover some of the extraordinary profits made through the land acquisition process.

References

Ahmad, Niaz, and Ghulam Abbas Anjum. 2012. "Legal and Institutional Perplexities Hampering the Implementation of Urban Development Plans in Pakistan." *Cities* 29 (4): 271–77.

Anjleena, Suza. 2020. "Mr Ali Riaz Malik Biography—Entrepreneurs and CEO of Bahria Town in Pakistan." *Trendy*, May 27, 2020.

Bahria Town. 2020. "About." Bahriatown.com. Accessed September 12, 2020. https://bahriatown .com/.

Bhatti, Haseeb. 2018. "Supreme Court Finds Massive Illegalities in Land Acquired by Bahria Town for Housing Projects." *Dawn* (Karachi), May 4, 2018.

Citybook. 2020. "Top 10 Richest Man in Pakistan 2020." *Citybook*, March 15, 2020. https:// citybook.pk/blog/top-10-richest-man-in-pakistan-2020/

Dawn. 2012. "Profile: Malik Riaz Hussain." *Dawn* (Karachi), June 10, 2012.

Ellis, Peter, and Mark Roberts. 2016. *Leveraging Urbanization in South Asia: Managing Spatial Transformation for Prosperity and Livability*. Washington, DC: World Bank.

Emirates 24/7. 2022. "Pakistani Expats' New Realty Check." *Emirates 24/7*, March 5, 2022.

Government of Pakistan. 1956. *The Constitution of Pakistan*. Islamabad: Government of Pakistan.

Government of Sindh. 2014. "The Sindh Special Development Board Bill, 2014." Notification, October 23, 2014. Government of Sindh, Karachi.

Haque, Nadeem Ul. 2015. "Flawed Urban Development Policies in Pakistan." Policy Working Paper 119, Pakistan Institute of Development Economics, Islamabad.

Hafeez, Somaiyah, and Zafar Musyani. 2021. "The Battle over Bahria Town Karachi." the *Diplomat*, July 8, 2021.

Khan, Nayab. 2022. "Top 10 Richest People in Pakistan (2022)." *Phone World*, June 16, 2022.

Magnier, Mark. 2011. "Pakistan Gated Community Sparks Controversy." *Los Angeles Times*, October 6, 2011.

Mélange Magazine. 2018. "Malik Riaz: From Rags to Riches." *Mélange Magazine*, July 23, 2018.

Neate, Rupert. 2019. "Pakistani Tycoon Agrees to Hand over £190m to UK Authorities." the *Guardian*, December 3, 2019.

Newsweek. 2013. "Bahria Town, Gateway to Paradise." *Newsweek*, December 10, 2013.

Pakistan Today. 2012. "A True Rags to Riches Story." *Pakistan Today*, June 13, 2012.

Planning Commission. 2011. "Task Force Report on Urban Development." Government of Pakistan, Islamabad.

Qadeer, Mohammad A. 1996. "An Assessment of Pakistan's Urban Policies, 1947–1997." *Pakistan Development Review* 35 (4): 443–65.

Qureshi, Nadia, and Yue Li. 2021a. "Bahria Towns: A Case Study of Private Cities in Pakistan." Background paper, *Private Cities: Outstanding Examples from Developing Countries and Their Implications for Urban Policy*, World Bank, Washington, DC.

Qureshi, Nadia, and Yue Li. 2021b. "Private Cities in Pakistan." Background paper, *Private Cities: Outstanding Examples from Developing Countries and Their Implications for Urban Policy*, World Bank, Washington, DC.

UNDP Pakistan. 2018. "Sustainable Urbanization." *Development Advocate Pakistan* 5 (4). United Nations Development Programme Pakistan, Islamabad. https://www.undp.org/pakistan/publications/sustainable-urbanization.

CHAPTER 20

Pakistan | SIALKOT

Nadia Qureshi and Yue Li*

Sialkot, a well-known manufacturing center for centuries, declined with the partition of the subcontinent. However, thanks to a remarkably cohesive business community that took charge of urban development, it has become one of Pakistan's most important economic hubs.

Private actor

Sialkot has a long history as an urban agglomeration and was formally recognized as a city during British colonial times. Yet its private sector has filled a gap left by the government to develop and manage the large-scale infrastructure the city needed to thrive (Idris 2007).

The extraordinary clout of Sialkot's business community is a legacy of the powerful Biradari system, a strong societal identification based on common ancestry and lineage. The clans and families involved may not always cooperate, but unity emerges in difficult times. Elders and notables are highly respected, and their views bring the collective together (Nadvi 1999a; Tandon 1969; Tariq and Alamgir 2013).

The key private actor over the past few decades has been the Sialkot Chamber of Commerce and Industry (SCCI). Championed by local entrepreneurs since the 1970s and formally established in 1982, its goal is to advance the interests of the city's business community. SCCI has approximately 9,000 member firms, most of them export oriented (SCCI 2020a, 2020b).

*This private city snapshot is based on Qureshi and Li (2021).

Interaction with government

The government bodies interacting with SCCI include the local and provincial govern-ments but also, importantly, central government entities such as the Export Promotion Bureau, Civil Aviation Authority, Executive Committee of National Economic Council, and Local Government and Community Development Department (SCCI 2020a, 2020b).

The main vehicle for the private sector to influence local development is not just par-ticipating in the governing bodies of the city, but rather lobbying the central government at the highest level, bypassing local counterparts. The interaction with government also relies on creative arrangements such as trust funds, public-private partnerships, and matching grants. There is arguably a "shared governance" of the city, but in an entrepre-neurial rather than institutional sense (Qureshi and Li 2021).

Location and connectivity

Sialkot lies in the northeast of Punjab province, 125 kilometers from Lahore, its main urban center and Pakistan's second largest city. The partition of the subcontinent in 1947 also left Sialkot a mere 7 kilometers from the Indian border, a frontier that ever since has worked more as a barrier than as a gate.

The area is well connected to the rest of the country through a network of roads, motorways, and rail lines. The main railway station is located in the center of the city, linking it with Lahore but also with Karachi, Pakistan's biggest urban agglomeration and most important port.

Development time line

While the first human settlements date back 5,000 years, the town that developed there only became well known during the Mughal period. Its main reputation came from its paper goods—especially the white, bright, and strong Hariri paper—and its metal prod-ucts, including swords and daggers for the Mughal crown.

Sialkot became a city proper under British rule, when it became a manufacturing center. The leather industry boomed during the 1870s, propelled by British demand for tennis, football, and hockey items (Atkin et al. 2017). The establishment of a mission hospital around 1890 boosted the demand for surgical instruments, which the local blacksmiths were quick to respond to. Sialkot gained a reputation for high quality and started exporting to other British colonies.

This remarkable growth cycle came to a sudden end in 1947, with the partition of the subcontinent. Being so close to the new international border, communal rioting was particularly violent (Chatta 2009). Large numbers of Hindus and Sikhs departed for the India side of Punjab, and close to 200,000 migrants arrived from Jammu.

By some accounts, 80 percent of Sialkot's industry was destroyed or abandoned by the time Pakistan became an independent country (Qureshi and Li 2021).

The city's comeback was slow at first. Small cottage industries developed, displaced populations were gradually absorbed, and local coalitions building on the Biradari system started to emerge.

In the 1960s, the central government supported this momentum by establishing an industrial area with land available at a 50 percent discount. However, despite repeated requests from the private sector, the government was reluctant to invest in a city so close to the border and, hence, so vulnerable in the event of a military conflict. This reluctance convinced the business community that it had to take urban development into its own hands (Qureshi and Li 2021).

An important step was the creation of Sialkot Dry Port Trust in 1982. With 52 reputed industrialists at the helm, it aimed to bring customs clearance to the city's doorsteps. In 1984, the government granted the necessary permissions and committed to match on a three-for-one basis the funding raised by the business community. Since then, the customs facility has been managed by the central government, and its operations by the trust (SCCI 2020b).

Next came the establishment of the Sialkot City Program, a resource-pooling initiative to upgrade local roads and drainage. In 1999, businesses agreed to contribute 0.24 percent of their export invoices to the program. The central government committed to a one-to-one fund-matching arrangement and the government of Punjab was to triple that amount. The program funded the construction of half a dozen of Sialkot's major roads (SCCI 2020a).

Another important milestone was the establishment of a public-private partnership to build an international airport. After SCCI unsuccessfully pleaded the case with the central government, more than 250 local firms endorsed the construction under the build-own-operate model. The initiative was officially approved in 2001, with the Civil Aviation Authority under the Ministry of Defense as its government counterpart. The airport was inaugurated in 2007 (Qureshi and Li 2021).

Other developments include the establishment of an export processing zone in 2002 and an industrial estate for tanneries in 2018 (figure 20.1). The biggest investment was for a motorway connecting Sialkot to Lahore, relying on a partnership with the government under the build-operate-transfer model. The motorway is more than 90 kilometers long, with four lanes, seven interchanges, eight flyovers, 40 bridges, and 70 underpasses. It cost US$258 million and was inaugurated in 2020 (Shehryar 2020).

Institutional status

While Sialkot's recent development has been led mostly by the private sector, administratively the city is run by the government. This tension has been a source

FIGURE 20.1 **Initiatives by the business community in Sialkot, Pakistan**

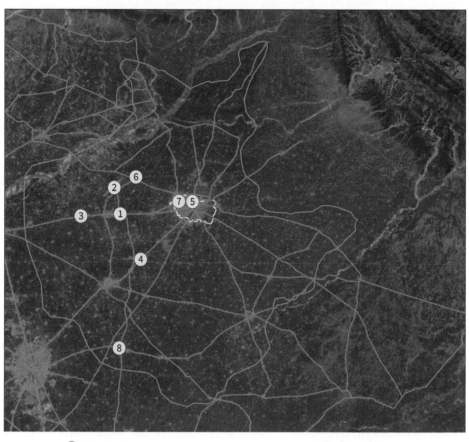

1. Dry port
2. International airport
3. Export processing zone
4. Sport industries development center
5. Business and commerce center
6. Tannery zone
7. Air Sial head office
8. Motorway exit

—— City boundary

—— District boundary

—— Main roads

Source: Original figure for this book, based on Qureshi and Li 2021.
Note: Initiatives are numbered in chronological order, starting with the oldest.

of considerable transaction costs. For example, gaining approval for the Sialkot City Program was a tedious process, and it was only after a major lobbying effort that a law was passed to allow its operation.

In parallel, the relationship between the administrative city and the central and provincial governments evolved considerably during this period. A significant change was the adoption of the Local Government Ordinance in 2001, during the government of General Pervaiz Musharraf (Cheema, Khwaja, and Qadir 2006). This devolution initiative transferred considerable authority to elected mayors, limiting the role of central and provincial governments. Budget funding was directly allocated to local authorities; participation by the local community in city matters was enhanced; elected authorities were given full autonomy over urban planning and implementation; and the granting of land permits was facilitated. These changes made it easier for the business community of Sialkot to carry out its initiatives.

The new decentralization arrangements were partially reversed in 2013 and 2019. However, in 2021 the Sialkot Development Authority was established, with the support of the local business community. This new entity is responsible for urban planning and has authority to coordinate water supply, sewerage, and drainage systems within the city (Adnan 2021).

Land assembly

Land acquisition was less central to urban development in Sialkot than in other private cities. The local business community focused mainly on infrastructure projects, and these required relatively limited amounts of land. Thus, 92 hectares were needed for the 2002 export processing zone, 405 hectares for the 2007 international airport, and 155 hectares for the 2018 estate park for tanneries.

However, the conversion of even small amounts of land was challenging. Under the Land Acquisition Act of 1894, only the deputy commissioner under the local government has the authority to assemble land for projects benefiting the broader community, and the land can only be transferred to a government entity.

Creative arrangements were needed for the transfer to benefit the business community. For example, land acquisition for the international airport was conducted by the local deputy commissioner but partially paid for by the business community. The land was then transferred to the Civil Aviation Authority, which in turn leased it to the company in charge of the airport—in practice under SCCI. Brokering such arrangements took time and involved complicated legal formalities (Qureshi and Li 2021).

Economic activity

Sialkot is by now the third largest economic hub in Pakistan and its second largest source of foreign exchange after the city of Karachi. Most of its industrial output is exported, generating over US$2 billion per year in foreign exchange. Its income per capita is among the highest in the country. The city also yields US$1,200 in tax revenue per person, more than any other administrative jurisdiction in Pakistan (Recorder Report 2019; Sanchez-Triana et al. 2014).

The main sectors of activity remain the same as in British colonial times. Sialkot is a top source of leather products, sporting goods, and surgical instruments. The city counts 264 tanneries, 244 leather garment factories, 900 plants producing sports goods, and over 120 brands of surgical instruments. Food products are important as well, with the city hosting 57 rice husking mills and 14 flour mills (Sanchez-Triana et al. 2014).

Sialkot's reputation for high-quality products also remains (*Economist* 2016). And it continues to rest on local clusters that support inter-firm cooperation and strategic vertical ties with both local subcontractors and external buyers (Nadvi 1999b).

With 928,000 inhabitants, Sialkot is one of Pakistan's most prosperous districts, with a dense network of upstream cottage industries ensuring that the benefits spread out. A relatively recent multidimensional assessment found that the poverty rate in Sialkot was 14.0 percent, substantially lower than the 38.8 percent national average (Government of Pakistan 2016).

Amenities

Urban amenities are less well developed. Colonial areas have wide streets and large lawns. But the core of the city is composed of old, densely populated neighborhoods. Most roads are narrow, and often congested. Many of them were upgraded under the Sialkot City Program, but their condition has deteriorated over time (Anwar 2014).

Telecommunication services are limited. Although the deployment of a fiber-optic network is under way, access to high-speed internet remains an issue. Some areas of the city even have limited mobile phone coverage. Gas shortages affect its manufacturing activities (Koh 2022).

The water supply network has greater coverage and provides better services than in other cities in Pakistan. About 80 percent of the local households have access to it, and among them 85 percent are current in their bill payments. But sewers are clogged in multiple places, and only one-quarter of the city's solid waste is collected (ADB 2017b).

Social and environmental issues

Despite its shortcomings, Sialkot is known as "the city of opportunities." Its vibrant business environment attracts people from all over the country (ADB 2017a). The migrants' ethnic diversity has not been a source of social tensions. And the city's literacy rates are among the highest in the country, standing out for their greater gender parity (Rehman, Jingdong, and Hussain 2015).

Like most cities in developing countries, Sialkot suffers from urban sprawl (Al-Rashid et al. 2021). However, its land consumption index—the change in land area for a given change in population—is below average (Government of Punjab 2018). This relatively good performance could be partly due to the historically compact and dense nature of the city (figure 20.1).

Pollution, however, remains a concern. Tanneries are a major source of environmental degradation, and a national clean production program failed to make a dent (Padda and Asim 2019). The establishment in 2018 of a dedicated industrial estate for tanneries, where effluents are actively managed, may offer some hope for improvement on this front.

Land value capture

Businesslike deals between the local private sector and the government have made it possible to share the surplus generated by the city between the public and the private sides in a mutually advantageous way. Contributory arrangements such as those underpinning the Sialkot City Program have made the business community internalize urban development costs, while the broader population has benefited from urban development.

These deals have helped overcome the absence of legal authority by the private sector over functions it has taken over from government, such as building roads. Instead, the business community takes ownership of the proceeds through financing arrangements.

At the same time, the business community faces significant risks from engaging in such deals. The operation of any privately run urban project—for example, the Sialkot International Airport—could indeed be shut down at the government's discretion. Some in the private sector fear that the approach chosen to make Sialkot thrive lacks stability, and no extent of lobbying can mitigate such risk (Qureshi and Li 2021).

References

ADB (Asian Development Bank). 2017a. "Sialkot Pro Poor Growth, Poverty and Social Safeguards, Annex-8." *Pre-Feasibility Study for Sialkot City*. Manila: Asian Development Bank.

ADB (Asian Development Bank). 2017b. "Sialkot Rapid Assessment Study, Annex-3." *Pre-Feasibility Study for Sialkot and Sahiwal Cities*. Manila: Asian Development Bank.

Adnan, Imran. 2021. "Punjab LG Draft Act Wins Cabinet Nod." *Express Tribune*, November 24, 2021.

Al-Rashid, Muhammad Ahmad, Muhammad Nadeem, Adel Shaheen Aldosary, Yong Adilah Shamsul Harumain, and Hafiz Syed Hamid Arshad. 2021. "An Integrated Approach to Analysing the Urban Growth Patterns: The Case of Sialkot, Punjab, Pakistan." *International Review for Spatial Planning and Sustainable Development* 9 (4): 116–38.

Anwar, Nausheen. 2014. *Infrastructure Redux: Crisis, Progress in Industrial Pakistan & Beyond*. Berlin: Springer.

Atkin, David, Azam Chaudhry, Shamyla Chaudry, Amit K. Khandelwal, Tariq Raza, and Eric Verhoogen. 2017. "On the Origins and Development of Pakistan's Soccer-Ball Cluster." *World Bank Economic Review* 30 (1): S34–S41.

Chatta, Ilyas Ahmad. 2009. "Partition and Its Aftermath: Violence, Migration and the Role of Refugees in the Socio-Economic Development of Gujranwala and Sialkot Cities, 1947–1961." PhD diss., University of Southampton, UK.

Cheema, Ali, Asim Ijaz Khwaja, and Adnan Qadir. 2006. "Local Government Reforms in Pakistan: Context, Content and Causes." In *Decentralization and Local Governance in Developing Countries: A Comparative Perspective* 2, edited by Pranab Bardhan and Dilip Mookherjee, 257–84. Cambridge, MA: MIT Press.

Economist. 2016. "If You Want It Done Right." the *Economist,* October 29, 2016.

Government of Pakistan. 2016. *Multidimensional Poverty in Pakistan.* Islamabad: Planning Commission.

Government of Punjab. 2018. *Punjab Cities Growth Atlas 1995–2015.* Lahore: Planning and Development Department, Urban Unit.

Idris, D. 2007. "Drivers of Economic Growth: Unleashing the Potential of the Private Sector." Unpublished manuscript, LEADS, Islamabad.

Koh, Ann. 2022, "Gas Shortage Hits Pakistan's Exports, Adding to Economic Stress." *Bloomberg News,* January 3, 2022.

Nadvi, Khalid. 1999a. "Shifting Ties: Social Networks in the Surgical Instrument Cluster of Sialkot, Pakistan." *Development and Change* 30 (1): 141–75.

Nadvi, Khalid. 1999b. "The Cutting Edge: Collective Efficiency and International Competitiveness in Pakistan." *Oxford Development Studies* 27 (1): 81–107.

Padda, Ihtsham Ul Haq, and Muhammad Asim. 2019. "What Determines Compliance with Cleaner Production? An Appraisal of the Tanning Industry in Sialkot, Pakistan." *Environmental Science and Pollution Research* 26 (2): 1733–50.

Qureshi, Nadia, and Yue Li. 2021. "Sialkot: A Case Study of Private Cities in Pakistan." Background paper, *Private Cities: Outstanding Examples from Developing Countries and Their Implications for Urban Policy,* World Bank, Washington, DC.

Recorder Report. 2019. "Golden Economic Triangle: Government Urged to Take Revolutionary Steps." *Business Recorder,* August 6, 2019.

Rehman, A., L. Jingdong, and I. Hussain. 2015. "The Province-wise Literacy Rate in Pakistan and Its Impact on the Economy." *Pacific Science Review* 1 (3).

Sanchez-Triana, Ernesto, Dan Biller, Ijaz Nabi, Leonard Ortolano, Ghazal Dezfuli, Javaid Afzal, and Santiago Enriquez. 2014. *Revitalizing Industrial Growth in Pakistan: Trade, Infrastructure, and Environmental Performance.* Washington, DC: World Bank.

SCCI (Sialkot Chamber of Commerce and Industry). 2020a. *Sialkot City Package.* Sialkot: Sialkot Chamber of Commerce & Industry. https://scci.com.pk/sialkot-city-package/.

SCCI (Sialkot Chamber of Commerce and Industry). 2020b. *Sialkot Dry Port Trust.* Sialkot: Sialkot Chamber of Commerce & Industry. https://scci.com.pk/sialkot-dry-port-trust/.

Shehryar, Muhammad. 2020. "Critical Review of Lahore-Sialkot Motorway." *Daily Times,* June 6, 2020.

Tandon, Prakash. 1969. *Punjabi Century, 1857–1947.* Berkeley: University of California Press.

Tariq, Shahnaz, and Muhammad Alamgir. 2013. "Impacts of Biradarism on the Politics of Punjab: A Case Study of District Khanewal." *Pakistan Vision* 14 (2): 182–94.

CHAPTER 21

South Africa | WATERFALL CITY

Yue Li and Martin Rama

South Africa's largest private property development ever, Waterfall City, is currently being built in the vicinity of Johannesburg, the continent's wealthiest urban agglomeration. Its unlikely land assembly, sizable economic potential, and religiously inspired regulations connect, in different ways, with Apartheid and its aftermath.

Private actor

Waterfall City is inextricably linked to Moosa Ismail Mia, a devout Muslim from Gujarat—nowadays an Indian state—who settled in the Johannesburg area in the 1890s. Together with his descendants, he built over time an empire of 70 companies. He did so despite apartheid laws prohibiting non-White people from doing business in White areas (IOL 2021).

In 1934, Moosa Ismail Mia purchased the land on which Waterfall City currently stands, and in 1940 he founded the Waterfall Islamic Institute to support underprivileged Muslim communities. The land is held by the institute, now a trust managed by the Mia family (Herbert and Murray 2015).

The corporate arrangements regarding the city are complex. Waterfall Investment Corporation (WIC) is the sole proprietor of the real estate component of the project. WIC has spun off about a dozen subsidiaries that take care of infrastructure services for the city and are cobbled together by interlocking directorships and partnerships. Rival companies are not allowed by WIC to have offices on the premises or to compete with its subsidiaries (Murray 2015).

WIC is fully owned by the Waterfall Islamic Institute, and two of its four directors are from the Mia family. The board of this umbrella organization oversees all operations by its affiliated companies and retains veto power on decisions related to Waterfall City, all the way down to the precinct level.

WIC also acquired 22 percent of the Atterbury Property Group, a major developer that had previously built 700,000 square meters of prime commercial properties across South Africa. In exchange, the Atterbury group got exclusive development rights for over 1.4 million square meters of rentable area in Waterfall City. Another major developer, Century Properties, is responsible for 600 hectares of mixed-use and residential components (Herbert and Murray 2015).

Interaction with government

In the 1990s, with the end of Apartheid, South Africa embraced a far-reaching decentralization process. The autonomy of local governments was enshrined in the constitution of 1996, followed by the election of local authorities in 2000.

Alongside this transition, single metropolitan governments were established in six major jurisdictions. Among them was Johannesburg, an urban agglomeration whose GDP is surpassed by only 7 of the 54 countries on the African continent. The consolidation of multiple local authorities into single metropolitan governments aimed to redress a legacy of spatial segregation and to enhance the opportunities of peripheral Black populations to access better employment opportunities.

Consistent with this vision, in the wake of the 2010 football World Cup, hosted by South Africa, an ambitious transit-oriented development strategy was adopted by the national government. A rapid bus system for 13 cities, including Johannesburg, was approved in 2007. Previously, an express regional commuter rail network called Gautrain had been launched for the Johannesburg region, also with the financial backing of the national government.

The availability of this new transport infrastructure, together with a mandate by the national government to prioritize economic growth and job creation, prompted the city of Johannesburg to envision new urban developments around the transit nodes being created (Pieterse 2017). As in other countries on the continent, the municipal authority could now become a partner—rather than just a facilitator—in the development of private cities (van Noorloos and Kloosterboer 2018).

Not all aspiring private cities in the Johannesburg area were endorsed by the authorities. In 2014, the Chinese group Shanghai Zendai Property proposed a new development toward the east, at a cost of US$8 billion. Spanning 1,600 hectares, the project was supposed to be completed in 15 years and create 200,000 permanent jobs. However, negotiations ended a few years later due in part to a divergence of views, with the city of Johannesburg preferring a less luxurious hub and a greater emphasis on affordable housing (Balkaran 2019).

In the case of Waterfall City, the Atterbury group and WIC negotiated with the authorities what became known as "a basket of rights." Under the terms of this deal, the private side agreed to build the connecting road infrastructure for the project and to turn it over to the city of Johannesburg. In exchange, it was allowed to develop the master plan for the entire area, provide services and amenities, and retain discretion on building specifications (Murray 2015).

Location and connectivity

Waterfall City is almost halfway between Johannesburg's central district and Pretoria, South Africa's capital city. It takes about 20 minutes by car to reach the former and some 30 minutes to get to the latter. The site is also within minutes of the satellite city of Sandton, the premier financial and corporate location in the country, often referred to as the richest square mile on the African continent.

In terms of infrastructure, Waterfall City is close to O.R. Tambo, Africa's busiest international airport, and to the country's major north–south highway system (N1), through which 120,000 vehicles pass in each direction every day. The site has its own Gautrain station and is close to three others (Herbert and Murray 2015; Murray 2015).

Development time line

The spatial development of the Johannesburg region was deeply affected by Apartheid, with the key milestones being the 1923 Natives (Urban Areas) Act and the 1950 Group Areas Act. Different places were set aside for each racial group, with over 1 million hectares of urban land being zoned on a race basis between 1950 and 1991 (Christopher 1997).

Legal frameworks were not the only drivers of spatial segregation. Some researchers have highlighted the continuity of trends around these two milestone acts and concluded that economic forces also played an important role. Others have pointed out the influence of modernist planners in shaping racially segregated cities (Maylam 1995; Parnell and Mabin 1995).

Crime was another important force at play. An extraordinary degree of urban violence has distinguished South Africa from the rest of the continent. Early Johannesburg was defined by its large concentration of Sub-Saharan African migrants housed in single-sex mining compounds. Together with prisons, these compounds served as dysfunctional socializing agents. Criminal activities flourished, with about 100 gangs being recorded just between 1940 and 1960. Violence even escalated after the end of Apartheid in 1994 (Dirsuweit 2002; Kynoch 2005, 2008).

Racial discrimination, economic forces, and the flight to safety made Johannesburg evolve from a monocentric city to a polycentric metropolis (figure 21.1). Most of the urban poor now live toward the south of the city, around townships reserved for the Black population under Apartheid. Among them is Soweto, which was officially

FIGURE 21.1 **Waterfall City, South Africa: Emerging as Johannesburg evolved from monocentric to polycentric after Apartheid**

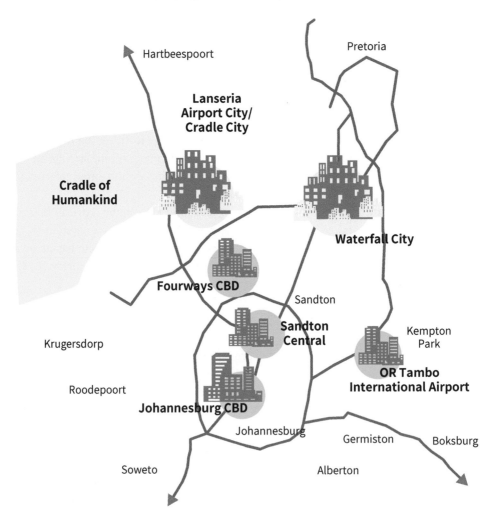

Source: Herbert and Murray 2015, © *International Journal of Urban and Regional Research*. Reproduced with permission of *International Journal of Urban and Regional Research*; further permission required for reuse.
Note: CBD = central business district.

recognized in 1963 and now has a population of over 1 million. Meanwhile, Sandton was incorporated as a separate urban area in 1969, launching the northward drift of wealthier population groups (Herbert and Murray 2015; Todes 2012).

In line with this trend, WIC envisioned its own urban development project north of Johannesburg in 1997. In the years that followed, the Atterbury group commissioned Boogertman and Partners Architects to design an expansive city from scratch.

Construction of the first residential estate started in 2006. By now the basic infrastructure of the city is nearly completed, and the health facilities, retirement villages, residential estates, and affordable housing are fully operational (Herbert and Murray 2015).

Institutional status

Waterfall City benefits from a long list of legal exemptions. Together with restrictive covenants, internal guidelines, and tight regulatory regimes, special rules have allowed WIC to maintain control over infrastructure services, bundling them into a single package, directly interacting with users, setting fees, and even establishing subsidies—as a local government would do.

Such administrative autonomy has transformed WIC into a city council of sorts. To fulfill this role, WIC created an independent subsidiary, the Waterfall Management and Operating Company, to manage daily operations and deliver essential services.

This unusual governance structure could be taken further by the Atterbury group, as it envisions creating a company to oversee the management of the commercial and business side of Waterfall City. This novel approach would include the appointment of a city manager—referred to as "the mayor"—who would act on behalf of the relevant stakeholders but not be subject to any public authority (Murray 2015).

Land assembly

Waterfall City spans 22 square kilometers of the formerly vacant land that Moosa Ismail Mia purchased from an insolvent estate in 1934. This oversized plot has been held by his extended family for almost a century, a remarkable accomplishment given Apartheid policies.

A 1932 law restricting land ownership by people of Indian descent was circumvented by issuing 50,000 bearer shares, which could be controlled by people of any race. Another, even more challenging 1948 law was overcome by donating the plot to the Waterfall Islamic Institute. And to rebuff subsequent attempts by the government to seize the property and close the institute, the Mia family started a quarry on the plot, since a legal loophole allowed non-Whites to hold mineral rights (IOL 2021; Murray 2015).

Economic activity

Waterfall City's population is expected to exceed 100,000. Its master plan envisions a compact urban layout, at odds with the trend toward unplanned suburban sprawl. The project is characterized by mixed land use and proximity between homes and work opportunities.

These features should contribute to higher productivity than in the surrounding areas (Herbert and Murray 2015).

Local authorities have expressed concern about the increased traffic congestion such a large project could generate in the broader metropolitan area. In response, WIC financed a traffic master plan to simulate traffic patterns within 20 kilometers of Waterfall City and committed to spend an estimated US$27 million on highway improvements (Murray 2015).

To support Waterfall City's economic growth, WIC has focused on three sectors of activity: health services, telecommunications, and education. However, the rapidly urbanizing area has also attracted investments in other sectors such as small-scale manufacturing and office parks (Herbert and Murray 2015).

In addition, the project includes a large warehousing center—the Waterfall Distribution Campus—aimed at providing logistic services beyond national borders. Among its tenants are a 30,000 square meter facility for the South African subsidiary of Walmart, and an 8,000 square meter distribution warehouse servicing fast-food companies such as KFC and McDonalds (Murray 2015).

Amenities

Because the local government did not have enough resources to cover basic services in the new urban area, WIC assumed responsibility for roads, water, sewerage, drainage, electricity, and 130 kilometers of optical fiber. The developers in charge of building Waterfall City had to commit that all services would be in place before putting properties up for sale.

Health services are provided through a business partnership with a company that operates the largest private hospital networks in South Africa and the United Kingdom. Plans include a fully serviced hospital, an oncology hospital, and the first private medical school in the country. Waterfall City also has six schools catering to an international clientele.

Local amenities include 150,000 square meters of retail space, encompassing a major shopping mall, casino complexes, and a conference and exhibition center. A recreational lake, a 300-hectare indigenous greenbelt, golf estates, polo fields, and horse-riding and cycling trails are also part of the package.

Affluent retirees are one customer segment specifically targeted by WIC. The project thus includes two retirement villages and what is expected to become Africa's biggest cemetery (Herbert and Murray 2015; Murray 2015).

Social and environmental issues

Because Waterfall City is geared toward the richer segments of the population, it embodies social segregation to an extent that may seem paradoxical in post-Apartheid

South Africa. Waterfall City is also separate in having its own set of norms on issues ranging from crime to religion (Herbert and Murray 2015; Falk 2012; van Noorloos and Kloosterboer 2018).

Security and law enforcement are handled by private companies, with residential zones surrounded by 4-meter-high reinforced concrete walls, topped with an electric fence and mounted with closed-circuit television cameras. Thermal detection and fingerprint recognition provide additional protection against intruders, with armed-response vehicles ready to intervene (Murray 2015).

As for religion, the strict devotion of the Mia family to an austere version of Islam has resulted in restrictive codes that businesses and households need to abide by. Alcoholic beverages are available in restaurants, but there is a strict prohibition on the establishment of liquor stores anywhere in Waterfall City. And while there is a mosque in the development, WIC banned the establishment of Christian churches, as well the public display of religious signs (Herbert and Murray 2015).

Land value capture

The land Moosa Ismail Mia donated to the Waterfall Islamic Institute is supposed to belong to Allah, so it cannot be sold and any returns from it must be used for charitable purposes. To build Waterfall City, the Mia family had to grant 99-year leaseholds to the Atterbury group and Century Properties, the two large developers implementing the project. These leasehold agreements are automatically renewed every three years, in effect perpetually transferring land-use rights to the two developers (Herbert and Murray 2015; *Mail & Guardian* 2016).

The Waterfall Islamic Institute receives a sizable monthly payment from the leaseholders. In addition, WIC—which the institute owns—derives income from cascading business arrangements, with many of its subsidiaries enjoying significant market power.

Thus, the Atterbury group—in which WIC has a 22 percent share—remains the owner of the commercial real estate it built, leasing its properties to business clients. And with the exception of standard commercial establishments, such as restaurants and mall outlets, business enterprises operating independently of WIC do not exist at Waterfall City (Murray 2015).

References

Balkaran, Sanjay. 2019. "Smart Cities as Misplaced Priorities in South Africa: A Complex Balance of Conflicting Societal Needs." *Journal of Management & Administration* 2: 1–30.

Christopher, Anthony John. 1997. "Racial Land Zoning in Urban South Africa." *Land Use Policy* 14 (4): 311–23.

Dirsuweit, Teresa. 2002. "Johannesburg: Fearful City?" *Urban Forum* 13 (3): 3–19.

Falk, Tyler. 2012. "How Satellite Cities Are Reshaping East Africa." *CityLab*, Bloomberg, May 9, 2012.

Herbert, Claire W., and Martin J. Murray. 2015. "Building from Scratch: New Cities, Privatized Urbanism and the Spatial Restructuring of Johannesburg after Apartheid." *International Journal of Urban and Regional Research* 39 (3): 471–94.

IOL. 2021. "Ode to Joburg Property Tycoon Sayed Mia as He Turns 75." *Independent Online*, March 5, 2021.

Kynoch, Gary. 2005. "Crime, Conflict and Politics in Transition-Era South Africa." *African Affairs* 104 (416): 493–514.

Kynoch, Gary. 2008. "Urban Violence in Colonial Africa: A Case for South African Exceptionalism." *Journal of Southern African Studies* 34 (3): 629–45.

Mail & Guardian. 2016. "Waterfall Development a R16bn City in the Making." *Mail & Guardian*, March 17, 2016.

Maylam, Paul. 1995. "Explaining the Apartheid City: 20 Years of South African Urban Historiography." *Journal of Southern African Studies* 21 (1): 19–38.

Murray, Martin. 2015. "Waterfall City (Johannesburg): Privatized Urbanism in Extremis." *Environment and Planning*, March 2015.

Parnell, Susan, and Alan Mabin. 1995. "Rethinking Urban South Africa." *Journal of Southern African Studies* 21 (1): 39–61.

Pieterse, Edgar. 2017. "Urban Governance and Spatial Transformation Ambitions in Johannesburg." *Journal of Urban Affairs* 41 (1): 20–38.

Todes, Alison. 2012. "Urban Growth and Strategic Spatial Planning in Johannesburg, South Africa." *Cities* 29 (3): 158–65.

van Noorloos, Femke, and Marjan Kloosterboer. 2018. "Africa's New Cities: The Contested Future of Urbanisation." *Urban Studies* 55 (6): 1223–41.

CHAPTER 22

Vietnam | PHU MY HUNG

Martin Rama

Phu My Hung—meaning "wealthy, beautiful, and prosperous"—was one of the trans-formative policy pilots attempted in the early years of Vietnam's economic transition. Aimed at testing the possibilities opened by strengthened land-use rights, the city has also been touted as a new model of urban civility.

Private actor

Lawrence Ting is widely recognized as Phu My Hung's visionary developer. Arriving in Taiwan, China, from the mainland when he was 10 years old, he graduated from the military school and trained as a US airborne ranger. He also studied at Columbia University before succeeding in the plastics industry (Macomber and Lau 2013).

In 1989, Lawrence Ting became the chairman of Central Trading and Development (CT&D), a corporation created by the Kuomintang to explore investment opportunities abroad. Despite its political dimension, CT&D was run as a family-owned business (Kriken, Lou, and Culvahouse 2017).

After visiting multiple locations across the developing world, Lawrence Ting set his sights on Vietnam. Cultural and social similarities with his own country—including Confucian values, a history of civil war, and high literacy rates—justified his choice (Jung and Lee 2017).

Lawrence Ting's activities in Vietnam grew from a logging project to the development of Phu My Hung to a close partnership with the local government of Ho Chi Minh City. These engagements earned him multiple civilian distinctions locally and the "King of Vietnam" nickname at home.

In 1993, in a sudden turn of events, the Kuomintang decided to divest its 75 percent share from CT&D and to withdraw from Vietnam altogether. A long battle for control of the corporation ensued, and corruption charges were filed. In 2004, shortly after meeting with his lawyers, Lawrence Ting leaped to his death from a 15th-floor window (Macomber and Lau 2013).

Interaction with government

The decade that followed the end of the war, in 1975, was a time of extraordinary hardship in Vietnam. A leadership more attuned to military strategy than to economic management had embraced central planning on ideological grounds, but the result was a blatant failure, with even food becoming scarce. Soon, provincial officials with unquestionable patriotic credentials started experimenting with market solutions at the fringes of what was politically acceptable. Their hope was that successful pilots would gradually lead to a new mindset, and eventually trigger deep economic reforms (Rama 2008).

A pioneering champion of this approach was Vo Van Kiet, one of the top communist leaders in the south during the war, who subsequently became the party secretary of Ho Chi Minh City and then, in 1986, the prime minister who led *doi moi*—Vietnam's renovation process. While in charge of Ho Chi Minh City, Vo Van Kiet brought together reform-minded advisers, including from the former regime, to discuss how to leverage market mechanisms and support faster economic development (Harms 2016; Rama 2008).

The group's discussions boosted the interest in building export processing zones (EPZs) and created the conditions for engaging international investors. Recognizing that the Vietnamese government did not have enough planning capacity to steer urban development, the group also helped develop the concept of new city areas (Harms 2016; Jung and Lee 2017).

Efforts to team up with foreign partners were punctuated by many false starts. But in 1988, the leader of Vo Van Kiet's discussion group finally connected with Lawrence Ting. After three years of conversations, an agreement between the Ho Chi Minh City government and CT&D to create the Phu My Hung Corporation (PMHC) was signed (Douglass and Huang 2007; Harms 2016; Huynh 2015).

Location and connectivity

Phu My Hung is located in Saigon South, an elongated 3,300-hectare area only 4 kilometers from Ho Chi Minh City's downtown. A salted marshland deemed unsuitable for building, this area had been left mostly untouched due to the strong presence of Vietcong guerrillas during the war (Harms 2016; Kriken, Lou, and Culvahouse 2017).

Saigon South is crisscrossed by navigable canals. A highway also runs through it, connecting its Tan Thuan eastern end on the Saigon River with Vietnam's main north–south highway on its western end. In addition, a subway line is planned to go through the area, with another one connecting it to Ho Chi Minh City's downtown (Kriken, Lou, and Culvahouse 2017; Nguyen 2012b).

Development time line

Building an EPZ in Tan Thuan was first considered by the government of South Vietnam in 1971. The inspiration was a successful model pioneered in 1966 by Taiwan, China, one of the southern regime's staunchest allies. An agreement was signed between the two sides in 1974 to conduct a planning study, with US funding, but not much happened as a result (Nguyen 2012b).

After the end of the war, the idea of building EPZs caught the interest of Vo Van Kiet's study group. In parallel, the development agenda that urban planners had set for Ho Chi Minh City was to build in the direction of the sea. This southward orientation made Tan Thuan a natural location for the country's first EPZ pilot (Harms 2016; Huynh 2015).

The Tan Thuan EPZ, with capacity to host 200 factories and employ 80,000 workers, was one of four projects covered by the agreement between the Ho Chi Minh City government and CT&D. Second was a thermal power plant with spare capacity to supply electricity to Ho Chi Minh City. Third was the highway connecting Tan Thuan westward to the main north–south highway, subsequently named after Vo Van Kiet. And the fourth and most ambitious project was to build a modern urban area around the highway (Kriken, Lou, and Culvahouse 2017; Macomber and Lau 2013; Nguyen 2012b).

The contribution of the Ho Chi Minh City government was to provide land. In Phu My Hung's case, the initial offer was for a 50-meter-wide strip on both sides of the highway. Lawrence Ting countered with a proposal for five large nodes (figure 22.1). Three of them would be residential, another would focus on international-quality health care facilities, and the fifth would host a central business district. Together the five nodes would accommodate 500,000 residents and help the broader Saigon South reach a population of 1 million. The counterproposal was accepted (Kriken, Lou, and Culvahouse 2017).

The master plan for Phu My Hung's central business district was chosen through an international competition. A high-profile jury was convened, assembling reputable international architects and planners, as well as representatives of the Ho Chi Minh City government. The proposal by the US firm Skidmore, Owings and Merrill was unanimously endorsed, because it delved in depth into the site as a river delta. However, given the exceptional pool of submissions, the jury decided to divide the work. Urban planning was allocated to Skidmore, Owings and Merrill, design guidelines to Koetter Kim (another US firm), and architectural projects to Kenzo Tangue (from Japan) (Kriken, Lou, and Culvahouse 2017).

Over time, CT&D invested US$10 billion into the project, and Taiwan, China, became the biggest foreign investor in Vietnam. The construction of the new central business district began in 1996, and the first housing project was launched in 1998. PMHC was in charge of much of the urban infrastructure while individual owners could build on their parcels of land but had to follow strict design guidelines (Harms 2016; Kriken, Lou, and Culvahouse 2017; Macomber and Lau 2013).

Institutional status

Vietnam's new urban zones are characterized by innovative economic and political arrangements between government authorities and land developers. In Phu My Hung's case, the Ho Chi Minh City government created an urban administration pilot under which management responsibilities were handed over to PMHC (Harms 2016).

FIGURE 22.1 **Land allocated by the government for the development of Phu My Hung, Vietnam**

a. Initial government proposal

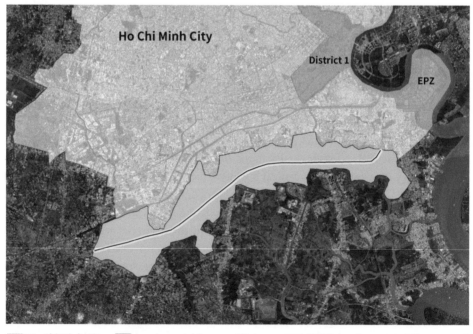

☐ Ho Chi Minh City ▣ Land assembly ── Highway ▨ 100M development strip proposal

(Figure continues on next page)

FIGURE 22.1 **Land allocated by the government for the development of Phu My Hung, Vietnam** *(continued)*

b. Counterproposal by CT&D

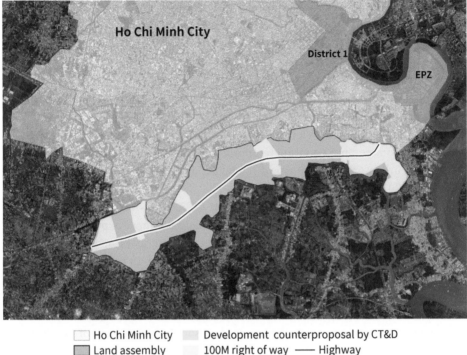

| | Ho Chi Minh City | | Development counterproposal by CT&D |
| | Land assembly | | 100M right of way —— Highway |

Source: Original figures for this book, based on Phu My Hung masterplan information and Kriken, Lou, and Culvahouse 2017.
Note: CT&D = Central Trading and Development; EPZ = export processing zones.

However, local authorities remained engaged in both oversight and facilitation. The government of Ho Chi Minh City appointed two vice presidents and one vice controller for each of the four PMHC projects. Their primary duties were to maintain the relationship with CT&D and to speed up government approvals, permits, and licensing (Kriken, Lou, and Culvahouse 2017; PMHC, n.d.).

Land assembly

The creation of PMHC was preceded by the introduction in 1993 of a new land law that became one of the key milestones of Vietnam's reform process. Under the new law, the state remained the owner of all land, but use rights by households and firms were made tradeable, admissible as lending guarantees, and transferable through inheritance (Rama 2014).

PMHC was granted rights on the land contributed by the Ho Chi Minh City government for an exceptionally long 99-year period. A special legal basis for land clearance was established in 1994, with a company under the Ho Chi Minh City government handling relocations. PMHC was also granted toll collection rights on the highway for a period of 30 years (Harms 2016; Kriken, Lou, and Culvahouse 2017; Macomber and Lau 2013).

Economic activity

Phu My Hung's economic success partly derived from its exceptional location. Ho Chi Minh City is not only Vietnam's main economic hub; with 19,000 inhabitants per square kilometer, not counting temporary migrants, its downtown is also among the densest urban areas in the world (Douglass and Huang 2007; Kriken, Lou, and Culvahouse 2017).

Phu My Hung's success also resulted from CT&D's vision for how to put it all together, as illustrated by land there being substantially more expensive than in the rest of Saigon South. An analysis of real estate transactions estimated that its location premium for comparable properties was a stunning 43 percent (Huynh 2015; Kriken, Lou, and Culvahouse 2017).

The outcome of the other projects undertaken by PMHC is more mixed. The Tan Thuan EPZ became highly profitable and was even rated the best industrial zone in Asia by *Euromoney*. And at one point, the power plant supplied 45 percent of the electricity consumed by Ho Chi Minh City. But running on fuel, its breakeven electricity price is three times as high as the tariff charged to industrial plants and 50 percent higher than the tariff for households (Huynh 2015; Macomber and Lau 2013).

Amenities

PMHC owns and operates utility infrastructure for the locality, delivering services to residents through a model that lumps all utility expenses into one. In some cases, such as electricity, retail distribution is assured under a licensing agreement with the public utility. In others, such as water treatment, proprietary infrastructure had to be built once it became clear that the government would not reliably provide it as planned (Kriken, Lou, and Culvahouse 2017; Macomber and Lau 2013).

PMHC also delivers a range of other urban services, including security, maintenance, street cleaning, and landscaping. It has even established its own bus company to provide commuter service to downtown Ho Chi Minh City. The ticket fare is three times higher than that of regular buses, but its service is much better and more reliable (Huynh 2015).

High-quality education and health care facilities are part of Phu My Hung's branding. There is a French hospital, which at one point was the best-equipped medical facility in Vietnam, as well as two international universities, from Australia and the US. There are also several prestigious schools, including the largest from Taiwan, China, in all of Southeast Asia. In addition, Phu My Hung counts among its amenities sports facilities, parks, and popular pedestrian promenades, and it hosts the most upscale shopping mall in Ho Chi Minh City (Harms 2016; Huynh 2015; Kriken, Lou, and Culvahouse 2017; Macomber and Lau 2013).

Social and environmental issues

Phu My Hung received a Progressive Architecture Award in 1995, an honor award from the American Institute of Architects in 1997, and a Global Excellence Award for livability and sustainability from the Urban Land Institute in 2012 (Kriken, Lou, and Culvahouse 2017).

The project's environmental performance is widely recognized as solid. The city is organized as a set of walkable islands separated by canals that continue to support waterway transportation and trade. The regular dredging of these canals facilitates their flushing by the region's often heavy rains. It also provided the sand-fill to raise the ground 1.5 meters above the highest tide level in preparation for sea-level rise (Nguyen 2012a, 2012b).

However, Phu My Hung is often depicted as an extreme example of social segregation. Its population is much wealthier than the Ho Chi Minh City average, and its distinct institutional status makes it largely independent from the local government (Douglass and Huang 2007; Waibel 2004).

In Phu My Hung's defense, only 7 percent of the residential stock of the city is gated, and 94 percent of the river frontage is accessible to everybody. Besides, being run by a corporation is arguably less damaging to democratic urban governance when citizens would have had limited power to choose their representatives anyway (Harms 2016; Kriken, Lou, and Culvahouse 2017).

There is, however, an important difference in the way public space is used. Social life in Ho Chi Minh City largely unfolds on sidewalks, where all segments of the population meet, eat, and trade. By contrast, Phu My Hung prides itself on its high levels of civility and cleanliness but is largely devoid of liveliness and conviviality (Douglass and Huang 2007; Harms 2016; Kennedy 2013; Kim 2015).

There is also an important difference between Phu My Hung and its surroundings. A management authority was established for the rest of Saigon South in 1997, but master plans were only partially implemented. Land was assigned to numerous developers without sufficient attention to coherence, infrastructure, or amenities. Together with spontaneous outgrowths, by 2006 these weaknesses had resulted in 10 times the population density of Phu My Hung (Harms 2016; Huynh 2015; Kriken, Lou, and Culvahouse 2017).

Land value capture

An evaluation based on several sources suggests that from 1998 to 2009 PMHC generated US$1.3 billion in revenue, leading to US$500 million in profits, of which 70 percent accrued to CT&D and the rest to the Ho Chi Minh City government. The internal rate of return during this period was estimated at 125 percent. Even discounting the cost of the highway in full, the annual return would be around 30 percent (Huynh 2015).

Land value has not been captured by PMHC alone. Roughly half of Phu My Hung's population is made up of expatriates, and most of them sublet from Vietnamese home-owners who acquired their plots in the early stages of the project. While precise estimates are not available, Phu My Hung has likely been a major source of tax revenue for both the national and local governments (Nguyen 2012b).

References

Douglass, Mike, and Liling Huang. 2007. "Globalizing the City in Southeast Asia: Utopia on the Urban Edge—The Case of Phu My Hung, Saigon." *International Journal of Asia-Pacific Studies* 3 (2).

Harms, Erik. 2016. *Luxury and Rubble: Civility and Dispossession in the New Saigon.* Oakland: University of California Press.

Huynh, Du. 2015. "Phu My Hung New Urban Development in Ho Chi Minh City: Only a Partial Success of a Broader Landscape." *International Journal of Sustainable Built Environment* 4 (1): 125–35.

Jung, Sanghoon, and Jae Seung Lee. 2017. "Korean Developers in Vietnam: The Mechanism of Transnational Large-Scale Property Development and Its Planning." *Sustainability*, May 4, 2017.

Kennedy, John. 2013. "Large-Scale Urban Planning, Culture and Environment: A Case Study in Saigon South Urban Area." Independent Study Project (ISP) Collection 1564, Hamilton College, Clinton, NY. https://digitalcollections.sit.edu/isp_collection/1564/.

Kim, Annette Mia. 2015. *Sidewalk City: Remapping Public Space in Ho Chi Minh City.* Chicago, IL: University of Chicago Press.

Kriken, John Lund, Ellen Lou, and Tim Culvahouse. 2017. *Building Saigon South: Sustainable Lessons for a Livable Future.* Novato, CA: Oro Editions.

Macomber, John, and Dawn H. Lau. "Phu My Hung." Harvard Business School Case 213-098, February 2013. (Revised February 2014). https://www.hbs.edu/faculty/Pages/item.aspx?num =44309.

Nguyen, Do Dung. 2012a. "Nam Sài Gòn - một lược sử quy hoạch - Trò chuyện với KTS John Lund Kriken, tác giả đồ án Nam Sài Gòn / Phú Mỹ Hưng." *Ashui*, March 12, 2012.

Nguyen, Do Dung. 2012b. "Phu My Hung." *Do thi Vietnam*, December 2012.

PMHC. n.d. "Phu My Hung." Phu My Hung Corporation. Accessed May 14, 2022. http://www .phumyhung.com.vn/en/.

Rama, Martin. 2008. "Making Difficult Choices: Vietnam in Transition." Working Paper 40, on behalf of the Commission on Growth and Development, World Bank, Washington, DC.

Rama, Martin. 2014. "Viet Nam." In *Handbook of Emerging Economies*, edited by Robert E. Looney, 339–63. London: Routledge.

Waibel, Michael. 2004. "The Development of Saigon South New Urban Area: A Sign of an Increasing Internationalization and Polarization in Vietnamese Society." *Pacific News*, no. 22, July–August 2004.

Milton Keynes UK
Ingram Content Group UK Ltd.
UKHW052338040823
426363UK00004B/58